The Ultimate Treasure Hunt

The Ultimate Treasure Hunt:

Finding the Child Inside

ADAIR N. RENNING

COVER ART BY ASIA RENNING

The Ultimate Treasure Hunt:
Finding the Child Inside
Copyright 1995 by Adair N. Renning

First Printing: November, 1995
ISBN: 0-9648773-0-9
Library of Congress Catalog Card Number: 95-92625
Cover illustration by Asia Renning
Cover design by Technological Insights
Book design by Adair Renning
Desktop published by J.A.M.A. (Jerry, Adair, Meghann, and
Asia)
Printed in the United States of America

**For my family,
with all my love,
Mom.**

Acknowledgments

I may have done the typing, but this story would never have become a book without the support of many people. I would like to thank my mother, who has always believed in my dreams, and still helps me achieve them. Mom, I love you. Jerry proofread every chapter for accuracy, at least twice, and tolerated one-sided conversations for the past three months. Asia grudgingly shared the computer with me, and Meghann, (who was the original inspiration for the book), was font, style, and photo consultant. You three mean the world to me.

Special thanks to Annabel Stehli, who jump-started my writing batteries and who kept me from letting the fear of failure stop me from trying. I tried to "make you *see* it," Annabel. Thanks for teaching me to spell numbers.

Joan Matthews used her practiced eye to find a home for all the homeless commas in the world and taught me to write in *italics* instead of **bold**-face type. In addition, she provided the technical information I lacked regarding the layout, margins, copyright information, and much more. Joan, you're wonderful.

Cleon and Lorena Seaver, and Marsha Hancock proofread and managed to find errors all the rest of us had missed. The weekend before taking the final manuscript to the printer, Murphy's Law ruled, and Marsha's calmness and humor kept me on track. Thanks, my friends.

When self-made computer glitches threatened my sanity, I called on my "computer gurus": Meghann, of course, and Jess

Spike (who made me laugh instead of kick the machine), Wayne and Kathy Johnson, (who make it all look so easy), Dan Spurling, (who has probably changed his phone number), and Bill and Jane Geiger. Without Bill and Jane I wouldn't even have the computer!

If I start listing all the people who have been important in Asia's life, we'll need to add another chapter. But a few in particular need to be mentioned. Without Teri Bacall (Bell, now) and Mrs. Choi in Korea, there might not be a story at all. Thanks to Dorothy Rappel for all her early support. Thanks and love to my sister, Cindy, for always being there and always knowing. Jerry's parents, Bud and Wim Renning, got us off and running twice, first with Touch and Tell, and then by giving us Doris Rapp's book, which started our search for alternative treatments. Barb Tostrup started Asia's progress, and always applauded the small steps. Her teachers over the years, Sheri VanAtta, Nancy LaPrairie, Maria Bolen, Carol Vollink, Mike Stanek, and Marsha Adams, have each risen to the enormous teaching challenge that Asia provided. Marsha continues to support and nurture Asia daily, and next to us, knows her better than anyone. Asia's speech teachers, Corrine Martinez, Sheri Larson, and Mary Underwood, have been wonderfully supportive, patient, and encouraging. Melissa Dertian, a very special young lady, was the first person close to Asia's age, outside of the family, who went out of her way to include Asia in play. Danette Talbot has offered both tutoring and friendship. Thanks to her cross-country coaches, Steven Porter and Cindy Hasselbring, for believing in her and giving her a chance, and to the Milan Girls Cross Country Team for their acceptance, encouragement, and friendship.

If I have inadvertently left anyone out in this list, please accept my profound apologies, and heartfelt thanks, and chalk up the ommission to my less than bionic memory.

Adair Renning
September 1995

The Ultimate Treasure Hunt:
Finding the Child Inside

Contents

Foreword by Teri Bell

Part I   The Story of Kim, Hee Young   1
1   She Will Be Pretty Like Flowers   7
2   The Arrival of the Silver Stork   14
3   Moving Right Along, Folks   20
4   Seoul Food   27
5   Every Picture Tells a Story   34
6   Playing the Waiting Game   49
7   Seoul Food, Part 2   64
8   "Twinkle, Twinkle, Little Star"   67
9   Cracking the Shell   78
10   More Milestones and Miracles   91
11   High-Speed Baby   98

Part 2   Unlocking Asia   109

12   The First Irish/Korean War   113
13   Doctor Hopping   118
14   Forward and Backward   125
15   ?????   131
16   The Move   136
17   Milan, MI 48160   141
18   Grilled Cheese Sandwiches   151
19   Shrinks   158
20   Shrinks Part 2   167
21   Re-Building   178
22   The Cold Turkey Diet   184
23   Changes   192
24   Mayhem at Middle School   200
25   AIT and Annabel   215
26   After AIT   221
27   The Last Chapter   234
Afterword--Kenyon Wilson   264
What to Read and Who to Call   266

Foreword

It had been approximately ten years since my last contact with Adair Renning, so you can imagine my surprise when she telephoned last July. I listened with interest as she filled in the time gap for me, and I held my breath as she began to tell me about Asia. This is obviously not a book on adoption, it is the story of one child, Asia Renning, and her family. However, I feel compelled to comment on it from an adoption social worker's point of view.

In every part of the world that I have traveled and worked, I have been asked why I place the children I do, who would want them, and why they would want them. The answers are, of course, as diverse and individual as the children and families themselves. I suppose the simple answer to the first question is Asia. Asia, for me, at this moment, represents all the children who waited and continue to wait for one person or one family to give them a chance. The people who want to bring a child with special needs into their family are not looking for problems; they are looking for a child they can offer their lives to, one who can hopefully benefit from what they have to offer. They don't look at their potential child as sick or handicapped; they see that child as someone they can share their love with who is challenged in some way. They are not adopting a disability; they are adopting a child. For some reason even she cannot explain, Adair was attracted to a particular child. She and Jerry felt compelled to bring Asia into their lives. Their hopes and dreams for Asia may have been different from the realities as they emerged, but they are her parents and she is their child-- that is what really counts.

In the United States I find that I am asked all the above questions with the same curiosity I have found in other cultures, but I am also asked, often with hostility, why I would participate in bringing children "like this" into our country when we have problems enough of our own. While I try to use this type of question as an opportunity to educate, I have come to realize that, for myself and the families adopting children in need, there are no geographical boundaries. I understand that this concept cannot easily be communicated to those who do not share this opinion of the world. It is my hope that this book will explain more than I can--by virtue of the fact that "adoption" is not the theme of Adair's story, but rather one of love, hope and determination.

The expectation of adoption is that a child will gain a family of his or her very own, a family that will love, cherish, and accept them no matter what the future brings. The greatest hope for an adoption social worker is that the child they are placing will be adopted by people who can accept the special, unique method by which their child entered their family, but who cannot see that it makes a difference. In reading *The Ultimate Treasure Hunt: Finding the Child Inside*, it was clear to me that Adair and Jerry have done just that. They see both Asia and Meghann as the daughters they will love, nourish, educate, stand by, discipline, support, encourage, and accept come what may-- in short, they are their own children.

Asia is a very special child. She is one of the many special children whose adoption I participated in during a time period which has spanned almost twenty-five years. As a social worker who assists in the placement and adjustment of international children with special needs, I occasionally find that I am listening with trepidation to parents whose children are now grown or on their way to being grown. The paths that some of these children have traveled have been difficult and often quite different from what their families had planned. In retrospect, I wondered if I had prepared the Rennings sufficiently for the possible pitfalls and long-term effects of parenting a child with Asia's special needs. Adair says I did, and that they knowingly made an informed decision to add Asia to their lives. I believe we did all we could to make it possible for them to become a family. We believed the Rennings were ready to handle their future with Asia. I know for sure that Asia's life is enriched by the love and determination of her mother, father, and sister.

When families come to me hoping to adopt an international child with special needs, I find it difficult to balance my desire to find that child a family with my need to be sure that the parent(s) understand what the realities are for this child. The adoption of a child with special needs is not something that potential adoptors are expected or encouraged to consider or a decision to be made lightly. It is a choice that some exceptional people make, although many of them cannot say why. It is wonderful to believe that the child who has not thrived in his or her homeland will respond once they have the love and attention of a family. While this has proved to be true in many cases, realistic expectations are a must, because unfortunately, *love does not conquer all!*

From my years in the field, from my observations and most of all from listening to the experts--the parents--I have found that there are specific issues which we as social workers can ask potential adoptive parents to look at as they make this lifetime commitment. For instance, a failure-to-thrive or institutionalized child, a developmentally delayed child, or a child with a parental history of substance abuse may not respond, catch up, or accomplish the dreams their family has envisioned for them. That child may always remain delayed or unstable. There are no guarantees in life as to the future of any child, whether that child is brought into the family by adoption or by birth. Many people can spend long hours, days, or months working with a child when they feel that the outcome will be a positive one. But it is important for families to know if they are capable of feeling that their new child is still a part of their lives even if the outcome is not as positive as they had hoped. The reality that our expectations for our children cannot always be fulfilled often becomes too clear after the fact. It's best for potential adoptors to examine themselves beforehand whenever possible.

International adoption differs from U.S. adoption (for the most part) because the information the adoptor receives may be scant or inaccurate at best. Adoptors must, however, take the information available to them, and, looking at the best and worst scenarios, decide if they feel strong enough to cope with whatever may lie ahead for them. I have included these issues as part of my foreword to this book, because it is important to understand the type of commitment made by Adair, Jerry, Meghann, their extended family, their friends, and those who supported them in their community. Many families have children with special needs born to them, and while the issues they deal with on a day-to-day basis are the same, the initial difference, the one of choice, is quite different.

The book Adair has written is really the story of Asia and what she has experienced since her arrival home. The majority of her initial experiences have revolved around contacts with the medical community. Actually for the parents of an internationally adopted child, their experiences with medical professionals begin even before their child arrives home. In her book, Adair refers to visits with doctors and other parents regarding Asia's medical problems before the child joined her new family. These contacts are essential for parents adopting a child with special needs. Even with a physician they trust, families can be frustrated and overwhelmed by their initial contacts with the medical community. It is often difficult to know what questions to ask once they meet with their doctor. Families who have the most success are the ones who have done their homework regarding any medical information they have received about the child. If the child being referred has a specific handicapping condition, the potential family should visit their local library and contact the appropriate organization to inform themselves about that condition. Involvement with parent groups that meet to discuss similar concerns is also very important. Families will be helped immensely as they attempt to put the medical information into perspective by learning about the day-to-day lives of children with specific challenges.

A wonderful aid in decision making for families is to spend some time with children who have similar physical challenges. This might include a visit to see the child at home and school. If the family is comfortable with what they have seen and learned at this point, one last tool to be sure they are making a good decision would be to visit a similarly challenged teenager and his or her parents. We all the images we have of ourselves are true. We look at the children and families that have "made it" and we say, "We can do that too." We want to see ourselves as strong enough and capable enough to endure whatever challenges life presents. It is important that families be realistic regarding their strengths and weaknesses. This time spent gathering information will better prepare adoptors to discuss the prognosis of the child they are considering with their doctor.

The majority of families who are choosing adoption of a special-needs child bring the medical community into their decision making process at some point. This isn't as easy as it may sound. There are many questions that potential adoptors will want to ask, and many questions a doctor may ask them. The doctor must understand from the outset that he or she is not being asked to make the decision for the family: that the decision to proceed with an international adoption of a special-needs child has already been made. The information and guidance offered at this time should be the same as that given to a family who enters the office with their birth child, asking the same types of questions. One of the last steps a family should take before making a final decision, is to evaluate all of the information received from the specialists and decide if any of this information contains any adoption bias. Unfortunately, physicians are capable of the same prejudices against foreign and special-needs children that others in the community hold. International adoption is not without controversy.

Adair relates her frustration with the medical community, which developed after years of disappointing doctors visits. I have heard these same feelings expressed with increasing frequency by other adoptive parents I have grown to respect. Some of these parents have left the mainstream of medical care and turned to alternative therapies, hoping they will provide them with help for their children. In response to what I had been hearing, I recently began reaching out for information from both the medical community and the organizations which represent some of the frustrated parents of challenged children. I have been surprised by some of the reactions I have encountered from both sides of this issue.

The families who have turned away from the established medical professionals, as well as those they have turned away from, each express valid issues which need to be considered. There are respected members of the medical community who feel that the practitioners of some alternative therapies are taking advantage of discouraged parents, who will be given false hope and expectations and then drained of their financial resources. These physicians truly believe that what the family needs to do is stop looking for answers or cures which don't exist and begin to accept the reality of their child's disability. The other side of the coin is represented by the parents, who tell me that because the "traditional" medical community has no answers for them, they must look elsewhere for help with their children. The main reason given is that after making the rounds of various specialists, trying a variety of therapies and/or medications, and having no success (sometimes experiencing setbacks or negative reactions), they feel there is nothing to be gained by continuing on this merry-go-round. At this time they seek help from outside "established" medicine.

I have come to believe that the parent(s) of developmentally challenged children need to have *hope* that things can improve for their child. Presently, some of the families of children adopted from Eastern Europe who were having a difficult time finding help for their post-institutionalized children are now discovering a variety of therapy interventions available to them. Some of these therapies have brought changes into the lives of these children and their families, and these same therapies have given no help at all to others. Some therapies are becoming more respected by members of the medical community, while others have been strongly rejected and discredited. For the most part, these families are aware that a "cure" does not exist for their children, but they are not ready to "give up" and "accept" that only behavior modification and a dependence on alternative educational planning will make a difference.

In attempting to find the best advice to give families who are seeking help on issues concerning their child's development, I find myself encouraging them to continue looking for the right team for their child. It is true that in the vast majority of cases there is no cure. Children's developmental lags can be caused by a variety of conditions which cannot be erased. Brain damage may have occurred before, during, or after birth. The child may be genetically predisposed to the developmental disabilities they are experiencing or may have experienced an attachment disruption which was severe enough to cause that child to be unable to develop appropriately. Whatever the reason for the developmental concern, there may be one or more ways to increase that child's ability to live life to his or her fullest potential. It is important for families to grieve for what may never be, begin to deal with what is, and then get on with what can be. I strongly encourage families to be cautious consumers when considering the inclusion of anyone as part of a child's overall treatment. Ask questions, expect answers (even if the answer is that they *don't have* an answer). Don't be intimidated, and be cautious of anyone who says they can "fix" a child.

My request for all of those involved with this issue is to keep an open mind. So much is unknown, and so much is being learned in this area, that we limit ourselves if we only look at any one side. A close friend of mine in the "established" medical community who has worked extensively with children with developmental disabilities feels that it is imperative to listen to the families' concerns and suggestions for alternative therapy. The doctors at the hospital in which she is both an administrator and a practitioner routinely ask the family for any information they have regarding the alternative therapy they are interested in. The doctors discuss what they know about this therapy with the family and accumulate whatever additional information is available. They then incorporate that therapy into their patient's treatment plan. This, to me, is the best of all possible worlds. I cannot believe that this particular hospital has the only doctors who practice using this philosophy.

Asia's story shows the difference a pro-active family can make in the life of one very special little girl. There is no end to this story, because Asia and her family have shown us that, with determination, hope, and especially love, there is no end to her potential.

Teri Bell
Special Needs Co-ordinator,
Americans for International Aid and Adoption
(AIAA)

Part 1

She Will be Pretty Like Flowers

THE STORY OF KIM, HEE YOUNG
by Miss Meghann Renning
(age three-and-a half)

Meghann: Once upon a time, a long way ago, there was a man and a lady in America that wanted SO BAD a little girl to be their very own daughter. So they went to a place called WHAT?

Mama: Children's. . .

Meghann: Home. . .

Daddy: Society.

Meghann: And they talked to a nice lady named WHO?

Mama: Mary Abbett.

Meghann: And she showed them some pictures and one of them was WHO?

Daddy: Kim, Hee Young.

Meghann: And the lady said, "She's the most beautiful daughter I've ever seen in the whole world and I'd know her anywhere." And the man said, "She's real cute but she has funny hair sticking up all over." So they talked to Mary some more and signed some papers and Mary said, "She's your very own daughter and she'll be home in a few months."

Mama: And then what happened?

Meghann: They went home and called all their family and all their friends and said, "We've got a baby in Korea who's now borned and she'll be home in a few months." And they started getting things ready for the baby to come. And they got diapers and a diaper pail and Wet Ones and formula and bottles and clothes and a rocking chair and a crib and made a quilt and got toys and a changing table. And they thought the time would NEVER pass by!!!

Daddy: And then what happened?

Meghann: One day they got a phone call from Children's Home Society and the lady said,

"She's coming, she's coming, she'll be here in
two days!!" So they called all their family
and all their friends again and said, "Our
baby's coming home in two days. Do you
want to come to the airport to meet her?"
They wouldn't want to miss that, for Heavens
no!! So there was the man and the lady and
Bruce and Terry and Brandie and Cindy and
Dick and Lynn and Kimberly and Dick's
mom and dad and Grandma and Grandpa
Renning and Kim and Marv and Marvis
and Kris Muller and Bill and Rosie and
Mike and Kris and Rick and Linda and
Jolene and Libby and Eddie and Tom and
Marleane and Jeep and Bruce and Faricy
and Meesa Munholland. And the plane
landed and the people got off and the
pilots got off and a nice lady named
Debbie went on the plane and got Kim,
Hee Young from Mrs. Han. And she
handed her to the Mama and the Mama
handed her to the Daddy and Kim, Hee
Young went potty all over the Daddy! And
the Mama put her in a clean diaper and
clean clothes and gave her a bottle and
Mama and Daddy and Meghann (Kim,
Hee Young) and Cindy all got in the little
red Volvo and went home, where they
lived happily ever after. The End.

Mama: No, Honey, it's not the end, it's just the
beginning.

June 12, 1995

This is Meghann's version of the bedtime story we told her about how she became our daughter. We had told it to her so many times that one night she decided to tell it to us. We were lucky enough to hide the tape recorder and tape it the night before we were to go to Minneapolis to pick up our second daughter, Asia. Meghann was three-and-a-half years old at the time. She is now almost sixteen.

Chapter One

She Will Be Pretty Like Flowers

KIM, HEE YOUNG: Born November 22, 1979, in Seoul, Korea. Her given name "Hee Young" means, "She will be pretty like flowers and could share happiness to all." That description and her picture leaped out and grabbed my heart as surely as a hand. It was the instant recognition of a mother seeing her child for the first time. But let me go back to the beginning:

My husband Jerry was thirty years old and I was thirty-two when we were married in August of 1978. We knew from the beginning that we would not be able to conceive children, so we began shortly after our marriage to make inquiries at local adoption agencies. In Duluth, Minnesota, where we lived at the time, the St. Louis County Social Service office was our first stop. As congenial as the social worker was, she gave us no encouragement for the adoption of a "local" (either Caucasian or Black or Native American) child for at least five years. But what about a child from another country we asked. The County Social Service office did not handle foreign adoptions; however they were able to give us a list of international adoption agencies which place children from around the world.

From the list we selected six agencies--two that were in Minnesota--Children's Home Society of Minnesota, and Lutheran Social Services--and proceeded to write letters explaining our circumstances and great desire to have a child. We wanted an infant, as young as possible, either sex, from Asia or India. Knowing that many of the children in other countries who are waiting for homes have medical problems, we listed the conditions that we felt equipped to deal with.

Within a few weeks we received replies from the agencies. Although all were encouraging about the possibility of adopting a child, after reading the volumes of information sent, the agency we felt most comfortable with was Children's Home Society in St. Paul. It was the beginning of a relationship that would expand and enrich our lives in many ways other than parenthood.

We were advised of an orientation meeting on November 28, 1979, at the agency's office in St. Paul and made arrangements to attend and spend the night with friends. At this meeting we, along with about twenty other couples, learned about C.H.S.M.'s policy and requirements for adoptive families, the ages and races of the children available, and the approximate time before we could realistically expect the placement of a child in our homes. We learned from Tom Regan, the Director of Adoptions, that those families wanting infants could expect an eighteen-month wait, that most of the children placed were Korean, and that proportionately there were more girl babies available than boys. (Fine, so where do we sign?) Although the agency also places children from India and Guatemala as well as U.S.-born-children, because of an especially close relationship with the Eastern Child Welfare Society in Seoul, the majority of the children come from there. There were (and still are) infants, toddlers, sibling groups, school-aged children, and special-needs children in orphanages and foster homes waiting for their "Forever Families." Every child's story is different, but they all have one thing in common: the overwhelming need for a permanent home and a mother and father to love them.

One of the first requirements for consideration as potential adoptive parents was that the couple be married for at least two years. Jerry and I had been married only fifteen months. Trying to push my heart out of my throat, I raised my hand. "Mr. Regan, Jerry and I have only been married for a little over a year," I stammered. "But if it counts at all, we lived together for two years before that." The room full of parents roared with good-natured laughter.

"That's okay, Mrs. Renning. By the time you'd be likely to get a baby, you'll have been married the required two years," he replied with a grin.

"But what about registering," I asked anxiously. "Can we still register with you tonight?" I wanted to sign and pay and get on with it. He assured us that he would attach a note to our registration form waiving the two-year rule. We registered with the agency at the end of the meeting with the understanding that we would receive an application within a few months. We left the two-hour meeting not knowing that the beautiful child who was to become our daughter was six days old.

The following day while shopping in Minneapolis, it seemed that every other child we saw was Asian, and I approached every set of parents with the same questions. . . "Where is your child from? What agency did you go through to adopt? How long did it take? Have there been any problems?" The parents were, without exception, enthusiastic about their Korean-born children. Most had adopted their children through the Children's Home Society, and had had a very short waiting period, in most cases less than one year.

We returned to Duluth and drove the postman crazy watching every day for our application to arrive. Finally, in February, the long-awaited brown envelope containing our application forms, personal questionnaires, medical histories, and schedule of fees arrived. We wasted no time in answering, signing, and notarizing forms, having physicals, and promptly returning everything.

Poor postman, here we go again! The next step in the process is notification of acceptance by C.H.S.M. and appointments with a social worker for a series of pre-adoptive counselling meetings.

Families in the Minneapolis-St. Paul area generally attend these meetings over a period of several weeks, but because of the three-hour drive from Duluth, arrangements were made for three families from our area to attend a two-day counselling session with our social worker, Mary Abbett. We would be finger-printed at the Immigration and Naturalization office in St. Paul the morning of March 20, 1980, a required step in securing a visa to allow the child to enter the country as a dependent, and also to determine if we had any criminal record. The next stop was the agency for the first day of our sessions.

Greg and Cindy Johnson of Grand Rapids, Minnesota, and Dick and Lynn Eckhoff, also of Duluth, were the other couples in our group. During the first day we shared with Mary and the other two couples our feelings about not being able to conceive children, how our extended families felt about our adopting a child of another race, what our home life was like, who handled the money, and many more questions designed not only to tell Mary who we were and what we were about, but also to bring up questions about ourselves that perhaps we had not thought of. As personal as the questions were, Mary's manner of asking them was not intimidating. By four o'clock that afternoon we drifted somewhere between exhaustion and elation--we were finally on our way to becoming parents. We left the session with "homework": thirty-three essay questions that left no stone unturned. Our childhood was examined, our relationships with our parents, our views on child discipline, why we wanted to adopt a child. How did we feel that this child would be accepted by our families. . .and on and on and on. Seven legal sheets (each) and permanent writer's cramp later, we tried unsuccessfully to sleep and prepare for the next day.

On Friday morning Mary gave us much more information about Korean children, the culture of the people, problems we could expect to arise, such as difficulty digesting cow's milk or cow's milk based formula, Mongolian spots (which look similar to bruises on the lower back and buttocks and have caused more than one uninformed baby-sitter to go into coronary arrest). Because of the time difference between Korea and the United States, the children's "body clocks" are out of sync, causing sleeping difficulties--for the new parents as well as the children. Also the children often have problems with both internal and external parasites, which in most cases are easily corrected. In Korea, babies are placed on their back to sleep, so frequently the backs of the babies' heads are quite flat when they arrive. Since mothers carry their babies on their backs everywhere, wrapped in quilts tied around their waists, frequently the infants are slightly bow legged. Both these conditions are self-correcting after a short time in their new homes.

Petite Lynn Eckhoff piped up, "So what you're telling us, Mary, is that we can expect a spotted, bow-legged, flat-headed baby with lice, and worms, who can't drink milk and sleeps during the day and is awake all night. Okay, so far. So what's next, Mary?" That took care of any remaining tension in the room.

The next step is to be given a referral of a child. Basically speaking, this is a picture or pictures of the child and as much personal, medical, and behavioral information as is available. This varies from child to child, but in most infant referrals, there is birth weight information, height, birth marks, hair and eye color, general appearance, health information, and the foster mother or social worker's comments about the child. If the names, ages, and educational backgrounds of the birth parents are known, these are also given. Being new at this adoption business, we asked Mary if she had any referrals we might see--just to get an idea of what to expect, you understand. After cautioning us that the pictures of the children we were about to see were only representative of the types of children available and not necessarily themselves available for adoption, Mary handed us a stack of six or seven referrals.

The first I saw was a young boy, eighteen months old, whose mother had recently died and whose father felt unable to raise the child alone. He was an adorable boy, but though we thought we wanted a boy first, I really wanted a younger child, complete with diapers, two A.M. feedings, teething, and all the rest of the fun. Mary handed me the next picture, telling me that the child had a slight, already treated medical problem, and had already been passed over by several families. I didn't let go of the picture for two days. There she was: Kim, Hee Young, one day short of four months old, a round face, fair skin, and a shock of jet black hair that reminded Jerry of a dandelion going to seed. I've tried on a number of occasions to describe the feeling I had when I saw her picture, and the closest I can come is *instant recognition*. She *was* our daughter. Now to convince Jerry and Mary. I was barely aware of the other pictures being passed around. I felt dizzy and light- headed, as if I were going to pass out as I clutched the black and white photo against my chest. I didn't even want to show her to the other parents, because she was *our daughter*. Although the other children were cute, they weren't Kim, Hee Young. I saw signs in the referral that were meant only for us, I was sure. "Kim," her family name, is Jerry's sister's name. Her birthday, November 22, is the day before Jerry's sister Kim's birthday. Her given name, "Hee Young," means, "She will be pretty like *flowers* (we worked in a florist/greenhouse in Duluth) and could share happiness to all" (no doubt about that).

Time for lunch. Feeling faint, I asked Mary if we could take two of the children (pictures, that is) to lunch. Oh, please God, we can't go home to Duluth without the picture of this beautiful baby girl. At lunch Jerry and I ate club sandwiches we barely tasted and talked about the children. How do you choose one child over another like that, I've been asked. Well, for me, there *was* no choice, and Jerry agreed that if it were possible for us to adopt Kim, Hee Young, we would convince Mary at our after- noon meeting that we were the best parents for the child. After picking apart the little tinsel-wrapped toothpicks in my sandwich and shredding two napkins, we left the restaurant and walked around the fairground trying to kill time until our 2 P.M. meeting with Mary.

We arrived back at the agency in time to meet Dick and Lynn Eckhoff just as they were leaving with the picture and referral information of their new daughter, one-month-old Kimberly, an adorable child they had seen in the stack of referrals Mary had let us look at. After exchanging telephone numbers with the Eckhoffs and promising to stay in touch, we sat down to wait. We thumbed through the photo albums in the lobby and talked about Kim, Hee Young. In Mary's small office, Jerry and I sat, holding each others hands and the black and white picture of the beautiful little dark-haired girl while we nervously answered a few more questions. Just when we thought the meeting was about over, Mary said, "I noticed you were rather taken by that little girl, Adair. What do you think?" *What do I think?* I was too scared to think.

"Well, she is available for adoption, you know," she said, with a little smile playing around the corners of her mouth.

"I know, you told us she was available, but I didn't think it worked that way. I thought I'd have to persuade you that I simply couldn't leave here without knowing we could adopt her."

Then she allowed the smile to shine as she told us that it would take several months to process the paperwork, but she was our daughter. We had expected to be sent a referral some months later, and here we were, taking home a picture and three pages of information about our daughter so far away. We hugged Mary and left the office, then drove to our friends' home to spend the night. During all the time, I never let go of the picture.

Chapter Two

The Arrival of the Silver Stork

WE RETURNED TO Duluth on Sunday, armed with more information about Korea, Korean children, lists of books to read, and the phone numbers of the Johnsons and Eckhoffs, who would become very dear friends in a very short time.

Back in Duluth, we called family and friends and told them our good news. Monday morning I rather reluctantly gave one of the two sets of pictures to a local camera store to have copies made. The grandparents, aunts, and uncles each **had** to have a picture and copy of all the information, and one set of pictures was hung on the refrigerator with magnets. We spent the evenings selecting and discarding names and trying to prepare our two six-year-old dogs for the day when they would no longer be our only "children." And we waited and waited and waited.

We had been told at the Immigration Office that fingerprints are usually approved and visas granted within six weeks, and until the visa is granted, the rest of the paperwork processing in Korea is delayed. I counted forty-two days on the calendar and vowed not to bother the postman until the forty-third day. That promise only lasted two weeks, and then I began meeting him at the door.

Our friends at Engwall's florist, where we worked, gave us a baby shower, and the neighbors gave us a crib, which we painted. Jerry's parents brought up a dresser and my best friend Cindy and I painted it and re-covered Jerry's grandfather's rocking chair in preparation for rocking our baby to sleep. I made a crib quilt and a baby afghan and spoke with our family doctor about child care classes. Being an only child myself and one of the youngest grandchildren, I had no personal "baby care" experience to draw from. Our doctor recommended a wonderful lady who came to our home several times and played "twenty questions" with me, reassuring me that my mothering instincts were strong and just needed some "hands on" experience.

I bought baby bottles, bibs, diapers, baby care books, and books on infant nutrition and development. My sister-in-law brought over clothes that her daughter had outgrown and the little dresser drawers began to fill.

We learned of an adoptive parents support group which had a chapter in town and attended a meeting and subscribed to their magazine. In one issue we read of several families in Duluth who had recently adopted Korean children, and I called them all. They were all helpful and encouraging, but one particularly fine lady named Dorothy Rappel became the calming force that helped see us through the waiting period. She answered my questions and calmed my fears and reassured me that things were proceeding normally and according to schedule.

But where was our visa approval? The other two couples had received theirs and my fingerprints had been returned approved, but Jerry's had apparently been lost. Fortunately the Immigration Office had taken two sets and resubmitted the second one. But I was horrified at the thought of another six-week wait. I called the Immigration Office in St. Paul almost daily. My fertile imagination took wings. What if all fingerprints really aren't different and Jerry's look like an axe murderer's?

We attended a Korea Day workshop at Children's Home Society which was conducted by a Korean-born social worker, Hyun Sook Han. Petite, with thick black hair and a smile that enveloped her whole face, Mrs. Han warmly welcomed each of us. We saw a slide show on home life in Korea, learned still more about their child-rearing practices, and had our first taste of Korean food. We talked with families who had recently received their children, saw their arrival pictures, and learned what to expect during the first few days.

On June second Mary called to tell me that both the Eckhoff's and the Johnson's babies were arriving on Wednesday June fourth. She knew how upset we would be that our daughter would not be coming with them, and wanted to tell us herself. But Lynn Eckhoff had already called and asked if we would go with them to the Minneapolis-St. Paul Airport, since they had no family in Minnesota. Although Mary thought it would be terribly hard for us, we felt we couldn't refuse, since they would have no one to take those precious arrival pictures if we didn't go. All the way to the airport a little voice kept saying, "It's just a mistake, she's really on the plane with the other two babies. You'll see." Or sometimes it would say, "They're all teasing you, they just want it to be a *big* surprise when they bring her off the plane." My fantasy went so far as to include a well-meaning friend who would slip a fully stocked diaper bag in the car without my knowing, so that I would be prepared for her arrival. Although I knew these were totally unrealistic expectations, I couldn't seem to chase them from my mind. It was one of the few times the little voice was wrong.

While waiting for the plane, Jerry and I called the Immigration office. . .still no word about his fingerprints. As the plane landed, I could feel my throat tighten, and by the time the escorts brought the babies off the plane, I was crying so hard that Jerry had to take the pictures. My little fantasy had been just that.

We came back home with Dick and Lynn and baby Kimberly, and by the next day I was in a state bordering on panic. We had heard that student riots and civil unrest were causing the Korean government to consider halting the adoption processes "temporarily." We had to get our baby out of there before the doors were closed. We called our congressman's office to ask for assistance.

In the middle of my near hysteria, Lynn Eckhoff called. "Try calling this number in Washington. It's the office of a Special Assistant to Vice President Mondale. She helped us once, maybe she can help you guys. It sure can't hurt."

We called immediately, and after explaining the urgency of our situation, we were told to send all the information in a mail-gram (remember, this was pre-fax and E-mail days), and she would try to help us. We learned that another plane bringing babies was coming on June nineteenth, and that Mr. and Mrs. Tom Regan and Hyun Sook Han from Children's Home Society would be returning from Korea and acting as escorts for the children. My mind was made up. That was the flight our daughter would arrive on. We sent the mail-gram and waited.

Our friends tried to discourage me from planning on the flight on the nineteenth, but I wouldn't be swayed. Two days later, while I was at lunch, we received a call from the Office of the Special Assistant saying that the fingerprints had been approved and that the visa approval had been cabled to Korea. With one giant swoop, she had cut through all the red tape. Children's Home Society also sent a cable, and later that evening Jerry and I sent a personal cable to Tom Regan begging him to please bring our daughter home with him.

C.H.S.M was scheduled to receive the list of children arriving on the flight on the nineteenth on Monday the sixteenth of June. Monday afternoon. . . .**no list!** (How our friends and family put up with us during this time, I'll never know.) Tuesday morning the seventeenth at 10:00 A.M. I was at work preparing to deliver some plants to a local bank when I was called to the phone. It was C.H.S.M., and on their list of arrivals was the name Kim, Hee Young. My scream brought people running from all over the greenhouse, and an announcement over the public address system called Jerry up front to hear the news.

I left work at noon that day, and after calling everyone with the long-awaited news, went out to shop. I was in such a daze that it was probably dangerous for me to be on the highway. I left my purse at the bank and forgot what to get at the grocery store. I ended up being guided through the store by a friend who had followed me, and somehow managed to make it home with soy formula, a diaper bag and enough food to feed an army.

June nineteenth dawned sunny and warm, and since it was possible that she would be arriving on a flight at 3:30 P.M., we were ready to leave for Minneapolis at 10:00 A.M. We traveled in caravan. . .Jerry, Cindy and I in our car, Bruce (Jerry's brother), his wife Terri and daughter Brandie in another, and bringing up the rear, Dick, Lynn, and Kimberly Eckhoff and Dick's parents, who had arrived to see their new granddaughter.

The 3:30 flight from Seattle was filled, so the babies and their escorts, who were flying stand-by, were scheduled to arrive on a flight at 9:30 P.M. We shopped, ate dinner and went to the airport about 6 P.M. to wait. There we were met by representatives from C.H.S.M. and the flight aide who would bring our daughter off the plane. We had a few last papers to sign, one of which asked what name we had chosen for our child--the moment of decision. After selecting and discarding probably one hundred names over three months, Jerry and I agreed on the name "Meghann Hee Young Renning." We both felt strongly about keeping her Korean given name as part of her new name. Jerry's parents and sister Kim arrived, and soon our party numbered twenty-eight excited greeters.

The plane was late, (no surprise there) arriving at 10:40 P.M., and after the passengers and crew deplaned, the flight aides were allowed to board the plane to bring off the babies. Although there were nine infants on the plane, I saw only one, and I would have known her in any nursery filled with babies. Foolishly I expected her to recognize me too. I had carried her dog-eared picture in my shirt pocket, next to my heart, for three months. We learned that she had so thoroughly charmed the passengers on the plane that many of them followed her escort to see which lucky family she was coming home to. After an eighteen-hour plane flight, Meghann smiled and cooed and flirted all the while as cameras rolled and flash cubes popped, and when I handed her to Jerry, he looked down at the growing wet spot on his knee and realized that he was a daddy, and Meghann Hee Young Renning was finally home.

Chapter Three

Moving Right Along, Folks

WE STAYED AT the airport for about another hour while we fed Meghann two bottles and changed her clothes. We learned that because of the delay in Seattle, the escorts had run out of formula and diapers, so all the babies were really hungry. Finally our party began to break up, (by now it was nearly midnight), and Jerry, Cindy, Meghann and I prepared for the long drive back to Duluth. Friends tried to persuade us to stay overnight in Minneapolis, but we really wanted our daughter to wake up in her own bed her first morning with us. It was on that long drive home that I realized how grossly unprepared I was. It is a well-known fact to mothers everywhere that "What goes in, must come out." In those days I was a strong believer in cloth diapers (Ha!) and thought that three would be enough. (Wrong, foolish woman!) Forty miles from Duluth, with no diapers left, we heard Meghann's first cry.

We finally arrived home at 3:30 A.M. Cindy left and Jerry and I changed Meghann and tried to get the three of us settled down for some sleep. We had heard that Korean babies often sleep with family members, and though we disagreed with the practice on a permanent basis, we thought it might help her feel more comfortable her first night with us. Wrong again. In Korea, the families sleep on pallets on the floor, not on waterbeds. With a howl Meghann let us know in a hurry that this was totally unacceptable. I left Jerry to sleep alone while I took Meghann into the living room to rock her to sleep. The sky was just beginning to brighten at 5 A.M. when I carried her to her crib and crawled to bed.

6 A.M. Daylight. Sunrise. Our male canary, McCartney, who shared Meghann's room greeted, the morning with a song that to me sounded as loud as the noon whistle at the fire station. If she can sleep through this, she can sleep through anything, I thought. And she did, for another hour anyway. Jerry and I were bleary-eyed and barely conscious but Meghann was raring to go. Time to introduce her to our two dogs who, until that day, had been our only two "children"--Hurricane, a semi-paranoid German shepherd, and Chinook, a slightly overweight Norwegian elk-hound. Hurricane let us know right away that he disapproved of the situation by refusing to come out of the room to say "Hello." Chinook, on the other hand, took one look at Meghann and thought "human puppy" (she had had twenty-three of her own). Meghann soon won them both over, though, and both dogs learned that she usually had food on her face and hands and the floor around her, so close to Meghann was a good place to be.

Three days after Meghann's arrival, we celebrated her seven-month birthday. Actually, all three days had been a celebration, with friends arriving in shifts to meet the newest Renning. I learned in a hurry that in order to preserve my health and sanity, I'd better plan to sleep when she did, at least until her body cl became adjusted to Central Standard Time.

Jerry had taken a few days off work to get to know daughter, so together we took her to our family physi well-baby check up. He confirmed what we already for a slight cold, she was absolutely perfect. She and developmentally normal. Dr. Day advised us of feeding schedules and little hints like using boiled or bottled water to prepare her formula for a few weeks to avoid any intestinal upsets. "The human body builds up a tolerance for the bacteria common to the water in their area but can react violently to a sudden change in water supply," he explained. Must be Minnesota's version of Montezuma's revenge. Soy formula was recommended until she was at least one year old, since lactose intolerance is so common among Asian children.

The next few days our parents called almost daily for progress reports on their new granddaughter. And Jerry and I told everyone how she slept, what she ate, what her newest accomplishments were. To us, everything she did was exceptional, and those same wonderful people who tolerated us during the pre-arrival traumas now indulged us through the New Parent Euphoria.

Jerry and I had bought a house on two lakes shortly before Meghann's arrival, and we were to move in the weekend of the Fourth of July. So the two weeks after Meghann's arrival, I spent every moment of her nap-time packing boxes. Our little trailer, which had seemed so spacious only two years before, was now impossibly crowded. Friends volunteered to help, and on moving day we left our life in the trailer behind us and led another caravan, this time to our new home in the country. Five cars, two vans, and one step van load later, we were semi-settled into our new house. It would be weeks before all the boxes were ___ but on a beautiful summer day at the lake, who would ___ unpacking bathroom supplies?

___ ___tiful summer that we'd spent in ___ fishing was good, and by the ___ I were nearly as brown as ___ eriod that Meghann and I also ___ things to do than wash and fold ___ disposable age." Now, in my later, ___ ears, I apologize to the Earth for

I had arranged to have the entire summer off work, with the exception of a few outside watering jobs for the greenhouse that could be done on our day in town. So I mentioned we had learned that Korean mothers carry their children on their backs by wrapping them in a quilt and tying it around their waist. One of our first acquisitions was a Snuglii baby carrier. The carrier had an adjustable pouch inside, to accommodate infants to young toddlers, padded shoulder straps. It tied around the waist and could be worn on either the front or back. I would arrive at the bank to water their plants, accompanied by a baby, a watering can, and a Snuglii The first time we caused a few raised eyebrows, but soon the sight of me watering the plants with Meghann strapped to my back went almost unnoticed. Meghann was so comfortable in the baby carrier that Jerry would often mow the lawn with her asleep on his back.

New foods were no problem for Meghann. She adjusted to most everything right away and liked all the fruits and vegetables we gave her. The only problem we were having was her sleeping schedule. She woke at 5-6 A.M., napped for an hour before lunch and one or two hours after lunch, went to bed at 8:30 A.M., and woke crying sometime between midnight and 4 A.M. Sometimes she was hungry, sometimes not. We were advised by well meaning friends to let her "cry it out." And cry she did. The record was six hours. Non-stop. I would check on her every half-hour or so. No diaper change needed, not hungry, not sick, let her cry "they" said. We would find her, exhausted but standing up, still awake in her crib at 6 A.M. We soon realized that letting her cry it out was not the answer, and the lack of sleep was making a wreck out of me. So we went back to plan "A" and would comfort and console her until she went back to sleep. At least that way I could get a little sleep too. We had read that children who had been in foster homes often grieve for their foster mothers, and possibly have nightmares about being separated from their new families. We'll probably never know for sure what her problem was, but by the time I was ready to go back to work part-time at the greenhouse, Meghann was sleeping though the night, and, thank goodness, so was I.

Going back to work presented a new problem--finding the right baby-sitter. Like most new mothers, I was reluctant to leave Meghann with "just anybody," so we asked friends to recom-mend someone. We were very fortunate to find a wonderful family only one mile from the greenhouse. They loved Meghann right away, and she soon began to feel at home there. Though it was hard to leave her in the mornings, we knew she was well taken care of, and that the Wiitas loved her nearly as much as we did.

My mother had been unable to come out from North Carolina for Meghann's arrival or during the summer due to health problems, but by November she was ready to travel. She planned to come for Meghann's first birthday and Thanksgiving. I'd love to have a picture of my mother's face when she came off the airplane and saw her granddaughter for the first time. They became best friends right away, and back problems or not, if Meghann raised her arms to Grandma Betty, up she went.

Meghann's first birthday was a wonderful day. Our good friends the Eckhoffs and Johnsons brought their beautiful daughters. It was a reunion of the three families who had started the long adoption road together eight months before. Meghann's godmother, Aunt Cindy, arrived with the hit present of the day, a sled with side rails to prevent little children from falling off in the snow. On Thanksgiving day the same group of friends celebrated again, realizing just how much we had to be thankful for: new children, new friends, and family ties strengthened by sharing the planning and preparation for and arrival of our wonderful daughter. She was certainly living up to her name-- she was and is pretty like flowers and shares happiness to all. Meghann made my mother's trip complete by taking her first step and speaking her first sentence, something like MAMADADAMAMADADA, before Grandma Betty returned to North Carolina.

In Minnesota, adoptive parents can apply for the legal adoption of their children six months after placement of the child in their home. Our social worker, Mary Abbett, came to spend an evening with us and very unobtrusively evaluate our adjustment to each other. In the five months Meghann had been with us, it was hard to imagine what life had been like before she came. She had blended so well into our life style that we went everywhere together. She was a regular at area florist meetings and amazed everyone by being better behaved than some of the adults.

Late in November we contacted a lawyer and began the arrangements for legal adoption. On December 16, 1980, Meghann Hee Young Renning became our daughter for the second time, this time in the eyes of the law. Although nothing could ever change the fact that she was our daughter in our minds and hearts from the day we first saw her picture, it was a wonderful feeling to have that legal milestone behind us.

Christmas time brought Jerry's parents and grandparents to Duluth to celebrate. The gifts spilled from under our table-sized tree to the floor beneath. By the end of the day Meghann was an old hand at opening packages, although the boxes sometimes held her interest longer than the contents.

Since March we had been receiving the "News of Ours," the adoptive parents newsletter. It was always exciting to read the other parents stories, read of the new arrivals and see pictures of the children. In the March 1981 newsletter, there was an urgent request for medical supplies and soy formula to be collected and sent to the orphanages in Korea. For a long time Jerry and I had wanted to do something to say "thank you" to the people who had cared for our daughter and kept her healthy before she came home to us. What better way than to pass it on, so other children could arrive healthy and well fed? We began immediately to contact our family doctor and other clinics and hospitals in the area for extra drug company samples they might have. The response was incredible, and within a few days we had collected three large boxes of children's aspirin, decongestants, vitamins, formula, diaper rash medication, and disposable diapers. We delivered them to Children's Home Society and, when we returned, acquired a list of all the drug company representatives in Duluth. Children's Home Society's Family to Family program had brought us in touch with other adoptive parents in Duluth who wanted to help. And so on the first anniversary of receiving Meghann's picture, during a conversation with Pauline Campbell, another adoptive parent with two beautiful daughters, our first Orphan Benefit Dinner was born.

Chapter Four

Seoul Food

BARB DALLEY FROM Minneapolis called one afternoon. "How would you like to head up a Family to Family group in Duluth, Adair?"

"Who, me? Organize a group? I can't even organize my kitchen cupboards. What would I need to do?"

"Family to Family's objective is to share our experiences with new parents-to-be who are at some stage of the adoptive process," Barb explained. "We can answer questions about the various steps in the adoption, share information about our children after their arrival, and be a sympathetic local ear when they need someone to talk to," she continued.

"In other words, do for other families what Dorothy Rappel did for me--calm their fears, right?" I asked.

"Exactly," Barb said.

"Okay, sign me up."

Adoptive counselors or social workers we were not, just new friends. But who knows a road better than one who's traveled it?

As Pauline and I talked, we discovered a mutual desire to

help the Korean agency that had made it possible for us to have our beautiful, healthy daughters.

Eastern Child Welfare Society in Seoul, Korea, is the agency that many of our local Korean-born children have come from, through C.H.S.M. The relationship between the Minnesota agency and the Korean one is so close that sometimes they seem to be branch offices. Eastern Child Welfare believes that children fare better in a family environment, and toward that end they employ several hundred foster mothers to care for the children until their placement with their Forever Families. Their facilities in Seoul were very small and impossibly crowded and in 1981 plans were begun for the building of Eastern Child Welfare Center. We decided that the money raised at our Benefit Dinner would go to Korea to help ECW build their new facility, and thus help them to help more children such as ours.

We patterned our dinner after the one held annually by C.H.S.M. At our first group meeting in March 1981, we set the date for May seventeenth, a scant six weeks away, planned the menu, and began to establish the program for the evening. We contacted C.H.S.M. and made arrangements for some authentic Korean items to sell at a bazaar table. We also talked to Mrs. Han, the Korean social worker about speaking on Korean adoption. The Lakeview Covenant Church graciously allowed us the use of their fellowship hall for the dinner and also for two food preparation sessions. Local grocery stores donated ingredients or sold them to us at wholesale prices.

Pauline and I spent several afternoons with our children in tow contacting merchants and arranging for donated door prizes. The posters were printed and distributed and the <u>Duluth Herald and News Tribune</u> wrote a beautiful article about us, our dinner, and our children, complete with pictures, which appeared on Mother's Day. With the help of Young Ju Kim, a Korean student at the University of Minnesota, Duluth, Pauline taught the young girls a traditional Korean dance and the younger children learned to sing "Twinkle, Twinkle, Little Star" in Korean. We arranged for Korean costumes for all the children, and when they entered the darkened hall following the dinner, dressed in their beautiful clothes and carrying candles, even some of the fathers were crying.

Our Korean food was well received, although some of the more sensitive pallets declined second helpings of *kimchi*. The national dish in Korea, *kimchi* is made with napa cabbage, onions, green onions, garlic, carrots, ginger root, and plenty of cayenne pepper. It far surpasses any Mexican food I've ever eaten for heat generation. However, once you acquire a taste for it . . .

Our Benefit Dinner was a huge success. We filled the church hall with one hundred and fifty people, and when all the bills were paid, we had raised $1,000 to send to Eastern Child Welfare.

We and several other families celebrated another milestone with our children in May 1981: the U.S. Citizenship Naturalization ceremonies for our children. Following the ceremony, each child (and new adult citizens as well) was given a Certificate of Naturalization and a small U.S. flag. Meghann was so proud of hers that she took her nap that afternoon with it clutched in her tiny fist.

To celebrate the first anniversary of Meghann's arrival, we planned a barbecue and invited all of the people who had been at the airport. Friends began arriving on Friday night and camped out in our yard. We had a cake decorated with the Korean flag and the American Flag, and enough food to feed a small country. One family brought home movies they had taken at the airport the night Meghann arrived, complete with the now famous wet spot on Jerry's knee. We ate, played volleyball, fished, swam, and ate some more. But most of all, Jerry and I remembered and re-lived and thanked God for our beautiful daughter.

It was nearly a perfect summer. Our home on the lakes had a small one-room cabin across the road with its own dock. Cindy was between apartments and needed a place to live temporarily, so she moved into the cabin, bringing her Samoyed husky,

Kochia. Our friendship with Cindy, which began sharing dog-sitting duties, had grown since we had moved to Duluth in 1978, and I considered her to be the sister I never had. Meghann called her "Aunt Sam," and delighted in exploring the contents of her purse. Cindy, in turn, *loved* to tell Meghann to "fix her hair" just when her hands were coated to the wrist with spaghetti sauce. Because the cabin was not winterized, when the leaves began to turn, Cindy moved back into Duluth, to a small house almost across the street from the greenhouse where we all worked.

Throughout that first year, Meghann went everywhere with us. She provided the perfect opportunity for us to talk about adoption in general and foreign adoption in particular. Most conversations began with the question "Is she yours?" Answer: "Yes." Question: "No I mean is she *really* yours?" Answer: "Yes, she *really* is our daughter. If you mean did we give birth to her, the answer is no." This usually led to questions of where she was born, how long the adoption took, what we knew about her birth parents, and so forth. One of my favorite questions was, "When she's old enough, will you tell her she's adopted?" Come on, now, people. Take a look at us. Jerry, with his blondish hair and light green (I still say they're blue) eyes, and me with brown hair and green eyes. Of course we'll tell her she's adopted, and tell her in a way to make her proud of it. In answering the questions about her birth parents, we tried to emphasize the unselfishness and great love of the Korean mothers who arrange for the adoption of their children. Instead of questioning the "whys" of her decision, we marveled at the strength she had to have to carry it out. We would love to be able to let her know that she made the right choice, and that her daughter, now our daughter, is healthy, beautiful, and very, very bright.

We soon discovered that there was another language to be learned here, a "politically correct" way of talking about adoption. There were "adoptive parents," and "birth" or "biological parents," not "real parents" or "natural parents." Such statements implied that families created through adoption were less "real" than biological families or that adoption was not a natural way to create or add to a family. No one was intentionally cruel, but many were insensitive, speaking about Meghann as though she were deaf, couldn't understand, or was not even there. Many people even asked what language she would speak when she started to talk. She was only seven months old when she arrived; of course, she would speak English. But we intended to attempt to expose her to Korean language, food, and customs as much as possible. Some of the questions made the hackles rise up on the back of my neck, but I reminded myself that a few years ago I was in their position, knowing what I wanted to ask but not how to ask it.

Since adoption was and still is one of my favorite topics, I was always happy to find interested listeners. One frequently asked questions was "Do you plan to adopt again?" The answer was always an emphatic **"Yes!"** Although blessed with many cousins, I was an only child, and I was determined that Meghann would have at the very least one brother or sister.

Our name was still on the waiting list with the St. Louis County (Duluth) Social Services Adoption Department, and every January brought a letter with a lower list number. Although we were approaching a point on the list where we would be considered ready for a home study, deep in my heart I was sure that there was a little Korean boy or girl who was meant to be our second child.

Every two months the latest "News of Ours" magazine arrived, and all work stopped while I poured over the pages of new arrivals and Waiting Children. Several times one of these little faces would call out to me, but after contacting C.H.S.M., I would find out that the child had already been assigned with another family. It was hard to be terribly disappointed, since I knew all the children would have wonderful homes, and after all, we had Meghann. My conscious mind said, "Don't be so greedy." But my sub-conscious little voice said, "The time isn't right yet. And when it is, the child will be there and it will all work out." I had learned a long time ago to listen to that little voice, so I waited, as patiently as I could, and still ripped the "News of Ours" out of the postman's hand to look at the Waiting Children.

Jerry and I had many conversations about the next child to become part of our family, and the talk often turned to the Waiting Children. These children have a variety of challenges facing them, from mental or physical handicaps, developmental delays,and surgically correctable and noncorrectable problems. Some just have the misfortune of being "too old" or past the "prime" age for adoption. Some are truly children without a country. Korea, the land of their mothers, considers them outcasts. And in many cases, their fathers from other countries have left either not knowing of their existence or conveniently "forgetting." Regardless of their situation, they are all children of pain, and both the pain and hope shine through their pictures.

Both Jerry and I were open to the idea of adopting a special-needs child, and had often talked about the challenges we felt that we, as a family, could accept. We agreed that we certainly could handle a condition which could be treated by surgery or therapy. I had often told Jerry that I felt drawn to autistic children, and thought that our home would be a good environment to provide the stimulation an autistic child would need. But I my instincts told me that I would "know" the child immediately, the same way I had known Meghann, and the medical condition would be secondary.

That summer I was contacted by the Duluth International Folk Festival committee to see if our group would be interested in having a Korean booth at the festival. The festival had begun over thirty years earlier as a way to bring the international community of teachers and students at the University of Minnesota at Duluth together for a summer picnic, featuring the foods from all their home countries. It had begun as a garden party in a beautifully landscaped rose garden by Lake Superior, and had evolved into an event that attracted more than 10,000 people and had food and crafts representing more than thirty countries. We were honored and excited, and immediately began planning our booth, which we called "Seoul Food."

The Lakeview Covenant Church once again allowed us to use their kitchen to prepare one thousand *mahndu,* Korean-style, triangular egg rolls, two gallons of *kimchi,* one with killer cayenne and the other for the wimps, and an authentic Korean orange punch.

Even before the festival opened at 10 A.M., the pungent aroma of garlic wafted across the fog-shrouded park. No one would have *any* problem finding us. We were completely sold out by 1 P.M., just in time for a torrential downpour. We laughed as five of us crowded under the corner of a neighboring tent just as that corner collapsed, dumping gallons of icy rainwater down our backs. We laughed as we packed our sodden, donated McDonald's napkins, greasy cooking tools, and deep fryer into disintegrating cardboard boxes. We didn't care, we had made several hundred more dollars to help Eastern Child Welfare.

Chapter Five

Every Picture Tells a Story

BECAUSE OF WORSENING asthma, I quit working at Engwall's in May of 1982. I had developed severe allergies to the pesticides and herbicides used in the greenhouse, and my lungs were terribly scarred. The previous winter had brought temperatures not even reaching zero degrees in the middle of the day for a month. When I went outside, I felt as though I was breathing razor blades. Our family doctor had told me to either leave the greenhouse or give up breathing. I chose to continue breathing and spent the summer regaining my health and enjoying the time with Meghann. In the middle of October, we were making plans for our second Orphan Benefit Dinner, and also for a televised special for National Adoption Week. I had contacted the OURS Headquarters in Minneapolis for assistance in preparing for the TV special, and they obliged by sending a generous supply of OURS balloons, pamphlets, and a stack of back issues of their magazine. "This is our fifteenth anniversary and we have a special issue with a glossy white cover, I'll send you extra copies of it," the OURS volunteer told me. Since our copy of the newest issue had not arrived yet, I was especially excited to get this package. In this issue, as in all others, there were pictures of the "Children Who Wait"--adorable children all, and certainly enough to tug at the heart of anyone with the sensitivity of an ant, but once again our child was not there.

Continuing on through the magazine, I came to an article titled "The Children of PACT Need You." PACT is an acronym for Partners Aiding Children Today, a nonprofit organization in Minneapolis. Through a sponsorship program of individual children by American, Canadian, Mexican, and Korean families, groups, and individuals, a great many children in Korea and India have been given a brighter future. Through their monthly donations, PACT sponsors provide for children whose prognosis is questionable. In many cases time and expert care is needed to determine the child's condition. If the child is an orphan, after enough information is gathered about his or her condition, he may be referred to the Waiting Child Program. Much of the formula and medical supplies and diapers we had gathered the past two years had gone to help the PACT children.

For me, no page of the <u>News of Ours</u> goes unread, at least twice, so I read on. The first child pictured was a three-year-old little boy with slow behavioral development. PACT was asking for sponsors to help give him a future. He had a face like an elf and looked like thirty pounds of energy on wheels. A fifteen-month-old, a twelve-month-old, and a five-year-old completed the page. All the children were appealing, and all in need of the time and care that PACT sponsorship could provide for them. I began toying with the idea of doing a fundraiser for PACT. Turn the page . . . Child Number Five. She was described as a beautiful eighteen-month-old girl with Hirschprung's disease, a failure of the nerve endings at the lower end of the colon to develop properly. A stoma (artificial anus) had been created shortly after birth to eliminate the possibility of total intestinal blockage. Her emotional development was of more concern to Teri Bacall, the social worker, than her physical problems.

The paragraph went on to say that, owing to her special needs, she had been placed in a "baby home" after her surgery until a foster mother could be found for her. She had not adjusted well to the orphanage and Teri was asking for sponsors to support her to see if time and the stimulation of a loving foster home would help her to adjust.

Jerry was at work and Meghann was napping, so I just sat there for a few minutes and reread the paragraph and stared at the picture. What can you tell from a rather dark newspaper copy of a wallet-sized black and white picture? *Volumes!* Squarish face with a prominent forehead, large almond eyes. Short dark hair combed to one side. She was looking at the person holding her and her mouth was slightly open. There was a slight sparkle in the sure-to-be black eyes. My heart was pounding--it was happening again--this was our child! I knew it as surely as I had known that Meghann was our daughter two-and-a-half years before. I had no doubts about this little girl, only my ability to convince everyone that I still had both oars in the water. But wait, there was another hurdle to overcome first, even before the money. PACT children needed sponsors first, then parents. She wasn't (I thought) even available for adoption yet. Well, that was okay. That would give us time to overcome obstacle No.2--*money*. At this point I wasn't even worried about convincing Jerry--*of course* he'd know that she was the one, and anyway, he's been through enough of my "intuitions" to know that *I* knew. I looked at the clock and realized that I had been staring at the picture for over an hour. It was time to get to work. Teri Bacall, who had written the article and had seen the child face to face was a social worker at C.H.S.M. (Hooray! One stroke for our team.) The first step, as the smaller, logical side of my mind took over, was to call C.H.S.M., talk to Teri, and find out everything I could about sponsoring her. Teri, as it turned out, was in Korea at the time, and one of the children she would be checking on was "our" little girl. I spoke to Bobbie Wiggins, who told me that Teri would be back in ten days (*ten days?*) I began machine-gun-firing questions at Bobbie. "Can we send clothes or toys? How about special colostomy supplies?" I knew next to nothing about colostomies, except that my dad had had an ileostomy before he died, so I figured it must be similar. "Can we earmark some of the formula we send to go to her? Are sponsors ever allowed to adopt the children they sponsor? Hey, wait a minute, is she even going to be *available* for adoption? Is there any way I could possibly get a copy of all available information on her?"

When I slowed down long enough to take a breath, Bobbie jumped in. "First of all, Adair, the name in the magazine is wrong," she said. "Her correct name is Oh, Kyung Hee and she was born on April 4, 1981. She was a C-section baby and her mother died later that month because of complications after the baby was born. Her father was a fisherman with two sons," she continued. Sons get top billing in Korea, because they carry on the family name. "The two brothers were sent to live with relatives after their mother died, but the father couldn't take care of a child with all of Kyung Hee's health problems, so he left her at the hospital and arranged for her adoption through Social Welfare Service." She had been ill for most of the last eighteen months, Bobbie said, suffering from a variety of skin problems, eye infections, diarrhea,and measles. She was described as very fussy, with slow physical and behavioral development. At eighteen months old, a time when most toddlers are into everything, learning to talk, and generally a bundle of live wires, Kyung Hee was only beginning to roll over onto her stomach, could not sit up without support, much less walk or crawl, and did not play with toys with her hands. It was felt, however, by the Korean social worker that once she had the surgery to reverse the colostomy, her health and development would improve rapidly. Teri's notes described Kyung Hee as "very irritable, with a possibility of retardation." Bobbie suggested that I call back in about two weeks and talk to Teri after her return from Korea. She would have more current information about Kyung Hee's progress since the last report.

All afternoon my mind raced . . . I was convinced that there was absolutely nothing wrong with that child that first her surgery, and then a loving family, complete with mom, dad, sister, two dogs, and an assortment of birds and fish, plus good food, couldn't cure. I began to make a mental list of the things we could send her . . . toys, clothes, pictures of us, a long letter which could be translated and read to her. I would figure out a way to come up with the sponsorship money for at least a couple of months.

Oops, the afternoon had slipped away, and it was almost time for Jerry to come home. Before starting dinner, I very carefully opened all six copies of the new News of Ours to the page with Kyung Hee's picture on it and left them in strategic spots around the house: the kitchen table, beside Jerry's chair in the living room, in the bathroom, on the bedside table. Our cabin was very small, so there was a picture in every room. By the time he tripped over the third one, he realized what was going on. I was afraid to say anything to Meghann yet, because she wanted a little sister so badly.

Jerry and I talked, and for a while at least, his stability prevailed. "Before we can even think about going any further," he said, "you have to check out our insurance policy to see if all this would be covered. It sounds like she'll need surgery plus therapy, and who knows what else." I agreed, and planned to call the insurance company the next day, *just in case*. Jerry has always been the more logical and level-headed partner in our marriage, while I operate best on a combination of intuition, blind faith, and optimism. Somehow we balance each other out. The next day I called our insurance company and was assured that any child we adopted would be covered the same as a birth child, including any necessary surgery. Whew! Another hurdle crossed. Then I called our doctor, who gave me the name of a local surgeon who could possibly perform the surgery to reverse Kyung Hee's colostomy. Before I called him, however, Dr. Day felt that we should have all available information on her. Okay, I can handle that. There was certainly enough stuff to keep me busy in the meantime.

We were still preparing for the taping of the National Adoption Week TV Special on November sixth, and my mother was due to arrive from North Carolina on November sixteenth. Knowing there was nothing else I could do until Teri returned from Korea, I threw myself in to preparations for the TV show. Pauline and I contacted the families to be present, prepared the food, and planned what points we wanted covered in the interview. The taping was held at Dorothy Rappel's house. Dorothy, who was preparing for the arrival of her second child, a two-month-old infant from India could well understand my anxiety. The dining room was decorated with a beautiful display of Korean clothing, artifacts, Christmas tree ornaments, food, etc., and around it all, information about adoption, the OURS Organization, and, of course, the latest copy of <u>News of OURS</u> with several copies discretely opened to page forty-three, Child Number Five.

The taping went smoothly, and the next few days were spent making Christmas gifts, housecleaning, getting ready for Grandma Betty, and thinking about Oh, Kyung Hee.

My mother arrived on November sixteenth and Teri was due back from Korea on November nineteenth. I had one day to let her settle into our home and two days to break the news to her. By this time I was convinced that nothing short of a national disaster could prevent us from adopting this child (who was not yet available for adoption). Mother took the news very well, that is, she didn't scream, or cry or faint. She just looked at me as though I'd lost the last remaining shred of sanity I'd left home with. We went through all the arguments: where would we get the money (I didn't know yet, but somehow we would), who would pay for the surgery (our insurance), what if she was retarded (she wasn't), what if the surgery didn't correct her problem (it would). By the end of the two days my mother was a little *less* sure that I was crazy and a little *more* attached to the picture of Kyung Hee. More than once I've wondered at the source of this blind optimism. I know now that when my heart tells me that something is right and true, my sensible side takes a back seat and lets my heart drive. It's always led me to the right place.

November 22, 1982. Meghann's third birthday. Her party was planned for Thanksgiving day, so not much was going on that Monday. Teri had returned from Korea but was not yet at the agency. However, she had given Bobbie an update on Kyung Hee's condition. "Teri found a wonderful foster home for her, Adair," Bobbie said. "They have four children of their own and the youngest is a six-year-old girl who absolutely adores Kyung Hee. She's been there for a month and a half, and Teri can't believe the progress she's made," she exclaimed. "She's not crawling yet, but she can stand up if someone holds her. She smiles a lot and her skin has cleared up and she has actually become chubby. Teri said that the whole time she was there Kyung Hee was babbling away to her foster mother."

All of this was quite a change from the nearly autistic child described in the July report. Teri's main concern at that point was Kyung Hee's inability to play with toys with her hands. Despite the fact that she could wave bye-bye, shake hands, and clap, she would deliberately drop or throw down objects and then push them along with her index finger, either unable or unwilling to pick them up. This was seen as a possible neurological problem in need of assessment. Although she still displayed some self-stimulation tendencies, such as waving her fingers in front of her eyes, she was happily responding to the foster family and making rapid gains in development--all of which confirmed my theory that all she needed was love and good food and she'd be okay.

"Now for the big news, Adair," Bobbie continued. "Teri's ready to place her with a family who can accept all her health problems and developmental delays. In other words, you can skip the sponsorship square and go straight to applying to adopt her." I almost dropped the phone. Before I could say anything, she said, "Mary Abbett is coming to Duluth on Wednesday on other C.H.S.M. business. She'll have all the information we have so far on Kyung Hee plus a bunch of pictures. Will you be around to talk to her or are you going out of town for Thanksgiving?"

After hastily assuring her that we would indeed be around and would welcome a visit from Mary on Wednesday, I hung up the phone in a daze. It was one thing to think about coming up with the adoption fees in two or three months, but I didn't have a clue how we could raise that kind of money right now. We lived from pay check until the day before pay check as it was. But before the cold, hard kernel of panic could take root in my heart, a beautiful sense of calm settled peacefully in its place. If all this was meant to be, our having a beautiful new daughter, Meghann having a little sister, and Kyung Hee, finally, having a family to call her own, then somehow the money part would work out. Come on, Mary!

Mary had always told us that if we heard she was coming by for a visit, she'd rather we bake cookies than clean the house, but I cleaned like a fiend (under the blanket excuse of Thanksgiving and Meghann's birthday party) and hoped I'd have time to bake later. Mary arrived in time for lunch and came with a sheaf of papers related to reapplying for adoption, a wealth of information about Kyung Hee, and about twelve color photos Teri had taken in July. While Mary and Grandma Betty visited and Meghann entertained, I blocked out everything else and devoured the pictures and pages. There were several pictures of the stoma (the artificial anus), which looked like an open red wound. The thing that struck me the hardest was the extreme thinness of her arms and legs. They reminded me of the pictures of Third World children who are severely malnourished. But the trunk of her body seemed plump, so her problem could be lack of muscle development, I reasoned. As sick as she'd been most of her life, it's doubtful if she had gotten much exercise. There was not one picture of a smiling Kyung Hee. In most pictures taken at the orphanage, she was expressionless or crying, and in several she reminded me of a deer who had been frightened by a car's headlights. There was only one picture where she looked the way Meghann had looked in a picture the flight aide had taken on the airplane--asleep on her back, head turned to the side, arms thrown over her head. There were two wallet-sized black and white photos of Kyung Hee with her foster mother. Kyung Hee's head had been shaved in an attempt to cure the continuous boils and skin disease she had suffered from for several months. I read the information, looked at the pictures, and cried. Jerry and I had agreed that there was no way that we could proceed with the adoption unless we could arrange the necessary adoption costs prior to signing the placement agreement. Mary was willing to allow us two weeks to figure out how we were going to come up with the money. She left the pictures and all the information with us and we sent her back to St. Paul with her car loaded with medical supplies we had collected to send to Korea.

As I went through the routines of the day, preparing meals and getting ready for Thanksgiving, all I could think about was Kyung Hee in Korea, and how we were ever going to be able to afford the adoption fees, then around $3,000. It had been barely two weeks since we'd first seen her picture and her place had already been established in our lives. For the past five or six months we had been telling Meghann "The Story of Kim, Hee Young," all about how she had come to be our daughter, as a bedtime story. It occurred to me that I could write the story and submit it to a magazine for publication and maybe raise some of the adoption fees. I wrote the first chapter, up to where we received Meghann's picture, and began making copies to send to various magazines. I talked to everyone I knew about Kyung Hee. One of Dorothy's housemates knew an editor at Harcourt, Brace, Jovanovich in Duluth, and after an excited phone call, I had arranged to meet him to discuss my story. Although it was doubtful that I would find a publisher for the story in time to meet the money deadline, his encouragement was the spark I needed to continue writing. As we learned more about Kyung Hee, I realized that the story would not be complete until her chapters had been added. Perhaps the finished work would show other families the joys to be found in adoption.

We celebrated Thanksgiving and Meghann's birthday with several family friends and their children and brainstormed with them to come up with money-making schemes.

The Monday after Thanksgiving I called a dear friend who owned a flower shop in Hayward, Wisconsin. I had a hunch that she might know someone who could help us. Jerry and I had known Verna for several years, and she had followed Meghann from first picture to new arrival. Verna had even given Meghann a *third* first birthday party at her store Wisconsin. She did, in fact, have a good friend in Minneapolis who had connections with several publishing companies. People have asked me how I had the nerve to call all these people I didn't know and ask for their help. The answer was simple: the life and future of our child was at stake, and there's nothing I wouldn't have done to bring her home.

Verna's friend Gary was a warm and caring person, and our plight must have found a spot in his heart. He encouraged me to send a copy of my story along with pictures and all available information on Kyung Hee and he would see what he could do to help. We didn't think of ourselves as being particularly special for wanting to adopt Kyung Hee, but apparently other people were beginning to.

My mother was still with us, and I worried about how little time I spent actually enjoying her visit. All of my waking time and energy was spent trying to make money grow on trees. The tension was incredible and it took its toll on all of us. We were all grateful for her patience and stabilizing influence during those agonizing two weeks of limbo. As guilty as I felt for not spending more time with her, I still realized how truly wonderful it was to have my mother be a part of this special period in our lives.

My optimism (some called it wishful thinking) knew no bounds. I entered contests and sweepstakes, and wrote to a television show which specialized in granting wishes. I'm not sure exactly when it happened, but at some point, a faith I'd been ignoring took over and made me realize that if Kyung Hee was truly meant to be our daughter, as I believed, then nothing and no one could prevent it. Conversely, if it was *not* meant to be, then there was absolutely nothing we could do to change that fact. But nothing could stop me from trying everything I could think of.

The two-week time limit, which was in Kyung Hee's best interest, was rapidly coming to an end, and we were not one dollar closer to our goal. We understood only too well how important it was to find a family for Kyung Hee, get her here, and get her on the road to recovery. We also knew that we were not the only family to call the agency about her, and those others were "on hold" until we had reached a decision. It was ridiculous to think that we were the only ones who could love her, but there were no doubts in my mind that she belonged with us.

While agonizing over our dilemma, another dream was born. In a time when there were staggering numbers of children throughout the world in need of homes and families to love them, and families who wanted to start or increase their families through adoption, it seemed inhuman to me that the only things standing between them was *money*!

How wonderful it would be to have a self-perpetuating fund for families who had already been accepted by an agency for the placement of a child, but who needed help with the initial adoption fees. Very few insurance companies include adoption expenses in their benefit package; therefore, the entire expense must be borne by the parents. To me, it seemed slightly discriminatory against couples who are unable to or decide not to have biological children. Many people who would be wonderful parents and could easily take care of the child after its arrival are discouraged by the cost of adopting. This is not to say that the fees are not justified in terms of the cost of caring for the children until placement, possible medical expenses, airfare to bring the children home, and agency costs, etc. But for many families, the expenditure would sap a lot of strength from the family reserves. In 1983, the cost was $3,000-$5,000; today it can be as high as $20,000. Insurance companies don't require reimbursement for maternity expenses. Why not a foundation that would help cover adoption expenses, until more insurance companies get the idea? All I could see was that with the help of some wealthy people with extra dollars, children would be taken out of orphanages and foster homes and placed with Forever Families. I even called my bank to find out how much money it would take to earn $5,000 in interest a year. That way we could either help one or two families a lot or give five families a thousand dollars each.

The weekend of December fourth and fifth was very nearly unbearable. My heart stopped every time the telephone rang. Gary, our new friend with publishing connections, had promised he'd call by Sunday evening to let us know if he'd had any luck with my story or if he had any ideas for raising the adoption fees. In an attempt to take my mind off the telephone, I began writing our annual Christmas card letter, ending it by asking our friends and family to pray for a miracle to allow us to adopt Kyung Hee.

A few moments later Gary called. With a mixture of hope and disbelief, Jerry, Mom, Cindy, and Meghann gathered around the room to listen to my side of the conversation.

"I've spent most of the afternoon with some friends who sympathize with your situation," Gary said. "They want to help you continue with your plans to adopt Kyung Hee. They'll take care of the financial arrangements in the form of a long-term, no- interest loan, which you will repay directly to Children's Home Society. Can you afford to pay fifty dollars a month?" he asked.

I was temporarily speechless . . . but only temporarily. "Who are these people? And what's the catch? This isn't a joke, is it, because if it is, Gary, even though I've never met you, I'll strangle you."

"It's definitely not a joke," Gary replied. "And the only catch is that they want to remain anonymous."

"Anonymous? They can't do that! I have to call and thank them. They don't know what they've done. We've never met them, or you for that matter, and they've just knocked down the single largest barrier to our adopting Kyung Hee."

"That was the whole idea," Gary said, but he was adamant. No amount of wheedling or bribery with cakes could get him to reveal the names. I can't begin to describe how humble I felt at that moment. By providing us with the financial means to adopt Kyung Hee, they were adding strength to our belief that ours was the family where she belonged. The only way we could ever thank them (besides paying them back, of course) was by proving them right in their assessment of us as a family. On Monday morning I called Mary to make an appointment for December fourteenth to sign the placement agreement and start in motion the wheels that would bring our daughter home.

On Tuesday my mother returned to North Carolina, taking with her every scrap of information we had about Kyung Hee, in order to question doctors there about her condition and possible treatment. During her two week stay with us, she had become as committed to this special child as Jerry and I were.

For the next week, in addition to making plans for our second Benefit Dinner, I called pediatricians, surgeons, and rehabilitation centers in order to learn as much as I could about Kyung Hee's various challenges. After a conversation with our family doctor, I called a local surgeon who had performed the type of surgery our daughter would need. If the translations of the medical records were accurate, she had Hirschprung's disease, and two operations would be needed to correct the condition. The first surgery would eliminate the portion of large intestine with no nerve endings, connecting healthy tissue to the anus. After approximately a six-week recovery period, during which time the colostomy would still be functioning, a second operation would be performed to re-connect the upper two portions of the large intestine and close the stoma that had been created when she was thirteen days old. He explained that the reason for the six-week wait between surgeries was to allow the first surgery to heal as much as possible before allowing food to pass through the bowel. The prognosis was excellent, with an

85-90% success rate. The surgeon asked to see Kyung Hee's medical records, and offered to have a Korean colleague translate one page still in Korean characters, in case it held important information. Once again, total strangers were going out of their way to help us.

We spoke with both physical and occupational therapists in an attempt to unravel the mysteries of Kyung Hee's inability to grasp objects. In all of the photographs her hands appeared normal, that is, not deformed. It was the opinion of the therapists that many of her problems stemmed from lack of stimulation. But until she was here, no one could accurately evaluate her condition. The translations were precariously uncertain and too much was left unsaid. Still, that wonderful little voice inside said, "Just get her *home,* and she'll be just fine."

Two of the many friends who had agonized with us in our attempts to raise adoption fees were Brad and Linda Habberstad. As parents of a Korean-born daughter, Brad and Linda understood our intense feelings about Kyung Hee. During a church youth group meeting one evening, the students in Linda's class were trying to decide what to do with the money raised by their "Christmas Card Angel." Every year, instead of sending cards to every member of the congregation, church members sent a card to the church, often with a donation inside to be used by the youth group. This year, after Linda told the group about Kyung Hee, they voted to use the money to help Jerry and me with our adoption fees. Once again the picture and story of a child in need had reached out and touched the lives of people thousands of miles away.

On December fourteenth, Jerry, Meghann, and I left for St. Paul for our appointment with Mary Abbett and Teri Bacall. Jerry and I fully expected to be quizzed, since the placing of a special-needs child is not a matter to be taken lightly. The last thing that child needs is a family that doesn't work out. Mary and Teri wanted to be sure that we had adequate insurance coverage to handle the surgery and possible physical and occupational therapy. Another concern was that we might be minimizing the seriousness of Kyung Hee's condition. "Listen, Mary, if I went through life *maximizing* every situation or event, I'd never be able to cross the street without shaking in my shoes," Jerry assured them. We tried to impress upon them the fact that although we were sure that with time and love she would be okay, we were prepared to deal with any problems if we were wrong, and love her just the same. The one thing we were not prepared for, however, was having to decide where Kyung Hee would have her surgery. We had assumed that it would be done here. After signing the placement agreement, as her parents, we were given the choice of having the surgery performed in Korea, or waiting until she was home with us to have the colostomy reversed.

Teri was full of extra information about Kyung Hee that had not been included in the referral sheets--personal observations and opinions. "She's really becoming a beautiful child," Teri said. "And she's made incredible progress in all areas except for the use of her hands." This was a primary concern for Teri, who mentioned again the possibility of neurological problems. My friendly little voice kept saying, "If a child has no mother's finger to cling to, then how can she learn to hold on?" We asked for some time to question the doctors and surgeons we had consulted before making a decision concerning the surgery. Neither Jerry nor I felt qualified to make that decision based upon our limited knowledge, and we felt too emotionally close to the situation to be objective. We left the agency promising to contact them as soon as possible.

Chapter Six

Playing the Waiting Game

ON DECEMBER 15, 1983, ten days before Christmas, we were the parents of a new daughter. Jerry and I felt profoundly grateful and Meghann was beside herself with excitement.. She had already begun to divide her toys and clothes into things she thought Kyung Hee could use or wear. The mail brought four new color pictures that Teri had taken during her trip to Korea in November. The changes were remarkable. Kyung Hee's cheeks were rosy, her eyes sparkled, and there was even a picture of a her smiling. In all four pictures, the foster mother's arm could be seen close by, within touching distance of the shy little girl. We immediately made copies of the best picture to share with Jerry's parents and grandparents during Christmas. It would be their first opportunity to hear firsthand the story of our newest daughter. Jerry's parents were enthusiastic about their new granddaughter, and encouraged us in our commitment to her. If they had any misgivings about her physical or emotional condition, they were careful not to overemphasize them.

We put together a box of Christmas toys and gifts to send to

Kyung Hee, and included pictures of us, her grandparents, and the room that she would share with Meghann. Teri promised to send the package with the next person returning to Korea. Our friend, Barb Dalley, another adoptive parent from Minneapolis, had recently returned from a trip to Korea. Because of all of her volunteer work for Children's Home Society and Eastern Child Welfare, she had been invited to tour the Korean agency, several orphanages, and foster homes. She shared traditional Korean meals with foster families and agency officials, toured Seoul and several other cities, and did her Christmas shopping as well.

The orphanage visits were the hardest because she wanted to bring all of the children home with her. All of her preexisting orphanage images were shattered. "I always thought the children would be shy, sad-eyed, shabbily dressed little things," she said. "But these kids were bright-eyed, happy, clean, smiling, and climbed all over me. The orphanages were immaculate, and no matter how tiny or sparsely furnished the foster homes were, they were clean, warm, and bright. On the walls at the orphanages were bulletin boards with pictures of the children who had already gone on to new families. Every child's wish was to have their picture put up there."

On the return trip, Barb and the other C.H.S.M. representatives had the privilege of escorting babies to their anxiously waiting families in Minnesota.

But as clean and neatly dressed and well fed as the children were, there were few toys. "There were probably sixty children at one orphanage we went to," Barb commented. "They were all ages, from tiny babies to young school-aged kids, but there was only a small kitchen cabinet's worth of toys to go around. Everything was shared. None of the kids had one toy to call their own."

Later that evening, as I was relating the story of Barb's trip to Jerry and Meghann and Jerry, Meghann stopped me at the toy part. "We can send them some of mine, Mommy," she said. "I've got lots I'm too old for (three years old), and you know I'm *real* careful, so they're not scratched or broken." As the tears threatened to spill over, I quickly faked a sneeze to have an excuse to grab a Kleenex.

"But honey, they don't have enough room to keep lots of toys."

"So let's send really little toys, Mommy." She ran off to her room and came back with a film canister, which she held up proudly. "How 'bout this, Mommy? It's **real** small." Meghann had carried the film canister for months, sometimes empty, sometimes with stickers or gum or some other tiny item inside. "You can send it like we send the medicines and diapers," she continued. How could I argue with three-year-old logic like that?

All through dinner the wheels in my brain were turning. Since I'm seldom quiet unless I'm sick, mad, or thinking, Jerry was immediately suspicious. "All right, what are you cooking up now? I know that look and, no, we can't afford to buy toys for all the children in the orphanage. Any extra will have to go toward adoption costs."

"I know we can't buy anything, but what if I could get stuff donated?" I asked.

"But you're still dealing with the space problem, and it would too expensive to ship."

"You heard Meghann. It would have to be *real* little," I replied, as I held up the film canister.

"You're going to send them empty film canisters?"

"No, Dad, we'll put little stuff in them," Meghann chimed in. She ran to her treasure chest and returned clutching a tiny, round, red pin she had gotten at a local jewelry store. The inscription on the pin was *I am loved.* It was the store's trademark advertisement. It fit in the canister perfectly. Then she stuffed in a balloon from our bank.

"How about a piece of sugarless gum?" Jerry asked excitedly, catching on. We all began thinking small.

The next day I called a photo processing store in Duluth. They had a huge box of canisters they were going to throw out, and they were mine for the taking. The jewelry store was happy to donate five hundred of their pins, and the bank gave several gross of balloons. (Free advertisement in Seoul, Korea). I called a novelty gag and gift dealer who, when I told him what we were trying to do, agreed to donate some things and let me buy others at wholesale prices. Meghann and I went that afternoon and picked out tiny erasers shaped like hearts and animals, high bounce super balls, and tiny matchbook-type cars. Then we got the idea to have both boys' and girls' canisters, with *boy* and *girl* written in Korean on the top of the canister. Each container had an *I am loved* pin, a piece of Trident Sugarless gum, a balloon, an eraser and several stickers. The boy's canister had a high bounce ball or a toy car and the girl's had lengths of hair ribbon, donated by Minnesota Fabrics, or small barrettes. Meghann and I spent several evenings assembling our tiny gifts.

Children's Home Society agreed to send as many of the canister as would fit in the escorts' luggage on the next trip to Korea, which would be before Christmas. It may have been a small thing, but we would fill as many canisters as we could, so that some of the children could have at least one thing of their own.

Before making a decision concerning Kyung Hee's surgery, Jerry and I spoke with our family doctor, the surgeon here, and other assorted pediatricians and psychologists. We had been assured by both Teri and Mary that Kyung Hee's foster mother would stay with her in the hospital. We spoke with a Korean neo-natologist in Duluth who was familiar with both hospitals where Kyung Hee had been treated previously. Jerry and I both felt that it would be far less traumatic for her to have the surgery completed in Korea, among familiar people, and recover in the now familiar surroundings of her foster home. Although we knew of no physical reason to hurry the surgery, we felt that she could not begin to make gains in other areas until her health was restored. Praying that we were making the right decision for our child, Jerry and I wrote Mary and asked that the surgery be performed in Korea, provided that it would be done immediately, in order to allow Kyung Hee maximum recovery time before coming home in March or April. By this time I had already decided that she would be home in time to celebrate her second birthday, April fourth, with her new family.

Everything had been going along so smoothly so far that it was time for a snag, just to keep us on our toes. It came, in the form of a letter from our insurance company advising us that Kyung Hee would not be covered by our policy until she had been legally adopted. In Minnesota, a child cannot be legally adopted until at least three months after placement. This was exactly the opposite of an earlier letter they had sent to us stating that she would be covered from the day she arrived. The letter went on to state that any surgery to reverse the colostomy would be covered only after she had passed ninety treatment-free days for that condition, or until she had been covered by the plan for one year. Even though we had requested that the surgery be done in Korea, there was always the possibility that for some reason it would not be, and if that were the case, it was possible that she would have to wait a year before the reversal could be performed. According to this letter, she would not have medical coverage for any other illness or accident until she legally became our child. The claims agent reasoned that we could bring *just anyone* into our house and try to claim them as a dependent in order to obtain insurance coverage under our group policy. *How absurd!*

After recovering from my hysteria, I called Mary to advise her of this new development. C.H.S.M. requires a letter from the adoptive parents' insurance carrier guaranteeing dependant status effective with the arrival of the child. I was absolutely terrified that she would say that this letter would mean that we couldn't adopt Kyung Hee. What she did say was, "Rubbish!" And then wrote a letter to the insurance company telling them, in effect, the same thing. In the letter she clarified our legal and financial responsibility toward Kyung Hee, effective upon her arrival. "It is discriminatory," she said, "to make a distinction between entering a family through birth or adoption." She further assured them that it was quite routine for insurance companies to cover children placed in families for the purpose of adoption from the day of placement. Mary didn't seem the least bit upset, and assured me that everything would be fine. Although she succeeded in calming me, at least temporarily, neither of us knew that this was the first of several white-knuckle days we would experience before our baby was finally home.

Early in January, Jerry and I received a medical update and four more pictures of Kyung Hee that had been taken in December. All of the information was positive. She was gaining strength and her skin conditions had completely cleared up. According to the Korean social workers' statement, since coming to the foster home, she was bright and responsive, and no longer had a "feeble, vacant" expression. She was able to move around in a walker and in general had lost many of the autistic tendencies she had displayed in the orphanage. What a testament to the power of *love!* She was obviously adored by her foster family. Kyung Hee was beginning to blossom and thrive under the loving care of this wonderful family. Several of the pictures showed Kyung Hee in the walker, playing with toys at her feet, and in one picture, her foster mother, Mrs. Choi, was kneeling beside her. I felt I had to write a letter to this special woman who had, in all probability, saved our child's life by giving her a home and love. I wrote, telling her everything I could think of about the three of us, our animals, our extended families, how we spent our spare time, anything I could think of that would make her feel more comfortable about the family Kyung Hee was coming home to. We were sure that she would be affected by the loss of this child to whom she had given so much of herself. We felt that perhaps knowing a little about us would help to make the parting easier. Since we had been told that correspondence between foster parents and adoptive parents is not customary, we were quite surprised to receive a warm and wonderful reply early in February. She reassured us that she would take good care of our daughter until she came home to us.

She also said that her youngest daughter, who was Kyung Hee's best friend, would be very sad when she left.

While continuing to prepare for the arrival of our daughter, we were also working on finalizing plans for our benefit dinner. We were still attempting to raise some of the adoption fees in advance, even though the generosity of our unknown friends had taken the pressure off for a while. For some time, close friends had been encouraging us to do the benefit dinner, at least in part, for our own adoption. While we would not hesitate to do a fund-raising effort to help someone else adopt, somehow it seemed wrong to be the beneficiaries ourselves. However, after being approached by several other friends with the same idea, we slowly began to change our minds. As friends and I brainstormed one evening, we decided to make ours the test case to see if the plan would work. If it did, then we would make ourselves available to organize another event for the next family in need of help with adoptions fees.

In our case, we wanted to divide the money three ways, giving one third to PACT, without whose help Kyung Hee's survival would have been questionable, and one third to C.H.S.M. After receiving assurances of help from Pauline, Dorothy, Cindy, and Linda, I called the Radisson to approve the dinner menu. The dinner date was set for March 19, 1983, in the Great Hall of the Radisson Hotel. The posters were taken to the printer and things appeared to be rolling along rather smoothly again. The group of families working on the benefit dinner grew with the addition of Patsy and Dick Wyler, who had recently adopted a six-month-old boy from Korea. The Wylers wholeheartedly supported the idea of a benefit dinner that would help other families adopt, and Patsy pitched in with the planning.

Our fingerprints and visa approval were due at the Immigration Office by January twenty-fifth, a Friday. I "graciously" allowed them several days before I called them. In view of our previous problems with fingerprints, I planned to be more aggressive earlier, and not allow Kyung Hee to be held up by technicalities on this end. By Monday morning, January twenty-eighth I could wait no longer. Four phone calls finally produced the frustrating news that Jerry's fingerprints had been returned marked "illegible," and mine had not returned at all. The Immigration officer suggested that we both be re-printed at the Immigration Office in Duluth, rather than drive all the way to St. Paul, where the printing was usually done for adoptions. We were both advised that even our new sets of prints were very poor, probably because of Jerry's chemical use in the greenhouse and my housecleaning products, but the Immigration officer submitted them, and we all hoped for the best. "You might want to plan on wearing gloves twenty-four hours a day for the next ten days just in case you need to be printed again," he suggested. Ha! Not bloody likely.

In mid-February we received a letter from our insurance company advising us that because of the additional information Mary had sent, they would consider Kyung Hee our eligible dependant as of the date of her arrival. However, her coverage was still subject to the preexisting condition limitation. Before major medical could cover her surgery, she would have to remain treatment free for that condition for ninety days. I called them immediately to see if the ninety day period immediately preceding her arrival in the United States would count. It would! This was a monumental decision, and only required confirming letters from Kyung Hee's physicians in Korea.

The first week in February, Jerry, Meghann, and I went to Minneapolis for the annual Jaycee convention. I had arranged a meeting with Teri to exchange medical supplies that we had collected to go to the orphanages and pick up Korean-made brass figures and dolls that PACT was providing for our benefit dinner. We were concerned because we had not heard from Korea about Kyung Hee's surgery. We had asked to be notified of her condition if and when any operation was performed. Teri had received no word, but reminded us of the Korean "no news is good news" philosophy. By February eleventh, with Kyung Hee's arrival expected within two months, Jerry and I called

Mary and requested that she send a cable to Korea and ask for an update on Kyung Hee's condition. We learned then that Teri had not seen the letter we sent requesting that the surgery be done in Korea, so we had to assume that the Korean agency was also unaware of our wishes. Knowing the length of time required even for cable correspondence between the United States and Korea, we decided that one week was the maximum amount of time we could wait before requesting a telephone call to Korea at our expense. It was a long and sleepless weekend.

Ever since signing the placement agreement, Jerry and I had been discussing possible names for our new daughter. I wanted to decide on her name as soon as possible, since, for me, it would make her even more ours. Jerry, on the other hand, wanted to wait until she was here to decide on which of our choices *fit* her. (We'd already been through this with Meghann, including the discussions on spelling, and I'd won!) The one thing we agreed on was to keep her Korean name as her middle name as we had done with Meghann. With the new and very disturbing turn of events concerning the fingerprints and Kyung Hee's surgery, we needed all the optimism we could muster, so we decided to agree on her name right away.

On any car trip longer than half an hour, one of our games to amuse ourselves and Meghann was selecting and discarding names. We didn't count barns or cows or train cars, we evaluated the merits of this name or that. Since many of the names we favored were overused now, and since we couldn't name her for either grandmother without offending the other one, we decided to name her in honor of the single most important person in her life at the time, her foster mother, Mrs. Ae Ja Choi. I reluctantly agreed to change the spelling to Asia, for school convenience, but not before I had made a crib quilt with her name on it, spelled AE JA. Her name became Asia Michaela Kyung Hee Renning. It was a mighty big name for such a little girl, but we knew she'd grow into it. All Jerry could think was, "What if she has to write it on the blackboard one hundred times?"

Finally Teri called to tell us that the Korean agency wished

Asia's surgery to be done in the United States. At first we were very,upset, since for two months we had thought that everything had been taken care of in Korea. But we soon came to realize that, as usual, things were working out for the best, and that we could decide after she was home when was the best time for her to have her surgery.

On February twenty-sixth our Visa approval came in the mail. With Meghann's adoption, nine days after we received visa approval, she was home! Time to finish the quilt, rearrange the bedroom, put up the crib . . .

In my continuing search to learn everything possible about Hirschprung's disease and related illnesses, I once again called area pediatricians, this time in search of a local family who had a young child with a similar condition. I wanted a mother's viewpoint of the day-to-day life of a child with a colostomy. Although I realized that in no way would our experiences be identical, I needed another mother's perspective to balance out the clinical details of the illness and the surgery. One pediatrician knew of a four-year-old little boy who had Hirschprung's disease, and she agreed to ask the mother to call me. I had expected that days would pass before I'd hear from the boy's mother, but twenty minutes later I was talking to Kathy Young. Kathy's youngest son had been diagnosed as having Hirschprung's disease when he was two and a half years old. He had suffered from constipation since birth, and according to Kathy, "He was constantly drinking prune juice. The poor kid was slowly being poisoned by his own body's waste, and his skin had begun to turn gray before the doctors finally discovered what the problem was. We were at our wit's end sure that he was going to die."

Kathy and I talked for nearly two hours, and she explained everything she had learned about the disease, the surgery and the recovery. Then she listened with compassion and concern while I told her Asia's story. Kathy's young son is now a healthy, normally functioning four-year-old, who exhibits no trace of his former illness, except for a reluctance to show his fading scars.

This was the only apparent area where the six months of poking and prodding by dozens of doctors and nurses had taken their toll. Kathy kindly asked me for any progress reports we received, and even offered to come and sit with me during the surgery. Her encouragement was contagious, and I hung up with renewed hope and a new friend.

The next two weeks were filled with final benefit dinner preparations. The programs were printed, last-minute details ironed out concerning entertainment, raffle items collected, and sale items priced. We were expecting a call from Mary Abbett any day telling us when Asia would be on her way home. Instead, she called to say that there had been two anonymous telephone calls questioning the agency's wisdom in placing Asia in our home. The callers went on to say that Jerry and I were not prepared, either financially or emotionally, to parent a special needs child, and that not only was the adoption causing problems between Jerry and me, but our parents were said to be totally against it. "I really hate to tell you this, Adair, but the adoption proceedings will have to be held up until you and Jerry can come to St. Paul to discuss these accusations," Mary said.

The callers also in some vague way questioned our fund-raising practices. My first reaction was stunned disbelief. "I don't know anyone cruel enough to do such a thing. How can anyone who knows us possibly believe such horrible accusations?" The one thing that kept running through my mind was the statement about "questionable fund-raising practices." Could all this be a result of the way we were planning to divide the proceeds from the benefit dinner? Several years ago, long before we even knew that Asia existed, we had proposed to a group of adoptive parents that we'd like to raise money to help a family adopt a child. We had no particular family in mind at the time. It was one of those "Wouldn't it be nice if . . ." ideas. We were shocked when the response of several members of the group was, "We had to pay full price for our child, let them pay full price for theirs," as though we were talking about a cantaloupe, not a child. I couldn't understand at the time how people could be so heartless. There was not one of them who wouldn't have jumped at the chance for financial help while they were adopting. How could they deny the same joy to another family . . . deny the same love and security to another child?

I tried unsuccessfully to calm myself before calling Jerry at work. We arranged to drive to St. Paul the next morning to meet with Mary and Tom Regan, the Director of Adoptions. Then I called Dorothy to see if she had heard anything that would give us a clue as to the identity of our accusers. She had heard nothing, and was appalled to think that anyone we knew would do something so mean-spirited. As soon as we hung up, Dorothy called Mary to offer her support of us as a family and our adoption of Asia. She was the first of many, many friends and family members to rally to our defense.

For several weeks Patsy, our newest dinner volunteer, had not been returning my phone calls. I hadn't really thought too much about it. After all, she had a new baby boy and her days were full. I called Patsy after dinner and put the call on the speaker phone so that Jerry and I both could talk to her. As soon as we asked her if she had heard anything about the accusations against us, she hung up without answering. By now Jerry and I had run the gamut of emotions, from shock and disbelief, to fear and now *anger*. Someone was trying to stop our adoption and we wanted to know who and why. Jerry called back and Patsy's husband Dick answered. Jerry told him in no uncertain terms that, while we were accusing no one, we *would* find out who was doing this.

Jerry and I put Meghann to bed early in preparation for a long and taxing tomorrow. We stayed up until the wee hours talking and picking apart the entire situation. Was the idea of raising money to help specific families adopt so radical and offensive to someone that they were trying to stop our dinner? Had we inadvertently said or done something that had given someone the wrong idea about us? Had someone heard about our earlier problems with insurance coverage and unreadable fingerprints, but didn't know that both had been solved? Or was there some deeper psychological motive that we couldn't begin to fathom? Was it because Asia wasn't (at least not yet) physically perfect? Did this person feel that if he or she was not equipped to parent a child with challenges, how could we possibly be? We racked our minds, but came no closer to answers. One thing we were certain of, however, was that nothing and no one would stop this adoption without a fight. We had come this far and were not about to give up our daughter easily. I finally fell into an exhausted half sleep, only to awaken several times from nightmares of people without faces who were trying to take our daughter away.

Icy roads and car problems slowed our departure Tuesday morning, but we ate sandwiches in the car and managed to arrive in time for our meeting with Mary and Tom. We had prepared a list of personal references and a chronological diary of events since we had first seen Asia's picture. We harbored no ill feelings toward C.H.S.M, for they were only doing their jobs. As a child placement agency, their first responsibility was to the children. They were obligated to investigate any charges of this nature against prospective adoptive parents.

We also knew that this was a difficult situation for both Mary and Tom. We had known both of them for three years. Mary had been our social worker for Meghann's adoption, and Tom and his wife and Mrs. Han had escorted Meghann home from Korea.

We answered all their questions as calmly and accurately as possible, and it wasn't until Tom said that their decision could take two to three weeks that I fell apart. "I really feel terrible about all of this," he said "but staff time is at a premium, and it will take at least that long to call all of your references."

"Tom, you may as well send me to Moose Lake Sanitarium right now, because I swear that I will be a certifiable basket case with gray hair and a twitch over one eye if it takes two weeks to resolve this," I declared. "Can't anything be done to speed things up?"

"Well, you could have the people on your list call or write us instead," he said. "That would definitely help."

Mary assured us that they did not need to notify the Korean agency yet, so the paper work processing on that end would not be delayed. Mary vowed to call us as soon as their decision had been made.

We drove away from the agency and stopped at the first pay phone we saw. I got change while Jerry began calling our Minneapolis friends, who then started a phone chain, calling other friends and explaining our desperate situation. We then drove back to Duluth in time for a florist meeting, with Jerry's parents in attendance from Rochester. After the meeting, over strawberry pie at Big Boy's, Jerry's dad offered to give us the equivalent of whatever our one-third share of the profits from the benefit dinner might be. If that was the thorn in someone's side, then he was going to remove it. Always the practical businessman, Jerry's father had overwhelmed us with his generosity. We absolutely refused to cancel the dinner. No matter how much money we raised, it would help a child or children for a while, maybe long enough for their "Forever Family" to find them and bring them home.

Since Dorothy was one of the volunteers for the dinner, I called her to see how she felt about splitting the money between C.H.S.M and PACT. Dorothy, in turn, called the president of the local parent group and advised him of the change in the division of the Benefit Dinner proceeds. Two days later, Dorothy and all the other members of the group, except Jerry and I, received in the mail an announcement of an International Family Night Dinner, scheduled the same night as our International Benefit Dinner. So the dinner was at the heart of it, after all, and this was someone's attempt to draw attendance away from it.

For the following week, Jerry and I called everyone on our list of references, explained our situation, and asked for their help. Everyone, without exception, either called or wrote letters on our behalf. It was an amazing show of love, friendship, and support on the part of our friends and family. For two weeks, even after their decision had been made, C.H.S.M. was besieged with telephone calls, telegrams, and letters.

We spent an uneasy weekend, hoping for a call that didn't come. Although in our hearts we were confident that everything would be resolved soon and that Asia would be on her way, our emotions were on a roller coaster. Our parents called daily offering love and encouragement. Finally, on Tuesday, March fourteenth, Mary called, saying, in her most official voice, "We've found no evidence to support the charges against you, and you both have our unconditional support. And by the way, you can tell your friends they can stop calling now." She also said that Tom had called the people who had made the accusations, advised them of C.H.S.M.'s decision, and suggested that they call us. She refused, however, to reveal their names to us, or confirm our suspicions.

Now the realization began to sink in that Asia could arrive any day. Her visa had been approved weeks ago, and we knew that there were potential escorts in Korea at the time, so all that remained was her preflight physical, and assigning her to a flight. What if she arrived on Saturday the day of the long awaited, very controversial benefit dinner. We could hardly say, "Gee, we're really busy that night, can you bring her another day?" Now could we?

Chapter Seven

Seoul Food . . . Part Two

THE NIGHT OF the benefit dinner had been chosen five months earlier, and was picked because of its significance to Jerry and me. Three years earlier, on the same weekend, we had first seen the picture of Kim, Hee Young. Unfortunately, it was also the same weekend for several other social functions, including the hastily planned International Family Night. Our ticket sales were considerably lower than we had hoped, but many friends and family members who were unable to attend had sent donations. Jerry, Meghann, and I arrived at the Radisson Great Hall at 3 P.M. and began setting up the bazaar table. During the past week, C.H.S.M. had requested that we give all the proceeds to PACT, which was fine with us. Had it not been for PACT, our new daughter might not have survived to come home to us. PACT had given us three large boxes of Korean dolls in traditional dresses, many pieces of Korean-made brass, as well as dolls and jewelry from India. C.H.S.M. friends drove up to attend and hinted that there might be a flight arriving within the next week to ten days. As our friends began to arrive, I felt my tension disappear. It was going to be a wonderful evening, and no one could say we hadn't done our best.

Our good friend, John Summer, who was at that time the evening news anchor for the ABC affiliate in Duluth, was our Master of Ceremonies. The Radisson catering staff had prepared a fine international menu, with foods representing Korea, China, India, Mexico, and South America. Raffle tickets and bazaar table sales were brisk and before we knew it, we were into the entertainment portion of the evening. A newfound friend was demonstrating Middle Eastern belly-dancing and Dorothy's daughter Ellie, at the ripe old age of four, was treating us to a violin solo. PACT had given us a slide presentation on their organization, showing before and after pictures of some of the children who had been helped by their programs. A local band had donated their evening to play wonderful blue-grass music for us, and Meghann, Jerry, and I were going to tell Meghann's favorite bedtime story, "The Story of Kim, Hee Young" We finished the evening by drawing for door prizes and raffle items and held our breath while we counted the money and paid the Radisson. After paying all of the bills, we had a $500 profit to send to PACT to enable them to continue their dedicated work. Needless to say, we were elated.

On Sunday, the feeling was stronger than ever that Asia would be home soon, and several times Jerry caught me sitting and staring at her pictures. I couldn't help wondering what this beautiful little girl was really like, and how our lives would change once she was finally home. The amount of suffering and pain she had experienced in her two short years would have worn down some adults. Maybe she hadn't *thrived,* but she had *survived,* and in spite of all the obstacles in our path, she was coming home to us.

The following Saturday we were all to be in the wedding of Cindy's roommate, who was also our dear Korean friend, Sun

Cha Kim. Sun Cha and Cindy had been roommates for nearly two years and through her we had learned much about Korean cooking, traditions, and family life. She had asked Meghann to be her flower girl and Jerry to give her away, since all of her family was still in Korea. In addition to helping make food for the reception, I was planning to take pictures of the wedding.

On Tuesday, March twenty-first, while I was putting the finishing touches on Meghann's peach, dotted-Swiss flower girl dress, Mary called. Asia would be arriving at the Minneapolis-St. Paul Airport on Saturday, March twenty-sixth. I had a mental picture of Mary holding the phone away from her ear to avoid the scream that she knew would follow. After congratulating us, and giving flight arrival information, she promised to try to be at the airport with us. I called Jerry, then Sun Cha. We knew that she would be sorry we could not be a part of her wedding, but that she would be rejoicing with us for the arrival of our daughter.

Cindy came out to celebrate with us, Jerry brought home a bottle of champagne, and we spent the rest of the evening calling all the wonderful people who were anticipating the arrival of this special child. During the next three days we finished all the last- minute preparations, packed the diaper bag, and reread every scrap of information we'd received about Asia Michaela Kyung Hee Renning-to-be.

Chapter Eight

"Twinkle, Twinkle, Little Star"

SATURDAY MORNING'S SNOWFALL in Minnesota was not causing problems for flights leaving Seattle, so Jerry, Meghann, and I left at noon, promising to meet our flight aides, Barb and Ken Dalley, at the airport by 4 P.M. Barb was the flight aide co-ordinator for C.H.S.M., a volunteer position that is responsible for assigning flight aides to individual families. Other respon-sibilities include maintaining contact with the airlines for information about the children to relay to the Immigration Office in Seattle, the port of entry into the United States.

Flight aides are normally assigned, but Barb was a personal friend, with a vested interest in seeing this particular baby united with her parents. As we walked up to the arrival gate, she greeted us with, "Adair, sit down. Everything's all right now, but I've spent the last two hours on the telephone with the Immigration Office at the Seattle Airport." My knees buckled, dumping me into a contoured plastic airport chair. "One of the babies on Northwest Orient flight No.70 arrived without the documents needed to enter the United States," she continued. "I knew, before he said it, that it was Asia."

Barb did exactly what I would have done under the circumstances--she burst out crying. I have a feeling that she was just beginning to threaten the poor man with bodily harm if he denied this child entry into the United States, when he agreed to send her on to Minneapolis with a temporary visa, valid for two weeks. Hopefully this would be sufficient time to forward the necessary documents to us.

By this time nothing would have surprised us, so as friends began arriving at the airport to greet Asia, the stories they brought of the rotten weather conditions outside only made us laugh. Everyone offered us a place to stay for the night, but once again, Jerry and I felt the best thing for Asia was to go home, so she could wake up in her own bed in the morning.

Our flight had been assigned to a gate with a waiting room the size of a postage stamp. Our group consisted of thirty-three excited "baby greeters". There were eight other children arriving on the flight, with family and friends waiting to welcome each child. As the room filled with people, the temperature inside rose, and the level of excitement became almost tangible. The families, like ours, who were there for the second time, knew what to expect, and that made it all the more exciting. When the plane landed, the flight aides advised the parents to stay in their seats, so they would be easier to find when the babies were brought off the plane. At Meghann's arrival, I had sat frozen in my seat, afraid to move, for fear that our flight aide would miss me. This time I was a seasoned veteran, so when Barb waved for me to "stay put" as she went on the plane, I bolted to my feet, on tiptoes, watching for the first glimpse of our daughter. Jerry had taken the front position with the camera and Meghann was perched on our friend Gary's shoulders with her eyes glued to the jetway opening. Gary was as anxious as anyone else, but not only because of Asia. He and his wife Karen were planning to adopt, and would soon be going through their homestudy. As the other flight aides began to deplane with their joyous little bundles, I could feel my vision narrowing to include only the opening of the jetway. The other voices in the room became background noise as all my senses were focused on the pathway from the airplane that held our daughter. And then, there she was!! Barb was holding her up for me to see from the other side of the passenger gate and I was crying as I pushed my way to the front of the crowd. Jerry was by my side to guide us back to our seat as Barb handed the poor frightened little girl to me. Barb was saying something about a rash that had Asia's escorts concerned, but all that really registered with me was the incredibly pained expression and huge black eyes of the child in my arms. She was absolutely terrified of the strange-looking people, bright lights, and loud noises of the airport. Mrs. Han and her husband had come to the airport to act as interpreters for the older children, and they rushed up to introduce Asia to us in Korean. Asia appeared not to hear or recognize their words. Friends were pushing closer, cameras were flashing, and Asia began to cry. It was the sad, frightened cry of a child who at some primitive core of her being realized that her life had just changed again, and she was pretty sure she didn't like it. She was too tired to cry for long, however, and soon was sitting quietly on my lap with a rather blank expression on her face, not really reacting to anything. Her escorts arrived to tell us how she had fared during the eighteen-plus-hour flight from Korea. The entire group of children had been escorted home by young servicemen, returning from a tour of duty in Korea, and several of them had scoured the area in a vain attempt to find colostomy bags for Asia. In fact, due to the expense and lack of funding, *Asia had never even worn a colostomy bag,* something that had never, in our naivete, even occurred to us. Korea was a progressive country, of course they had colostomy supplies. But the sad truth was that they were prohibitively expensive for some of the smaller, more remote orphanages. In Korea, a cloth diaper had been used to cover the stoma, the surgically created opening for the large intestine, and a three-laced binder, similar to an old-fashioned corset, had been used to hold that diaper in place. Asia was then diapered in the normal manner. They explained that Asia had been very quiet for parts of the trip, but occasionally had begun to cry inconsolably. She was, we believed, grieving for the loss of the foster mother whom she had come to love and trust.

One of the flight aides, a nurse, kindly offered to come with me to change Asia's diaper and check on the rash. Wim, Jerry's mom, offered to come too, but I told her I was fine. I really didn't want anyone to see how shaken I was. My hands were trembling as I pealed off several layers of clothing and put them in a plastic bag to take home. None of my reading had prepared me for the first sight of our daughter's colostomy. It looked like an incredibly painful open wound. The irritation caused by the diaper covering the stoma had made the delicate skin bloody and raw. And the smell was atrocious--worse than any dirty diaper I'd ever smelled, or so it seemed to my out-of-practice nose and already nervous stomach. But after the questions raised about our fitness to adopt Asia, I felt that I had to appear confident and in charge, when, in fact, I felt like crying myself. Somehow we managed to get through the diaper change. Meghann rubbed some lotion on Asia's dry, itchy skin while I got her clean clothing ready. The soiled binder had to be put away, and we hoped that a disposable diaper would sufficiently cover the stoma until we got home. Patty, the nurse, saw nothing to be concerned about in the rash on her stomach. What we didn't realize was that the escorts had seen hives, which had temporarily disappeared.

Dressed and dry, Asia appeared to rally a bit, but I was a complete wreck as I tried to mix a bottle of formula for her. She was so much frailer than we had ever imagined. Her arms and legs were as thin as willow branches, and her muscle tone was so poor that when we picked her up under the arms, her arms would fly up over her head as she slid out of our arms. There was no resistance at all in her shoulder muscles. All ten fingers were constantly crossing and uncrossing in all sorts of impossible combinations. She appeared to be double-jointed in her hands. She made strange croaking noises in the back of her throat, and ground her teeth together. She had little interest in her bottle or any of the stuffed animals that friends had brought as arrival presents. She only appeared comfortable when Jerry's mother was rocking her. We gathered our belongings and slowly began to make our way back through the airport terminal to the exit and our car. Despite all the warnings of bad weather and offers of places to stay for the night, Jerry and I were determined to make it back to Duluth. The snow was blinding and the highways treacherous, giving new meaning to the words "hazardous driving conditions," and nearly two hours later we were only on the north side of Minneapolis. We still had at least three more hours to go. Asia was terrified of the car seat, and because of the weather, I was equally terrified not to have her in it. She sobbed and screamed in anger and frustration and strained against the car seat straps, only calming when Meghann and I sang "Twinkle, Twinkle Little Star" over and over in Korean. The disposable diaper didn't reach high enough to cover the stoma, so we stopped at a gas station and bought a roll of toilet paper and a package of napkins to fashion something resembling the corset she had been wearing. The bathroom was out of order, so I brought in her blanket and changed her on the floor, while the attendant watched us warily. As we left in the blizzard, I looked back to see him shake his head. Jerry drove slowly and carefully home through the blizzard as Meghann and I sang.

We arrived home and unloaded the car about midnight, and while Jerry and Meghann acquainted Asia with her room and the rest of her new home, I called friends to let them know we were safe. We were all so wound up with excitement and tension that it took a while to settle down. Asia got acquainted with the dogs, and her eyes were constantly moving, taking in everything. How different it must have seemed to her. She had experienced so much pain and loneliness in her young life. And here in the space of twenty-four hours she had been taken away from the one person she had ever been able to call her own, her foster mother, the woman who had taught her what life could be like when you were loved. She had been put on an airplane with total strangers who talked funny, and looked funnier, had flown for eighteen hours, had been met at another airport by some more strange-looking people who flashed lights in her face. And now she was in a house where only one person looked right (Meghann) and was being sat on by a rather large, hairy black dog who insisted on washing her face. All that would have been enough to send some seemingly stable adults over the edge, but she appeared to be taking it all rather calmly now. What we didn't realize yet was that Asia had a very strong self-protective instinct that took over during times of high stress. Many times over the next few weeks we would notice her occasionally "blank out" when things became too intense for her. But during the first few hours of this first night home, we thought she was amazingly calm.

We finally got both girls settled down about 2 A.M. and Jerry and I collapsed into bed. We doubted if Asia would sleep through the night, but we were not prepared for the terrified screams that woke us about an hour later. Asia was completely disoriented, needed a diaper change in the worst way, and was scared to death of me. The disposable diaper/cloth diapers combinations were not working without the corset, so I ripped up old sheets to make one. Asia would not allow herself to be rocked to sleep, so I made a bed on the floor for the two of us, and tried to calm her by singing "Twinkle, Twinkle" Korean style. The magic song would work for minutes only, she would doze, I would doze, then the screaming would start again. She would thrash around on the floor, making a complete circle with her head at the center, and her feet beating a path on the floor around her. I tried to hold her tightly, praying that the love I felt for her would somehow get through.

Sometime around dawn, realizing that sleep was out of the question for Asia and me, I decided to try feeding her. Because of the paperwork mix-up, we had received none of her preflight physical information or social workers' statements of her eating and sleeping habits, but I thought I'd be safe with good old Gerber's baby oatmeal. *Wrong!* Asia screamed, threw her head back, and resolutely clamped her lips shut. I could do nothing to persuade her to try the cereal, and it would be several days before we realized that this was apparently her first experience with any other food or method of feeding than formula in a bottle.

We had learned from our earlier information that Asia hated taking a bath, but, like it or not, that was next on the day's agenda. *Hate* was much too mild a word for what Asia felt about bath time. Although the stoma itself should not have been painful, I had read, the raw irritated skin around it probably was. She alternated between total rigidity and total limpness, screaming all the while, and from time to time, rolling her eyes back in her head as though going into shock. All the commotion woke Jerry and Meghann, and between Jerry and me, we managed to dry Asia and dress her. Dressing Asia was a lot like trying to stuff cooked spaghetti into clothing. Her feet were so small and limp that even Meghann's tiniest baby shoes would not stay on, so we settled for warm socks, which wouldn't stay on either, unless held in place with loose rubber bands.

After all this torture, Asia was ready for some fun, we thought, so Meghann began bringing out her favorite toys. The first quickly became Asia's favorite--a musical strawberry that required nothing more that pushing a small pad with her finger tips to produce a sound. Since this was the only way Asia knew how to play with toys, it suited her perfectly, and she and Strawberry became inseparable. It brought about the first smile we'd seen since her arrival the day before.

Because the surgically created stoma had no sphincter muscles of its own, Asia had no bowel control, and was almost constantly in need of a diaper change. We knew the importance of cleaning her frequently, but immediately would have been more accurate. The strong digestive enzymes in her intestines didn't know the difference between human skin and hamburger and within minutes would begin their work, digesting, causing searing pain. We had an appointment with an enterostomal therapist at the Duluth Clinic on Monday to have Asia fitted for colostomy bags. We were sure that this modern convenience, so taken for granted here in America, would go a long way toward making her more comfortable. In the meantime, we gathered soft cloths to make into the fresh binders needed with every diaper change.

The experience of having a new child in the house was both exciting, and more than a little overwhelming, so Jerry and I were grateful when both girls fell asleep about noon. Asia woke in about an hour, screaming again. Her neck was covered with huge red welts, and she was clawing herself constantly. While Jerry held her hands, I placed an emergency call to our doctor, who phoned in a prescription for a mild sedative to calm her and relieve her hives. Her screaming gave us an opportunity to check her teeth, which were yellow and crusty and her breath smelled. The next call was to our friend and dentist, Carter Johnson, for advice. He suggested rubbing her teeth and gums with a soft, wet washcloth until she would allow us to use a toothbrush. This newest form of torture brought on more hives, so we promptly stopped, bundled everyone up, and left for town to pick up the prescription.

Had our family, complete with new addition, not stopped by Dorothy's house, she would have disowned us. Since Dorothy's new daughter, Anna, was much too small to need a walker yet, she was loaning hers for Asia. We sat in her warm kitchen as Asia and Meghann played bumper cars, with Asia in the walker, smiling as Meghann pushed a toy grocery cart. Meghann had already found so many ways to relate to her new sister, and not once had we seen any signs of jealousy.

Back at home with Asia's prescription, we tried to get everyone ready for bed early, in preparation for a normally hectic Monday. But once again Asia woke in pain and panic, and she and I spent another fitful night on the living room floor.

Monday morning we could see that Asia's hives were worse instead of better, so we made a hasty appointment with our physician. We tried the process of elimination to determine the cause of the hives and finally decided that they were stress related. Considering all that she had been through, who had more reason to feel stress? Next stop, our appointment with Margaret, the therapist, to have Asia fitted with the colostomy bags, and for me to get the basic instruction on the care and feeding of a child with a colostomy. So far in her young life, Asia's experiences with doctors were all related to pain, so she expected nothing less from this young woman in white. But Margaret knew how to work with panic-stricken children, and quickly and efficiently measured and fitted Asia with her first colostomy appliance. We left the clinic armed with books to read and a list of local pharmacies to call concerning necessary supplies.

Shortly after dinner Monday evening, Asia woke from a nap and was so completely covered with hives that her face was hardly recognizable. Her eyes were nearly swollen shut, and her neck was swelled even with her ears. She had already clawed herself so badly that she looked like the victim of a lion attack. It took Jerry and me both to hold her arms and legs (she was trying to scratch with her feet as well as her hands). It had all finally become too much for her, and her body was producing hives at an alarming rate. The greatest danger was suffocation due to hives in her throat, so while Jerry called our doctor and Meghann sobbed, I stuffed Asia into loose-fitting pajamas and a snowsuit for the fast ride to the emergency room. Jerry stayed home to try to calm Meghann, who was terrified that her new sister was dying, and I sang that old stand-by, "Twinkle, Twinkle, Little Star" to this poor frightened child with the swollen-shut eyes. At St. Mary's emergency room we were met by nurses with a gurney who whisked Asia inside while I parked the car. I had brought Hurricane, our German shepherd, along for protection, so I didn't bother to locking the car before I ran inside. The nurses already had Asia stripped down on the table and were taking her temperature while we waited for the doctor. While the sympathetic nurses did all they could to make Asia comfortable, I told them what we knew of her life before coming home to us. The doctor arrived and, after some preliminary investigation, decided on two adrenaline injections, one fast-acting and one long-lasting, to combat the hives. The poor little thing didn't even know me enough to hold on to me while the nurses gave her the shots. The shots would take effect within ten to fifteen minutes, the doctor said. Then, as if by magic, the shiny swelling began to diminish, and Asia's face began to resemble that of a child again, instead of a polished apple. The drugs also had a positive effect on her spirits, and she became a little giddy and actually started flirting with the nurses. My relief left me weak; she was going to be okay. Asia was asleep before we reached the car, and didn't wake up until 10 A.M. the next day. It is said that there is something good about every negative thing, and in this case it was that Asia's body clock completely adjusted itself in two days, and she was sleeping, waking, and napping at normal times. All thanks to a case of hives.

Asia wasn't out of the woods yet, however. On Tuesday she not only refused to eat, but rejected her bottle as well. She had slept on and off for most of the day, and by late afternoon she had still had nothing to drink. Cindy arrived to meet her newest niece, and while I held Asia, Cindy looked in her mouth with a flashlight. Asia's gums and the inside of her lips were covered with sores, probably a side effect of the stress and hives. Her mouth was so tender that even the nipple of the bottle hurt. The last thing Asia needed was to have to be hospitalized for dehydration, so Jerry, Cindy, and I took turns feeding her eight ounces of formula with an eye dropper. It took four hours.

Because it was impossible to constantly watch Asia to keep her from scratching, the nurses at the hospital had fashioned mittens for her from soft elastic bandages, and taped them on her hands. Asia's fingers had been her only toys for so long, that she was literally lost without them. Every few hours we'd remove one mitten at a time, and she was overjoyed to have her "friends" back. She would joyfully cross and uncross her fingers in complex patterns, and wave them in front of her eyes. When the rash had cleared and both mittens were removed, she spent at least an hour crossing and recrossing her fingers, and matching her two hands.

Chapter Nine

Cracking the Shell

THE DAYS THAT followed brought about changes in Asia that were nothing short of miraculous. Because of the convenience of the colostomy bags, she was, for the first time in her life, pain- free. The bags and appliance attachments kept all irritating material away from her skin. Gradually the hives faded away and her eyes lost their haunted expression. Although she was still terribly weak, and was content to lie on the floor most of the time, she was alert to all around her, and would visibly brighten when Jerry or Meghann came into the room. I, on the other hand, was the enemy. I was the one who bathed her, changed her colostomy bag, and tried to make her eat that vile stuff that didn't come in a bottle.

As the pattern of our days began to take shape, it became clear that Asia's short six months in her foster home had only begun to crack the "institutional shell" that enclosed our new daughter. She was absolutely terrified of any new experience, no matter how nonthreatening it seemed to us. The weekend after she arrived, Easter weekend, we had planned a trip to Rochester to visit Jerry's parents and celebrate Asia's second birthday. Asia's documents had arrived from Korea, so we detoured through St. Paul to pick them up at C.H.S.M. As we walked through the doorway, I could feel Asia's body begin to tense. We took her coat off first, but before we could remove ours, we were greeted by Bobbie Wiggins, bringing our daughter's overdue arrival packet, and two lovely gifts from Social Welfare Society in Seoul. In all the commotion, Jerry, Meghann and I still had not removed our coats and Asia, fearing that she was going to be left again with strangers, stiffened and began screaming and sobbing uncontrollably. We didn't realize the problem at first, and went through the routine of checking all possible trouble spots: wet diaper? No. Hungry? No. Tired? No, she'd slept all the way from Duluth. It was not until we put her coat on to go that she finally quieted and began to relax. She was going to leave with the same people she'd come in with, after all. When we arrived at Jerry's parents, the same thing happened. We brought her in the house and after taking her coat off, sat her on Grandma Renning's lap while we unloaded the station wagon. Her howl of disapproval reached us in the garage. Then we made the connection. It would be many months before she would be free of the fear that she was going to be taken somewhere and left with strangers to start all over again.

Settled back in the car with Jerry driving, I began to read the preflight information packet that should have come with Asia the week before. As I read and reread the page, it became clear that Asia's primary food had been formula in a bottle. No wonder she had so strongly resisted being spoon-fed cereal. It was just another new torture we were constantly thinking up for her.

During our visit with Dr. Day earlier in the week, we had discussed diet. "It won't hurt her to be on formula for a few more days," he said. "But you should try to start introducing new foods soon. Pretend she's eight months old and start with cereals."

"You've got to be joking. I tried cereal already and she screamed and let it fall out of her mouth in clumps. She wanted no part of it. She just throws herself back in the high chair, as far away from me as she can get."

"You're creative," he said with a smile. "You'll come up with something. Just remember, cereals, then fruits and yellow vegetables, then meats and green vegetables. Only add one new food every three to four days in order to avoid possible allergic reactions. Good luck." I didn't know if he was talking to Asia or to me.

Even though Asia had nearly all her baby teeth, she had never had to use them. Even though she was two years old, until she learned to chew, all her food would need to be baby-food consistency.

Since the bottle was a friend and this thick goo in the bowl was the foe, mealtimes became a contest of wills and a challenge to my patience. Asia didn't just resist eating, she became hysterical. Each spoonful of temperature-tested new food just hung in her mouth while she screamed until it fell out onto her high chair tray. She hated, hated, hated everything. "Um-m-m-m, this is good stuff, honey. Open wide, now," I tried, pretending the tiny spoon was an airplane flying into the hanger. "Rice cereal, Asia, you'll like this."

Her eyes said, "Not a chance, lady."

Once again Meghann came to the rescue, and a new mealtime ritual was born. When any new food was offered to Asia, Meghann would act as the "queen's taster," taking the first bite, pronouncing it fit to eat. Then Asia would try it, and in most cases devour it. All this was done with very solemn and elaborate pantomime, and the practice continued until we had worked Asia through all the food groups, and several combinations of foods. We felt very strongly that, second only to love, good nutrition was most important to Asia's recovery and future development. As I had done with Meghann, I began to prepare all of Asia's baby food. One day a week would be spent cooking various vegetables from our garden, grinding and then straining them and freezing them in ice cube trays, to be thawed out as needed. As meats were added to her diet, I mixed combinations of foods, adding noodles or rice occasionally for a change of consistency. Her appetite was phenomenal and required attention as soon as her eyes opened in the mornings. Mealtime was rapidly becoming her favorite time of the day. Scratch one area where Mom was the bad guy. But we still had bath time, teeth brushing, and colostomy bag cleaning and changing. The latter was my least favorite. The process, while not complicated, did require some timing and preparation, so Meghann's job became Official Gatherer of Colostomy Supplies, a responsibility she took quite seriously. While I bathed Asia, Meghann would assemble the changing cloth, skin wipe preparations, cotton balls, tissue, adhesive wafer, colostomy bag and clip, and a small bowl of warm water. The trick was to bathe and dry Asia and attach the fresh bag before mealtimes, when the stoma was less likely to be active. We didn't always make it, but Meghann and I became experts at the procedure in a few short weeks.

Because of my continuing asthma problems, I had still not returned to work at the greenhouse. I was, however, continuing to water the plants at several local businesses, and Meghann usually went with me. Several times we tried to take Asia with us, but she was not yet ready for so many new experiences. Shopping centers and grocery stores terrified her, and she would scream until we left. I had always looked a little smugly at mothers whose children screamed at the grocery store, because Meghann was always so well behaved. Now I raced through the shortest check-out line with my child screaming bloody murder, certain that this was "almost instant" karma.

It became necessary to leave Asia with a baby-sitter for several hours a week, long enough to do any shopping. The practice of leaving her and returning to pick her up reinforced her attachment to us and, we hoped, would help to convince her that she was not going to be uprooted again.

When Asia had first arrived in the United States, she could

not stand, walk, or crawl. She could not roll from front to back or sit unsupported. She could suck from a bottle, but did not bite or chew. Her muscular development (except for her lungs) was virtually nonexistent. As she grew stronger, she began to sit up for short periods of time. Because her stomach muscles were so weak, she had a very unusual way of getting into a sitting position. She would roll onto her stomach, and then with both legs stretched behind her, she would push up with her hands. Then she would bring her legs around, one on either side, completely flat on the floor, full circle, until they were both in front of her and she was sitting up. This feat, combined with the constant crossing and uncrossing of her fingers, gave further evidence that she was double-jointed.

She still strongly resisted holding any toys. If we placed one in her hands, she would scream and throw it behind her as though the offending item were electric. Although we had been told that she could hold her bottle to feed herself, it must have been a mis-translation, because she seemed to have little strength to raise it to her mouth. Or if she dropped the bottle, she would not voluntarily pick it up, preferring to wait for Jerry or me to hand it to her and then hold it for her. Was she testing us to find out if we were worth the time and effort to learn to trust us, or was she physically unable to lift and hold a bottle herself? I had to know.

Although we had not planned to take Asia to Nat Polinsky Rehabilitation Center (UDAC). for an evaluation until after her surgery, we decided to get a little advice from the United Developmental Achievement Center. After three weeks' time I felt we could give the therapists a thumbnail sketch of her strengths and weaknesses, and perhaps get some pointers on what to do next. There had been suggestions of autism in Korea, and occasionally we would see Asia "blank out" or spend lots of time playing with her fingers. She would stand in the walker and rock from side to side and stare into space for long periods of time. We believed that because of the long months spent in the crib in the orphanage, Asia had developed many of these self-stimulation actions as literally a means of survival, and perhaps as a way to escape from the pain.

As mentioned earlier, Asia's stoma had no sphincter muscle control, and since colostomy bags were not used in the orphanage, she was probably not the most fragrant child there. Her personality and disposition had been formed from pain. The croaking noises, teeth grinding, and lip smacking were her means of communication, and head banging and rocking from side to side were her answers to frustration. In all respects she functioned on a very primitive level. Her strongest instinct was survival, and everything else was secondary. These activities took all her available resources, and there was nothing else left over with which to branch out into the world. So she remained contained in her "institutional shell," unable to crack it by herself.

I learned at UDAC that part of Asia's inability to grasp and hold objects stemmed from hypersensitive nerve endings in her hands. At the age when most children are crawling on every imaginable surface, and thereby toughening the palms of their hands, Asia was confined to a crib, too weak and sick to crawl. The first thing to do, then, was to return Dorothy's walker and get Asia back on the floor to crawl. The crawling would also strengthen Asia's arm and shoulder muscles, equally important in lifting, holding, and manipulating. Not being able to crawl had also caused Asia to miss another important developmental step--bringing things to her mouth to explore. This, coupled with the almost liquid diet, had eliminated any possibility of learning to bite or chew. I left the meeting with a renewed admiration for the spunky little girl who had survived so much, and an even stronger determination to give her every chance to break out of that shell.

The next trick was to find something that would be absolutely irresistible to her, something she would *want* to pick up. That part turned out to be amazingly simple. Ever since Asia's first day at home, she had been drawn to a picture of my mother which hung near the fireplace. She would stare at the picture, then laugh and wave at it. If picked up, she wanted to be taken to touch the picture. She would constantly get her bearings in the room by first spotting the picture of Grandma Betty, whom she had not yet met. It was as if she recognized Grandma Betty, but how was that possible?

One morning in late April, Meghann dug out a small, clear plastic bottle that she had carried around as a baby. Inside the bottle was a wallet-sized picture of my mother. I casually dropped the bottle on the floor within Asia's reach and waited. Out of the corner of her eye she must have caught the motion of the bottle falling because she stopped playing with her fingers and stared at the bottle. Slowly, she looked from the bottle to the picture on the wall and back again. Here was a picture she could touch anytime she wanted to. Meghann sat on my lap and we both held our breath as Asia reached out and picked up the little bottle and brought it closer to her face for a better look. Satisfied that the two pictures were the same, she planted a kiss on the face in the bottle, and crawled off, bottle in hand, to a quieter spot to examine this new development more closely.

I was almost afraid to speak for fear of breaking the spell. But I've never been afraid to speak for too long. My excitement got the better of me, and I called Jerry first, then all our friends, and especially my mom, with the good news. That one basic action, when performed by Meghann, had thrilled us, but for Asia, it was an even bigger milestone. It meant, to me at least, that there was no physical reason for slow development in this area, only a lack of stimulation and opportunity, both of which we would see that she had in abundance.

As Asia's strength grew and she began to crawl more and lie on the floor less, we devised all sorts of exercises to strengthen and tone her muscles. For her weak eye muscles, we played "Wily Eye." We'd sit her on the sofa beside us, put our cheek as close to hers as possible, and lock our eyes to the side she was on, with her doing the same, and then switch sides. Silly and simple, but it worked. For her arms and legs, we played "Rock, Rock." With Asia standing in front of us, holding our thumbs, we would rock her back and forth and from side to side, and occasionally dump her on the floor with a tickle. We soon learned that the rougher we played, the better she liked it. She loved to be tossed in the air by Jerry, carried over his shoulders like a sack of potatoes, and thrown on the waterbed and tickled until she was weak. If Meghann did it, Asia wanted to try.

When Meghann was two, she had decided she wanted to take gymnastics. Most of the schools I called insisted that she was much too young and didn't have the attention span for an hour-long class, but they were dealing with a force beyond their comprehension. I finally persuaded one teacher.

"Just let me bring her in for one session," I begged of Nancy Anderson. "If it doesn't work, we'll come back in six months."

"Okay," Nancy said. "But just bring her in sweats. No need to buy a leotard until you know." I told my mother about the coming class and a leotard arrived the next week, in time for the lesson.

Meghann was younger and smaller than any of the other students, but determined. She was so agile that she could fold up like a piece of paper, and had no trouble following along. After that first class, Nancy said, "Well, I really hadn't wanted to discourage you, because it doesn't often work with kids her age. As long as she can keep up, bring her in." Meghann never missed a class.

When Meghann began practicing headstands and forward rolls for her gym class, there was Asia, ready to try. With a little help from me she, could do a darn good somersault, and scramble back across the floor for more.

Although her progress in four short weeks was astonishing, there were still several areas that concerned us. Asia appeared to have no idea how to chew food. She showed no interest in feeding herself with her fingers. If given anything with more texture than baby food mixed with a little rice, she would scream. The concept of biting food was unknown to her. We can only speculate why Asia had been fed formula almost exclusively. It most certainly was not cruelty or neglect. As we talked to more and more therapists and physicians, we learned that the nutrients in the formula were absorbed higher in the digestive tract, leaving little residue to be eliminated by the stoma. The stoma itself would not have prevented Asia from digesting baby foods. However, the more solid wastes there were, the more the stoma was active, and the more pain from irritation and constantly messy diapers. Oh, how valuable colostomy supplies would be in situations like Asia's. I vowed to try to locate some to send to Korea, along with the other medical supplies.

Asia made no attempt to imitate sounds or words in either Korean or English, and would only stare at us blankly if we tried to encourage her to speak. Her only voluntary forms of communication were screaming and crying if she was hungry, tired, or wet, much as a newborn baby would do. Bath time still terrified her, and she was afraid or unwilling to get her hands dirty or wet. She would willingly handle very few objects for a short time, then throw them down. We needed to know how much of this behavior was a form of regression due to trauma, and how much was due to developmental delays. More than anything, we wanted to make sure that we were not doing the wrong things out of ignorance or haste.

In addition to not walking, Asia didn't seem to know what to do with her legs when we carried her. I was used to Meghann wrapping her legs around my waist automatically when I picked her up. Asia's legs dangled like jelly-fish tentacles. When I tried to wrap them and hook them to my sides, they just slid back down. This seemed so basic to me that I was really stumped. Could it be that she had been held so seldom that she never learned how to hold on? Even babies carried on their mother's backs in Korea have their legs free to wrap. That's why we had been told by Mary that the babies are sometimes slightly bowlegged. But then, Asia had only had a foster mother for six months.

We arranged to have Asia's development evaluated by a team of physical and occupational therapists at Nat Polinsky Rehabilitation Center, where my friend Dorothy worked. It was decided that a speech evaluation was not appropriate at the time, since she didn't really have any speech to evaluate. Asia had been with us for barely five weeks when we went for the evaluation. For all Asia knew or cared, the two therapists were just playing with her. They didn't look like doctors and the room was designed like a giant playroom, so she loved it. They had all sorts of wonderful things to look at--a mirror to smear lotion on, with the therapists' help, balls and rings to swat, and balls large enough to sit and bounce on. But all the while, the quality of every movement Asia made was being noted and assessed. The therapists felt that Asia's overall developmental age was between seven and nine months of age. However, because of the quality and variety of her movement patterns, they believed, as Jerry and I did, that her delays were the result of a lack of stimulation, rather than a permanent condition. Both therapists felt that although Asia's behavioral and physical development was significantly below her age level, the prognosis for normal development in all areas was good. We left with a long list of at-home activities to help strengthen Asia and improve her muscle control, and new allies in our commitment to our daughter. We were encouraged to call with questions or to ask for advice, and tentatively planned to return for a reevaluation after Asia's surgery was completed.

Meanwhile, we watched Asia begin to blossom like an exotic hot-house flower that was finally in its own element. She began to play with objects with her hands for longer periods of time and loved anything that made noise. Her eagerness to keep up with her sister led her to other rooms in the house, and before long, she became quite the explorer on her own, although she crawled with her fists clinched. Soon she began pulling herself up by the sofa and taking a few hesitant sideways steps. Her ankles were very weak and rolled inward, but we were sure that the more she was on her feet, the stronger and straighter they would get. She played less with her fingers, ground her teeth less, and had fewer of the "blanking out" spells--she was simply too busy.

The biggest change was in her disposition. She seemed genuinely happy most of the time. Sometimes she would throw her head back and laugh from the joy of feeling good. She became a hopeless flirt and had quite an array of comical expressions she would use quite suddenly and send us into fits of laughter. Putting Meghann in the bathtub with her helped, and soon Asia forgot that she didn't like getting her hands wet and was splashing around in the water in imitation of her sister.

Her progress amazed friends who saw her only every couple of weeks. She was adjusting so well that we decided to investigate the possibility of starting her surgery early in the summer, in order to allow maximum recovery time during the "nicer" months of northern Minnesota's year. Always optimistic, I had geared myself for surgery in late May or early June, a one-week hospital stay, a one-month recovery, a one-week hospital stay again, and the rest of the summer to rebuild and fatten up our little girl. It never occurred to me that life didn't operate by my personal timetable and that the reality might be completely different.

We made arrangements for a preliminary examination by Dr. Phillip Eckman and notified my mother, who was planning to fly out to keep home and hearth together while I stayed in the hospital with Asia.

Although the original diagnosis we had been given was Hirschprung's disease, several other possibilities had been mentioned in documents we had received from Korea. In order to determine the exact condition, Dr. Eckman ordered barium X-rays of Asia's large intestine. This procedure could be performed at the clinic in a few hours. Anyone who has undergone this particular test knows that, at best, it is uncomfortable, but for a child with Asia's history and language limitations, it would be terrifying. Dr. Eckman agreed that Asia could be given a mild sedative.

Mother planned to arrive on May sixteenth and the X-rays were to be done on the following day. After Asia's reaction to my Mother's picture, I couldn't wait to see how she would respond to the real thing! As mother walked off the airplane,

Asia raised her arms to the grandmother whose picture she had carried in a bottle. Grandmother and granddaughter may have just met face-to-face for the first time, but they were not strangers. Mother had followed Asia's progress by phone calls, letters, and pictures for nearly six months, and Asia had used my mother's picture as an explorer uses a compass to chart unknown territory. No, they were never strangers.

Our instructions were not to give Asia anything to eat or drink after midnight Monday night. Withholding food would not cause too much problem, but Asia expected her bottle as soon as her eyes opened in the morning. We counted on the novelty of having Grandma Betty around to take her mind off her missing bottle. We arrived at the Clinic at 8 A.M. and were taken to the X-ray department almost immediately.

"There are no orders for a sedative on the chart, Mrs. Renning," the nurse said. "For some reason, Dr. Eckman had must have changed his mind. Let's just get started and see how she does. We'll be done in no time," she said, confidently. Against all my instincts, I let them go ahead.

By the time the first part of the test was completed, Asia was hysterical. No one could believe how incredibly strong this tiny, frail-looking child was. It took four adults to hold her for the test. "Please, please, call Dr. Eckman. Tell him this isn't working," I begged. "Ask if you can't give her *something*. This is beyond cruel."

Finally, they agreed, and I tried my best to calm Asia. We walked, bounced, patted, sang, and hummed, but as soon as I stopped moving or came too close to the examining table, she screamed and clung to me. The nurses came back with the welcome news that Asia could have a mild sedative, and while we waited for it to take effect, I sang that old standby, "Twinkle, Twinkle, da-da-da" in Korean and rocked Asia as she fell asleep.

Asia was sleeping so lightly from the sedative that when we moved into the X-ray room, she woke up. She was just groggy enough to be disoriented, and no amount of comforting would calm her for the barium enema and X-rays that would follow.

We were told that Dr. Eckman would call us the following day with the test results. The X-rays showed that, except for the colostomy, Asia's bowel was intact, complete with anus, which eliminated one diagnostic possibility. To be completely sure of Hirschprung's disease, however, a biopsy would be performed just prior to surgery, to determine the amount of large intestine with no functioning nerve endings. Surgery was scheduled for Wednesday, May twenty-fifth at 7 A.M. Asia and I were to check into St. Mary's Hospital on Monday afternoon for tests beginning on Tuesday.

We spent the rest of the week getting organized for Mother's stay and acquainting her with the household routines. Having her here made it so much easier for me to be away for at least a week, knowing that Jerry and Meghann's home life would not be too disrupted. Meghann understood the reason for my staying in the hospital with Asia, and was handling the prospect of our first- ever separation quite well. However, there was no way to prepare Asia for what was about to happen. She had spent so much of her short life in hospitals, in institutions, and in pain. We could only hope that her time with us had helped to dim some of those memories.

Chapter Ten

More Milestones and Miracles

ON MONDAY AFTERNOON Asia and I (armed with a cooler of Coca-Cola and my needlepoint) left Meghann and Grandma Betty and drove to the hospital to meet Jerry. Asia was admitted and we were taken to a four-crib ward on the pediatric floor. The nurses had arranged for a large, fold-out chair-bed beside Asia's crib for me. That functional, no frills crib was the first place where Asia began to sense that things were not quite as they should be. When she had to put on pajamas in the middle of the day, her suspicions grew. And when Jerry left and we stayed, she knew that something was definitely up. Asia's prescribed liquid diet until surgery also caused her disposition to drop a few more notches. In the past five weeks, she had learned that there was more to life than her bottle, and that the stuff I fed her with a spoon wouldn't kill her after all. The pediatric floor's well-equipped playroom included some of Asia's favorite toys, however, and helped take her mind off where she was. By bedtime she was tired enough to sleep in the crib.

On Tuesday we both began to slip into the hospital routine of breakfast, bath, doctor's visit, play time, lunch, nap, etc. The anesthesiologist stopped by to give us the schedule for Wednesday. We spoke many times with Meghann, Mother, and Jerry. Other friends and family called with good wishes and prayers. When Dr. Eckman came by just before Asia's bedtime. he brought news of a possible change in the plans for the surgery.

"There's a chance that I may be able to perform both operations tomorrow," he said. "I won't know until I'm in there, so there won't be any way to let you know. But if the surgery lasts longer than three to three-and-a-half hours, you can figure we're doing both."

This would eliminate the need for a second operation to close the stoma. It was almost too much to hope for. Although Asia didn't understand the significance of Dr. Eckman's news, I slept better that night than I would have ever thought possible.

Dawn. The sun was rising over Lake Superior and the huge "salties," the ocean-going ships, were moving in and out of the harbor, sea gulls swooping and diving in their wake. The nurses woke me early to shower before waking Asia. Again, she wasn't even allowed the comfort of a bottle that morning, so we rocked and tickled and sang until the nurses came with a sedative to prepare her for surgery. As the drug began to take effect and Asia's eyes lost their focus, the reality of the day hit me. Our poor little baby girl had already gone through more psychological pain than many people experience in a lifetime. She had lost her birth mother to death, and lost her father and brothers to the pressure of a society with no room for single parents. She had suffered surgery, pain and illness with no mother's arms to hold her, no father's knee to bounce on, and no sister to bring her toys or teach her to do somersaults. She had been taken from the only family she had ever known and sent with total strangers to live halfway around the world in a new life that she couldn't begin to understand. And now, just when it seemed that this new life might not be so bad after all, here she was again, back in the hospital again, going through surgery *again,* headed for pain *again!* I ached to be able to explain to her, to reassure her that, God willing, this would be her last surgery, and that no matter what, she would not be uprooted again. I longed to tell her of the wonderful life she had to look forward to, full of love and good health, and free of pain. But all I could do was hold her, and rock her limp little body while I sang "Twinkle, Twinkle" and tried not to cry. As the nurses wheeled Asia's crib to surgery, another mother from across the hall came over, put her arms around me, and cried with me.

I called Jerry at work and Mother and Meghann at home to let them know that the long wait had started. By 10 A.M. I was almost halfway through the needlepoint picture I was doing for Asia's room in our "someday" larger house. The picture was a mother swan leading two cygnets through a cattail-filled pond. Fat, white clouds floated overhead in a blue bowl of sky. "I could live there," I thought. There had been no word about the surgery. 10:30, then eleven o'clock came and went, and after calling Mother and Jerry and telling the nurses where I'd be, I went for a visit to the newborn intensive care unit to meet a Korean doctor I'd heard about. Dr. Pi knew of Asia through Dr. Eckman, and had assisted in translating some of Asia's medical documents before her arrival. The unit was alive with activity as doctors and nurses cared for the impossibly tiny infants, who were so hooked to monitors that they looked like miniature octopi. Still, it was a room full of life and hope. Dr. Pi was concerned and sympathetic, and promised to visit Asia after the surgery.

Shortly after returning to our room, Kathy Young and her fiance, Gene Powers, came to wait with me. Kathy had been through this with her own son Garrett. A few minutes later Dorothy arrived, and while we were in the middle of introductions, Dr. Eckman came in with the news that the surgery was over. He had removed approximately six inches of lower bowel with no nerve endings and had rejoined the large intestine and closed the stoma. Barring any complications, no second surgery would be necessary.

What a wonderful gift he had just given us and our daughter. I had to kiss the man! Asia was in recovery, he said, and would be back in the room in about an hour. Enough time for me to make the necessary phone calls, Jerry first, then Mother and Meghann, who was thrilled that her sister no longer needed the colostomy bags. Meghann, always thinking, said we should send the bags and other supplies left over to Korea. What a kid! I then called Barb Dalley, who relayed the good news to C.H.S.M. and several friends in Minneapolis.

Asia returned from recovery to a bedside table filled with flowers and helium balloons floating in the air above her crib. She slept the rest of the day and most of the next. Because of IVs and catheters and nose tubes, I was not able to hold her yet, so I sat in the chair and talked and sang to her while she was awake, and worked on her picture when she slept. In order to allow maximum healing time for the large intestine, she was allowed no food for several days, and received her nourishment through the IV. Her temperature was monitored, her diaper changed and she was given occasional shots for pain. The nurses who cared for her so tenderly were crushed when she greeted their appearance with screams. Dr. Eckman, though, had no such problems with her. He would arrive dressed in street clothes or surgical greens, anything but the hated white, and Asia would go right to him.

Asia's recovery was rapid, and by Saturday she was considered ready for a liquid diet. The suggested first clear liquid was a red colored fruit punch, which would have been greeted enthusiastically by most American youngsters, but it sent Asia into fits. She was so thirsty that she finally drank it, only to have her system reject it. It went in one end and immediately came out the other, with the same color, and I thought she was bleeding to death. Okay, we'll try again tomorrow.

"Can't we try giving her half-strength soy formula?" I asked the nurse. "It's all she's really ever had to drink, and her body is used to it." What a radical idea, mothers making suggestions to the doctors. Who do we think we are, anyway? But they got permission to try one ounce of formula every two hours. When that stayed with her, we were given the green light to try two ounces every two hours. The formula was working where the red liquid hadn't. The nurses tried to let me sleep through several of the middle-of-the-night feedings, but Asia would not allow them to give her the bottle. It was such a relief to see her drinking that I didn't mind waking up to feed her. With the liquid diet now a success, it was time to try Asia on cereal, which she ate with relish, and her system handled it well. By Tuesday morning we were both champing at the bit to be out of the hospital, and on Wednesday, after the surgical staples were removed, Asia and I left for home.

It wasn't until the second day at home that we began to see the terrible toll that the hospital stay and surgery had taken on Asia's emotional well-being. She almost completely reverted to the nearly autistic child who had arrived from Korea. Only this time, it was even more frightening, because we'd seen how far she had come. She would lie on the floor with her back to us, rejecting us completely. It was as if she were saying, "I loved you, and I trusted you, against my better judgment, and look what you did to me." She refused to smile, steadfastly ignored any attempt to play, and retreated into the security of her finger play, her teeth grinding and her bottle. As frightening as this was for us, our experience with Asia so far had taught us that this was her way of handling an incredibly painful situation, and when she was ready, she would come back to us. We only hoped it would be soon. By Saturday, Asia began to show a little interest in Jerry and Meghann wrestling, and on Sunday morning when she pulled on my thumbs and wanted to play "Rock Rock," we knew we had our daughter back. I shuddered to think what would have happened to her had I not stayed in the hospital with her.

One week following her release from the hospital, Asia was pronounced recovered by Dr. Eckman. "These are totally new sensations for her body, so it will be some time before she has bowel control, but the surgery was completely successful."

"Do we have to watch what we feed her?" I asked. "Are there special diets for children with Hirschprung's disease?"

"No, she can eat *anything* she wants. The diseased part of her large bowel was removed, and there are nerve endings in the rest," Dr. Eckman assured me. "Just feed her normally. She'll be just fine."

Her only problem was an insultingly red, painful, but totally normal diaper rash. By the time Mother left on June eighth, Asia was almost back up to speed, crawling again, and even trying to stand up by herself.

Having Asia's surgery completed in one step left us with an decision we hadn't previously considered--when and where to take our vacation. We checked with friends in Colorado and made plans to drive out for a two-week stay. It was our first trip in five years, back to the mountains where we had met, and the first time for any of our friends there to meet our children.

We arrived in Colorado after a twenty-six hour drive, and after taking the children into Don and Lori's house, Jerry and I returned to the car to start unpacking. Asia began crying the minute we left the room, even though Meghann was there. As Lori picked up Asia to comfort her, her cries turned to screams. We had wrongly assumed that Asia's adjustment was complete and that she knew as well as we did that she was our daughter. In her mind her worst fears had been realized--she had been left again, to start over with a new family. The constancy of the past three-and-a-half months had been a lie. Jerry and I ran back into the house and swooped Asia and Meghann onto our laps. Unpacking the car could wait. Later, as I calmed Asia, and Meghann explored the house with Don and Lori's daughter Heather, Jerry and Don unpacked the car. We watched Asia relax as she saw familiar things belonging to *all* of us being brought into the house. She finally began to realize that we were *all* staying.

In spite of the withering heat and the long drive, the trip was just the break we all needed from the tensions of the past few months. Asia recovered from her surgery, Meghann rode a horse for the first time, Jerry caught the world's most expensive trout, and I added shades to my suntan. On our return trip, as we made the last two turns to our house, Asia, from her car seat perspective, recognized the tops of the tree by the road, and she knew she was on her way home. She bounced in her seat, squealed and clapped her hands. It was another breakthrough for her. She had left two weeks earlier, stayed in many different homes, slept in many different beds, but always with Jerry, Meghann, and me. And now we were all coming home together.

We returned to a garden full of squash that threatened to take over the neighborhood and weeds intent on conquering the world. The unusually hot summer and fresh garden vegetables gave Asia a healthy glow, and we watched her grow stronger by the day. She began to take steps between Jerry and me if encouraged to. But she didn't have the strength yet to stand alone. I began holding her feet steady on the floor while she would pull herself to a standing position, thereby strengthening her stomach muscles. Meghann would take her hands and they would walk through the house, with Meghann pointing out and naming things for Asia. Finally, on August twentieth, at twenty-eight months of age, Asia stood up in the middle of the floor and started walking. She walked to the kitchen and back several times, never once falling. She held her arms up and slightly out, as though holding on to an invisible bar above her head for balance. After "forward" was mastered, she decided to try her hand at right-angle turns. Down the hall she went, laughing all the way. Next she tried out her brakes, and began to practice sudden starts and stops. She walked for two hours, continuously, until she was wringing wet with sweat. But she never fell. Holding our breath, Meghann and I had watched her in total amazement, and when she was through, I could contain myself no longer. Jerry was at a Jaycee meeting, so I called both grandmothers with the good news, then started on local friends.

Chapter Eleven

High-Speed Baby

LEARNING TO WALK opened both physical and mental doors for Asia. She seemed to gain confidence in her ability to learn other things. She started on a learning spree that I can only describe as "Fast Forward." Now she went everywhere at a trot. She was constantly on the move, and within a few days she was climbing onto and over everything in sight. She and Meghann played chase, and if Meghann was busy, Asia would run laps between the living room and the kitchen.

We had started several weeks before to encourage Asia to ask for things that she wanted rather than cry for them, and with the achievement of walking behind her, we hoped that talking would begin to come easier. She was required to say "up," or "puh" in her case, rather than scream to get out of bed in the mornings or after a nap.

Once she had mastered the word and knew what it meant, only once did she refuse to say it. It was her way of testing to see if we were as strong as we were. I must admit that there were times when I wondered that myself. Fortunately, we didn't have anywhere to go that day. I brought her bottles, but no toys. At first she was content to lie there and drink, but soon she became bored and began screaming, which I ignored until she stopped.

I walked into the bedroom, and as soon as she saw me, she scrambled to her feet and began to scream again. "Asia, if you want out of bed, say 'up,' honey." I said. I waited a few minutes, and when the screaming didn't stop, I left. The next time she stopped screaming, I went in again. "When you say 'up,' you can get out of bed, Asia," I repeated.

Asia stayed in her crib until 2 P.M. that day until she finally decided to say "up." On some instinctive level I knew that if I gave in, just once, she would continue to test every time. It was time, we decided, for Asia to begin to take some responsibility for her daily existence, and she resented it. Who wouldn't? Of course it was much easier to cry and expect people to anticipate your every need. We didn't expect her to learn volumes of words at one time, but we did sort of expect a response when we asked a direct question, complete with pantomime. "Do you want up?" "Are you hungry?" Blank, vacant looks and crying temper tantrums were not acceptable. Eventually we succeeded in getting her to repeat Mama, Dada, Agn (Meghann), and a few animal sounds, but they were all whispered, or distorted, sounding like someone who was deaf trying to learn to speak. The doctors, however, assured us that this was because of the adjustment, language differences, etc., etc. And we bought it, for a while.

Occasionally it seemed that for every two weeks of progress that Asia made, she would regress one week. Things that she had previously done well, she resisted. New accomplishments were out of the question. Regardless of the rewards, hugs, or consequences (no "ba-ba," no bottle), she would refuse to do anything.

Eventually we saw a pattern forming. Asia's progress would be put on hold at the beginning of any illness, no matter how minor. Because her system could not digest cow's milk, she had been drinking soy formula since her arrival. We gradually tried to introduce more milk into her diet as we had done with Meghann, but in Asia's case, the changes brought drastic digestive upsets. The digestive problems, in turn, resulted in developmental lags. Physical discomfort was met with intellectual indifference. She would revert to the old habits of "survival first." Until her health was restored, Asia would not practice new achievements or repeat old ones. But as soon as the physical condition was cleared up, her attitude improved and the learning would begin again.

When Asia had been walking for about a week, she had her second appointment at Polinsky for a reevaluation. This time it was the therapists turn to be amazed at her progress. In four months' time, she had gained eight months in development. Her surgery and recovery had hardly slowed her down.

There were times when I think the visits to Polinsky were as much for me as they were for Asia. Occasionally Jerry and I felt too close to the situation to be able to evaluate Asia's progress objectively. On the one hand, we didn't want to over-emphasize the gains she had made or read too much significance into her new accomplishments, while on the other hand, we didn't want to miss areas which needed more development. The visits to Polinsky left us properly encouraged with our collective successes and gave us new goals to work toward.

In early September C.H.S.M. had a summer picnic at a park in Minneapolis. Since Jerry had promised to help a good friend build a new patio that weekend, he was unable to attend, but Meghann, Asia, and I packed up the car Saturday morning, met Barb Dalley and her two children, and drove to the picnic grounds. It would be the first opportunity for many of our Minneapolis friends to see Asia since her surgery.

We hoped that Teri Bacall would be there. All of our efforts to get together since Asia's arrival had failed, and although we had sent her pictures and reports and had spoken on the phone, we were anxious to have Teri to *see* Asia. Of all the people at the agency, she would best be able appreciate the many and varied changes in her. Teri had seen Asia at her lowest point, and had seen a spark that told her that Asia was far from the hopeless case that the orphanage described. Shortly after we finished lunch, Bobbie Wiggins found us and led us through the trees to where Teri was sitting. Teri saw us coming, but didn't recognize us until we were almost to the large oak she was sitting under. When she recognized Asia, she couldn't get up fast enough. Teri was nearly in tears as she knelt on the grass and marveled at how well Asia looked. Teri grabbed a fistful of grass and held it out on her palm to Asia, who neatly flicked each blade away as expertly as a champion marble shooter. Asia had refined her earlier method of pushing things with the tip of her index finger and had added a deadly aim. Teri was planning a trip to Korea at the end of October, and promised to take pictures and a glowing report of Asia to her agency, and hopefully also to Mrs. Choi, Asia's foster mother. Here were two of the many people to whom we felt indebted for our daughter's very life. Had Teri not found Asia in the orphanage and seen that indefinable "something" in her eyes, who knows what would have happened. Had Mrs. Choi and her wonderful family not opened their home and hearts to Oh, Kyung Hee, in spite of her physical and emotional challenges, she probably would have had to stay in the orphanage, where she would surely have died, not from lack of food or medical attention, but from a lack of the one thing she needed most, her own family. We only carried on what the Choi family had started, and gave that spark that Teri had seen a protected, sheltered place to catch fire.

Also in September, Meghann began her first year at a Montessori preschool and her second year of ballet and gymnastics. The hours Meghann was in school gave Asia the opportunity to see what life was like as an only child, and though she enjoyed my undivided attention, she was always happy to see her sister.

At the beginning of October, Asia's legal adoption was completed. Although Jerry and I had managed to put the negative events of March behind us most of the time, it was a wonderful relief to know that Asia was now legally our daughter.

No October would have been complete without C.H.S.M.'s Korean Orphan Benefit Dinner. This annual event is sponsored by volunteers for C.H.S.M. to raise money to help Eastern Child Welfare Society. Since Meghann and so many of our friends' children are "Eastern kids," we welcomed the opportunity to attend and add our support to the Korean agency that had brought us so much joy. This year, in addition to the outstanding entertainment provided by the Korean Institute of Minnesota, a dozen or so C.H.S.M. children were going to perform a song from the musical <u>Annie,</u> called, "You're Never Fully Dressed Without a Smile." Meghann had been invited to join them. At the end of the song, Mrs. Han, the Korean social worker, was presented with a bouquet of roses. As the children gathered around this wonderful lady and she stooped to embrace each of them, there wasn't a dry eye in the room.

And now we had come full circle. It was November again, exactly one year since our hearts were first captured by the picture and description of Oh, Kyung Hee. A year ago, she was a dream, and now that picture had become a very real little girl. A year ago we had asked for our friends' prayers to "pull off a miracle." And it worked. A year ago I had begun writing a "short" story, in an attempt to raise money to bring our daughter home to us, and now look what had happened. As I watched our two daughters playing, I could not help feeling blessed. Asia was babbling constantly, bringing her bottle when she was thirsty and her diaper when she needed to be changed. She had added several words to her vocabulary and many hearts to her list of conquests. She was beginning to have bowel control, and like all survivors, had an incredibly strong will.

Instead of playing with her fingers all the time, she started to play with her sister, relying less on self stimulation and more on interaction. She was comfortable at the baby sitters', and blew kisses to me as she trotted off to play with the toys in the big trunk at Pat's. She had turned into a fish in the bath tub.

Although clinically Asia's future developments were not

certain at that point, what we had seen had told us that there are no limits to what she can achieve. At a picnic late in the summer, we watched as Asia walked off, on her own, unafraid, to explore the surroundings. She would stop from time to time to check our location, then march up to a tree and laugh. For a while, at least, her trials were over, and her scars were fading, both the physical and psychological ones.

For every gain that Asia made, Jerry and I learned volumes about ourselves. We were pushed to levels of patience that we didn't realize we possessed. We learned to gear down our expectations and to be thrilled with what others might consider modest accomplishments. We learned that the basics--food, and love, not necessarily in that order, really are the most important to a child, and everything else is secondary. We learned that we can do twelve things at once. And we'd do it all again.

Instead of causing jealousy, Big Sisterhood gave Meghann a maturity beyond her years. She was ever watchful of her baby sister, and never failed to remind us of the rights and privileges that went along with her responsibilities. Jerry had attained the enviable status of *Hero in Residence* and scarcely made it through the door before being pounced on by two adoring daughters.

The original purpose of this book was to chronicle Meghann and Asia's early history for my family and friends. However, if even one family who reads it decides to start or add to their family through adoption, I'll be thrilled. And if someone, somewhere out there finds it in their hearts to "take a chance" on a child that someone else has labeled "hard to place" or even "hopeless," I'll consider this attempt at writing an unqualified success.

Written in 1983-84

Meghann at thirty-five days old.
This is the first picture
we saw of her .

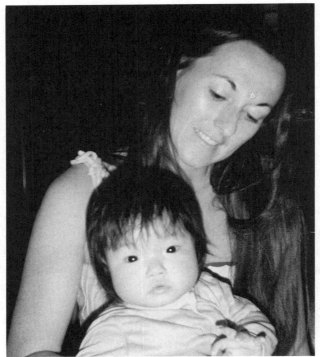

June 19, 1980 Minneapolis-St. Paul Airport
The aide had just handed her to me.

Meghann and Grandma Betty.
November 22, 1980
Meghann's first birthday.

Meghann's first birthday.
November 22, 1980

Meghann and all three grandparents. My mom, Betty
Nichols and Jerry's parents, Bud and Wim Renning.

The first picture we saw of Asia, in <u>News of Ours.</u>
She was about fifteen months old.

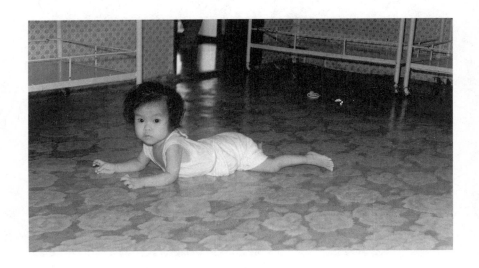

Asia in the orphanage in Korea.
Notice how thin her arms and legs are.

Adair, Asia and Meghann at Asia's arrival, March 26, 1993.

Part II

Unlocking Asia

And now, for the rest of the story . . .

IT IS NOW May of 1994, ten years since I completed what is now Part One of this story. At that point Asia had been with us for eight months. She had made many gains, more than some believed possible, and seemed well on her way to closing the gap between her developmental age and her chronological age. We foresaw a bright future for her.

My intention for the original manuscript, as I mentioned above, was that it be a history for our two daughters of how we all became a family.

But now, with all the twists and turns that Asia's, and consequently our, lives have taken, I feel compelled to begin writing again, to share all that we have learned, and perhaps save another child from some of the unnecessary suffering Asia has experienced.

With that goal in mind, I am going to attempt to reconstruct, as accurately as possible, the past ten years. At a time like this, hypnotic regression would be helpful, but I'll just have to rely on my phenomenal memory for dates, facts, and figures (no comments, please).

Chapter Twelve

The First Irish/Korean War

FOR ALL OF Asia's progress during her first year with us, there were still many things that concerned us. We weren't sure if we were expecting too much too fast or if we were playing ostrich, hoping the trouble would miraculously go away.

So far, Asia's personal plumbing seemed to be working just fine, and although she still didn't bite or chew anything, she had learned to eat most foods if they were cut into bite-sized pieces. But despite our elaborate and exaggerated pantomimes, she would or could not copy the act of *chewing* food. It went down the same size as it went in. Oh well, we figured, at least she was no longer undernourished. And, we rationalized, you can't fight on all fronts at once.

My incessant reading had taught me that children's skills need to be learned in a certain order, and that there are optimum times in a child's development for certain skills to be learned. If those "windows" are missed, then the skill will be more difficult to learn later.

Because of Asia's extended crib time, delayed crawling and tactile sensitivity, she missed most of the "hand-to-mouth" play that is not only a means of exploring the world, but a vital precursor to self-feeding.

So we actually needed to take her backward before she could go forward. She had to pick up the skills she had missed in order to fill in the gap.

United Developmental Achievement Center arranged for an occupational therapist, Barb Tostrup, to come to our house once a week to work with Asia on her fine motor skills. Since the theory was that she resisted holding objects because the lack of time spent crawling on different textures had caused the palms of her hands to be too sensitive, that was the place to start. And Barb's arsenal was limitless.

Because of Asia's fascination with small cars (she would spin the wheels for hours), Barb used them as bait. She brought ice cream buckets filled with a variety of items with different shapes and textures. One bucket had cotton balls, another dried beans, another popped pop corn, another with small erasers. Buried deep inside each bucket was a small car, and Asia would have to dig in to get her treasure. The one she absolutely refused was Jell-o cubes. No car made was worth touching that slippery, moving stuff. Barb brought texture boxes, blocks to stack, puzzles and games, and patiently worked Asia through different age-level skills. Barb's patience paid off, and eventually we had Asia building small towers and trains with the blocks, and putting simple puzzles together.

Through most of these sessions, Asia was essentially non-verbal. Barb tried the traditional "finger snapping, bell ringing" behind her head, and Asia would respond, but she made no attempt to imitate our speech. When Korean friends tried speaking to her, she seemed not to hear them any more than she heard us. We thought she might be afraid she would be taken away if she answered them.

Asia developed a fascination with abdomens--other peoples. She loved warm weather when people were in fewer clothes. She was only three, so when she patted their stomachs, nobody really minded. She would touch their stomachs and then look at her own. She was checking to see if they had scars like she did, and was overjoyed when she found someone that did. Only once did she carry this curiosity too far. Meghann, Asia, and I had driven to Minneapolis to pick up my mom at the airport. We were in the baggage claim area, waiting for her luggage to come around on the carousel, when Asia slipped free of my hand and wandered away. By the time I spotted her, she had cornered a very distinguished, very well-dressed man with a briefcase handcuffed to his wrist. (Perhaps he was a courier.) She had pulled part of his shirt out of his pants and was "scar searching" before I could open my mouth to yell. I threw up my hands and walked away, muttering under my breath, "Not my kid. I've never seen her before in my life." Meanwhile, my mom, (who's never met a stranger either), made excuses and apologized to the poor bewildered man. Someone with a gun he probably could have handled, but not a three-year-old with a scar fetish.

One day, in the spring of 1984, Asia refused her bottle. This was a child who not only ate to live but lived to eat, so bottle refusal was not normal. Not really believing it would work, I filled her brand new, never used Tommy Tippy cup with formula, and lo and behold, she *drank from it.* I was elated. No difficult weaning, just give up the bottle and pick up the cup. Who would have ever believed it? She hardly even dribbled. It was wonderful. It was too good to be true. Well, you know what "they" say about something that seems too good to be true: it probably isn't.

Not too many weeks later, I handed her her cup and she just held it and looked at me. I said (much to my regret months later), "Go ahead, Asia, take a drink, honey." From that day on, before she would drink from *any* cup of *anything* given to her by *anybody,* she had to be told "Go ahead, honey, take a drink." Then she would drink until finished.

After a week or so of this, I was totally exasperated, and talked it over with my friend Dorothy, who is a psychologist. "Can this be some need for reassurance, or is it fulfilling some other empty emotional slot?" I asked. "We know that she knows how to drink from this cup, but she just looks up at me expectantly, waiting patiently for me to tell her to drink."

"It seems like such a little thing to us, but maybe it's not so little to her, so keep it up for a while and see if she gets tired of the game," Dorothy said. So I continued, thinking she would soon feel secure enough and give it up on her own. *Wrong!* Three months later I was still saying, "Asia, take a drink." And by then she had added a new twist--she wanted to be told to take a drink before each sip. My Irish side came roaring to the surface. I imagined a fourteen-year-old Asia with a Tommy Tippy cup full of formula, waiting for her l'il ole grey-haired mom to say, "Go ahead Asia, take a drink, honey." And I freaked out. She was certainly getting plenty of love and attention, and she had mastered the skill of drinking from the cup months before.

She pointed to her cup and said, "Ba." (We hadn't progressed to the word "cup" yet). I filled it, put the top on, handed it to her, said, "Here, honey," and walked into the other room. It was the beginning of the first battle in the now famous Irish/Korean Wars.

She followed me from room to room, cup in hand, waiting for me to say the magic words, and I did everything else. I talked about what was on TV, when Meghann was coming home from school, what was for dinner, everything but what she wanted me to say. She cried. She screamed. I took the cup away and sent her to her room. The cup went into the refrigerator.

A few hours later, after time-out was over, Asia said, "Ba." I handed her the cup and walked away. She held the cup in my face, trying to *will* me to say the words. I refused. In case you didn't know, in addition to being superstitious, we Irish are also a *wee bit* stubborn. She cried. She screamed. I took the cup away and sent her to her room.

Time for dinner. I had fixed soup, in case the siege lasted much longer, so she wouldn't become dehydrated. I fed her the soup, which she slurped down happily, and handed her the cup after she got down from the high chair. . .fill in the rest with the above paragraph. I dumped the milk down the drain and washed the cup when she went to bed. Part of me said, "This is cruel. How can you refuse her such a simple thing? You are heartless and a poor excuse for a mother. Is it really so important?" But I *knew* that it was important. If I gave in, I was lost. I had to stand my ground or quit right then.

Two-and-a-half days, lots of time-outs, tears, and soup later, Asia took the cup from me and, screaming all the while, gulped down four ounces of formula, shoved the cup in my face and yelled "*More!*" She drank four cups of milk, each punctuated with, "*More!*" She developed other games later on, which, in turn, became other battlegrounds, but in this first war I had won. And so, in the long run, had she.

Cindy got married in August 1984. Her husband, Steve Eggleston, was in the Coast Guard, stationed at the Lake Superior Base. Having created so many spectacularly beautiful weddings for others, including us, Cindy chose a quiet wedding for herself and Steve, with a large reception several weeks later. At last--an occasion for Meghann to wear the beautiful peach dotted Swiss flower girl dress I had made for her to wear in Sun Cha's wedding. Asia wore a lime green dress with accordion pleats. They looked like sherbet children. The summer sun had left them both tanned and glowing. Cindy was radiant and Steve quietly, gallantly handsome. It was a grand celebration of their marriage with only one catch. Steve's tour of duty in Duluth was finished, and he and Cindy were moving to Portland, Maine. My best friend, my sister, who knew me with all of my warts and hairs and loved me anyway, was packing up, lock, stock, and Samoyed, and heading east. I was thrilled for her. She was beginning a new life with a man she loved, who adored her. They had already talked of adopting.

On Halloween, with Meghann dressed as a pussycat, we stopped to say good-bye. The empty house echoed as we walked through, checking for forgotten items. I would be lost without her. As friends go, she would be a tough act to follow.

Chapter Thirteen

Doctor-Hopping

ASIA'S ABJECT TERROR of doctor's visits knew no bounds, and we constantly had to come up with new routes to take to get there. Once Asia knew the way, she would recognize landmarks and begin screaming miles before we were there.

This did have one slight advantage, however, if you're into sick humor. We *never* had to wait in the waiting rooms. I could imagine the nurses saying, "Quick, get room twelve ready and don't put anyone on either side--here comes Asia." The drawback, however, was that no one ever listened to me when I tried to tell them that Asia's few attempts at speech were not clear, and that I felt that something was wrong with her hearing. They would look in her ears hurriedly and confidently tell me, "Well, yes, Mrs. Renning, her ears are red, but that's because she's screaming." (Of course she's screaming; she hates it here and she's scared to death of you.) "I'm sure her speech will clear up as soon as she adjusts a little more." The few words she did say, she had begun to whisper. She was such an incredibly quiet child that there were times when I would forget that she was in the car. Once I was halfway across the parking lot at the mall when I realized, "My gosh, I left Asia in the car!!" Jerry and I longed for the day when we could tell her to "Please be quiet, Asia."

Meanwhile, her teeth grinding habit was beginning to drive us crazy. It had escalated in both frequency and volume, and no amount of behavior modification could control it. Not, "Asia, please don't grind your teeth," or "Asia, thank you for not grinding your teeth," or "Asia, if you have to grind your teeth, please go in another room." Sometimes you could hear her from the other room anyway.

Dr. Day was no longer at the clinic we went to so finally, at the risk of being called a neurotic, doctor-hopping mother, I took Asia to another pediatrician. I chose the doctor Kathy Young used since she would be familiar with children with Hirschprung's disease. We warned the office in advance, and they arranged for us to be the last patient before lunch, to avoid traumatizing any of the other children with Asia's screaming. In order to thoroughly examine Asia's ears, the nurse strapped her to a "papoose board" (substitute junior strait jacket) and flushed out bloody earwax the size of Grape Nuts. She had a galloping ear infection and much fluid behind the eardrums. She was put on Amoxycillin on and off for eight months, after which not only was the ear infection cleared, but the teeth grinding miraculously disappeared and she began to speak instead of whisper. Her voice, however, still had the quality of a deaf person who has learned speech. Her words were garbled because that was the way she had heard them for at least a year, probably more. We suspect that she had probably had ear infections for the better part of her life. By grinding her teeth, she had been sort of scratching an itch in her ears. But she had managed to grind off most of the enamel on all four of her back baby teeth in the process.

Because of Asia's intense fear of anything even remotely resembling a doctor's office, and because of her inability to respond to the test questions, traditional hearing tests were out of the question. At. St. Mary's hospital, under mild oral anesthesia, a brain stem audiogram was done, and showed that not only did Asia have no hearing loss because of the long-term infection, but her hearing tested "10% *better than normal*." At the time, I thought, "Hey, that's really great!" Now I have a better understanding of what it really means.

It was about this time that I realized something which other mothers out there may identify with. None of the letters after a doctor's name spell GOD. But we have elevated them to deity status and allowed ourselves to be intimidated by them to the point of reverence. It began to make me sick. I found that doctors were threatened if I spoke in words of more than two syllables, especially if I was able to pronounce any of the words pertaining to Asia's condition correctly. And they became downright hostile if I knew what they meant! There was no teamwork in treating our daughter. I tried to be more discriminating about the doctors we chose. If they talked *with* me, gave me credit for having more than half a brain, and allowed for the remote possibility that I could and would continue to read anything and everything I could get my hands on that might help Asia, they passed. Otherwise, it was more doctor hopping.

Periodically, Asia would have "absence-type" spells. She would literally blank out for a few seconds--the lights were on, but no one was home. They happened so fast that if you weren't looking at just the right time, you'd miss them. Our doctor had us keep a diary of when they happened, what she was doing, what she had eaten, any unusual noises, smells, or storms, what she was wearing, all in an attempt to find a pattern for their occurrence. We found none, but I would sometimes record as many as fifteen in a five-or ten-minute period. There were never any seizures exactly, at least not what I thought of as seizures, but she was definitely *gone*. If I snapped my fingers, she would blink back, but would she have blinked otherwise? I don't know. Where did she go when she was *gone*? Did she even know she was *gone*? Could she control it, and leave whenever she wanted or needed to? Or were the spells totally out of her control? I wanted answers. Our doctor felt that an EEG would be useless, because, given her fear of any type of medical procedure, she would have to be tranquilized in order to perform it, and that would alter the results. Eventually they disappeared, at least temporarily. I would have to do without answers.

Barb, from United Developmental Achievement Center, continued her weekly visits, bringing with her a tackle box full of tricks to improve Asia's fine motor skills. We put pennies in banks, learned about zippers and buttons, worked on "in front of," "behind," "above," and "under." With the exception of a handful of words, Asia was still mostly nonverbal. But since regaining her hearing, we felt that she was beginning to understand more of what was said to her.

For gross-motor skills, and also because a friend who was into holistic medicine suggested it, we got Asia a small exercise trampoline. The theory was that it would not only strengthen the muscles in her legs, but would increase the oxygen supply to her brain. At first we held her hands while she jumped. Soon, she wore out one person, and we would switch. Before long, if we had company, we all took turns holding her hands, sometimes for one thousand or more jumps (yes, we counted--three hundred for each person, minimum). She could tire all of the adults in the room, who were only sitting, holding her hands, and not even be breathing hard herself.

Sometime in late 1983, Asia had begun having trouble sleeping through the night. She would wake several times, screaming and thrashing in her bed, sobbing. The first time terrified me, because it was exactly like the first few nights she had been with us. But she was bigger and stronger now. The first night Jerry and I both bolted out of bed at her first cry. "Her eyes are open but I don't think she even knows we're here," I cried as we carried her, kicking and screaming, out of the room to keep from waking Meghann. Her eyes moved around the room as if she didn't recognize anything. She was not seeing our living room but some nightmare landscape, populated by her own private monsters. And she had no language to tell us what terrified her so. "Go on back to bed, honey," I told Jerry. "You have to work tomorrow. I'll sit up with her." It would take an hour or more for me to calm her into exhaustion, only to be awakened again before dawn. We came to call these episodes "night terrors," and sought explanations for them from various professionals.

At first we thought that it might have been a fear of her crib (waking up and seeing the bars). We believe that she may have been physically restrained in her early life, because there were red marks on her wrists and ankles when she arrived from Korea that took months to fade. This may have been done to prevent her from hurting or clawing herself as she had done with the hives. There's so much that we'll never know. So we removed the crib and let her share the double bed with her sister. That only lasted for a few nights, because the "night terrors" continued and Meghann was falling asleep in Montessori school. On to Plan C. We put the crib mattress on the floor, Korean style, hoping this was the answer. Nope, wrong again. We tried keeping her up later and eliminating naps. Our pediatrician suggested giving her Benadryl before bedtime to calm her, but she woke screaming, thrashing, kicking, *and groggy.*

After many months of Asia's night terrors, I was exhausted, confused, and frightened. Was the rest of our life going to be like this? Finally, a child behavior specialist asked if, since these episodes had started, she had ever slept through the night. I really had to think long and hard about that one, but I remembered a night during the summer of 1984 when it was too hot to sleep in our bedrooms (yes, we still lived in Minnesota) so we all "camped out" in the living room, Jerry and I sleeping on the sofa bed, Meghann and Asia on the floor.

The specialist suggested that we try letting her sleep in the living room, on the floor. Jerry was dead set against it. But then Jerry could sleep through a re-enactment of the burning of Atlanta. "Living rooms are for living, not sleeping," he said. "That's why God made bedrooms."

"I'm the one who gets up with her every night, and personally, I don't care if she sleeps standing on her head in the bathtub, just as long as she sleeps." We bought a child's sleeping bag and at 9 P.M. made a pallet on the floor, where Asia promptly fell asleep. We tiptoed to bed about 11 P.M. and woke to the alarm the next morning, sure that Asia was dead. I had just had my second full night's sleep in nearly eighteen months. It didn't matter how many people were over, or how loud the TV or music was, she slept right through it.

At the time, we believed that it was an intense fear of small enclosed spaces that brought on these spells, since she reacted the same way any time we took her into any office or small room, day or night, doctor's office or not. But in reality, we'll never know. As with so much of her early life, we resort to speculation in an attempt to try to make sense of the peculiarities. Eventually (years later) she was able to accept small spaces if the doors were left open.

Chapter Fourteen

Forward and Backward

ASIA HAD ALWAYS been a difficult child to buy gifts for. Dolls and stuffed animals didn't interest her. Games and puzzles gathered dust. She couldn't care less about new clothes and wouldn't sit still long enough for us to read to her. The only games she would really play with Meghann involved rough housing and tumbling, but no Barbies or tea parties. Toy cars, however, continued to be her passion, spinning their wheels for hours . . . sometimes flipping over wagons and tricycles to spin their wheels. When friends came over in trucks, I watched her sizing them up, trying to figure out how to flip *them* over to spin those tires. I really wouldn't have put it past her to try.

She still loved her strawberry musical toy, since it only required one finger to play, so we needed something that worked on the same principal. The answer was a learning aid with a voice module by Texas Instruments called "Touch and Tell." I don't remember who told me about it, but if you're out there and you read this, "thank you," from the bottom of our hearts. This "toy" brought Asia into the world of words. The module that came with it was called "All About Me," and had pages with pictures of a face, another with a farm scene, another with articles of clothing. When you pressed a section of the picture, the voice would say, "You have found the_____(red car, blue truck, socks)," whatever. "Can you find the_____(tree, barn, cat, etc.)" You get the idea. Incorrect responses brought the reply, "No that is the_____. Can you find the _____?" It never raised its voice. It was never impatient (although it would shut off automatically after five minutes of unuse). It was always ready to play, with the touch of a finger. And best of all, it was Asia-proof. It was perfect.

For months, Asia randomly touched the pictures, and seemed to make no attempt to learn, in spite of all our efforts to help. We guessed it must be too advanced for her, and that we were expecting too much too soon. One afternoon, after the ear infections had been cleared up, I was washing dishes when, suddenly, all the answers were correct. "Yes, that's the blue truck. Yes, that's the brown dog," and on and on and on. I thought Meghann must be playing with it until I realized that she was at school. Asia had finally gotten it. I quickly put in another page, and after one try, she had it mastered. Eventually we bought all of the modules and really credit "Touch and Tell" with helping Asia begin to learn language. It went everywhere with us, and I have only recently found anything to equal it in durability and appropriateness for her stage of development.

Through Barb's patient therapy, Asia had begun to use pencils, crayons, and chalk, so we felt she was ready to begin eating with a spoon. Like all children, her first efforts were clumsy and awkward, but the end result was that the food got to her mouth without her having to touch it. And the dogs always waited patiently under the high chair for the morsels that headed toward the floor. Soon, she was doing a beautiful job of feeding herself, and we joked about getting a bigger spoon, say shovel size, to accommodate her appetite. One evening, we all sat down to eat, and I placed Asia's plate, with all the food neatly cut up, in front of her, spoon to the right (she used both hands equally). We began eating, but she didn't. She just sat, looking at me, until I said, "Pick up your spoon, honey. Let's eat." I didn't even see it coming. The next night, same thing. She waited for me to tell her to take every bite. She had me *again*! I couldn't believe it. So began the second battle in the Irish-Korean Wars. The following night at dinner I refused to tell her to take a bite, she refused to eat. She cried. She screamed. Her plate was covered and put in the refrigerator and she was sent to her room. When the tantrum had passed, we tried again. The food was reheated and put in front of her. She refused, I refused, and she went to bed without dinner.

Fortunately, this siege only lasted one day, and we only had one relapse. Each time either Jerry's parents or my mom came to visit, we had to update them on the rules of the newest game. My mom came for a visit, and we sat down to dinner before having a chance to tell her about the latest "Asia mind game." We began to eat. Asia didn't. Mom, being the grandmother that she is, picked up the spoon and began to feed Asia. Any self respecting Grandma would have done the same. We all screamed at once, "*Mom, put that spoon down*!" Too late. I detected a small gleam of triumph in Asia's eyes as she smiled sweetly at Grandma Betty, the unsuspecting victim in Asia's ongoing game of "How to Outwit the Grown-ups."

One "almost" second relapse occurred when Jerry's parents came for a visit. Asia seemed to need to constantly test the rules, especially to see if they still applied when we had company. Jerry's mom, Meghann, Asia, and I went shopping one day, and stopped to have lunch. I ordered chicken noodle soup and a grilled cheese sandwich for Asia. When it arrived, she looked at it, looked at me and then at Jerry's mom, waiting for Grandma to tell her to start eating. Luckily I had been able to warn her that this might happen. I cut the sandwich into bite-sized pieces and the rest of us began eating. An hour-and-a-half later, when the fat was starting to congeal on the top of the bowl of soup and the sandwich resembled cardboard, we left the restaurant. Asia got nothing to eat until dinner that night, and she fed herself.

This may sound like cruel and unusual punishment, but we *knew* that if we gave in, even once, and told her to take a bite, we would have lost the small bit of ground we had gained in the fight to help her develop. I could have given in at any time, but I knew if I did, I may as well let her go back to lying on the floor, spinning wheels.

Our neighbors on the east side, Scott and Sherry Seglem, already had three sons when Sherry gave birth to twin boys in the summer of 1994. As soon as Sherry was home, Meghann was over there, anxious to see the babies. She had watched as Sherry grew larger during her pregnancy, and we told her that Sherry was going to have a baby, but the news prompted no questions. That afternoon, after visiting the twins, Meghann crawled up on my lap and asked, "Mommy, was I a baby in your tummy like the twins were in Sherry's?"

We knew this question would come up eventually, but I still wasn't prepared when it did. "No, honey, you were a tiny baby in another lady's tummy in Korea," I replied, my mouth as dry as sand. "She was your 'Birthday Mom.'"

"Where is she now, Mommy?" Meghann asked, wide-eyed.

God, help me answer this right. "She's still in Korea, sweetheart. She loved you very much, but couldn't keep you with her, so she asked some people to help find you a new Mommy and Daddy who would love you as much as she did. And that's us," I said.

"Does she miss me, Mommy?" Meghann asked in a tiny voice.

"She misses you a lot, honey," I said. "But she's happy you have a home and a family that loves you."

"I love you, Mommy."

When Asia had been with us for about a year, we began to try to switch her from formula to regular milk again. We did it gradually, an ounce at a time, wait three to four days and add another ounce, until she was drinking straight milk. As it had with Meghann, the cow's milk made her constipated, so we added molasses, which had acted like Liquid Plumber with Meghann.

Unfortunately, Asia's system was already compromised enough, and could not handle the cow's milk yet, so we went back to soy. After her surgery had been done in 1983, we were told that she could eat anything. Other than providing her with a balanced diet, we were given no special instructions concerning foods which could cause intestinal problems. Nor were we told about the possibility of gastroenteritis, or the need for roughage foods in abundance. Shortly after the failed attempt to switch Asia from formula, she began having severe constipation. Days would pass without a bowel movement, and when they came, they were explosive. We sought the opinions of all of the doctors who had previously treated her. We asked the surgeon for advice. Was it remotely possible that there was still a section of bowel with no nerve endings to stimulate peristalsis? Answer: Absolutely not! We were afraid to take her too far from home until after the "blowout" because we never knew when one would occur, just that the spaces between them were getting longer . . . three days, five days, seven days. She still ate enormous quantities of food, but was beginning to lose weight. Her system was not able to process the food she was consuming. She began looking like a poster child for Ethiopia Famine Relief. Her pediatrician, who we later found had told the surgeon that in her opinion Asia was voluntarily withholding stools, told me to give her three tablespoons of mineral oil in a glass of orange juice, to clean her system out. At 3 P.M. I gave her a glass of juice with an oil slick on top. She drank it, and then took a nap. Six P.M. was dinner time, but Asia wasn't hungry. She didn't say so in words, she just wouldn't eat. And this time it wasn't a game. She got down from her chair and started to lie down on the floor just before she threw up the oil-slicked juice plus lunch.

We cleaned her up and changed her clothes, and spread plastic under her bed on the floor. She was limp and lethargic and her face was the color of guacamole. She couldn't even tell us that she felt sick. At 8 P.M. the diarrhea started. Oh well, I thought, they said this would clean her out. By 11 P.M. she was either vomiting or having diarrhea constantly. I had tried to reach the pediatrician, but she didn't return my calls.

Jerry and Meghann went to bed, and I set up camp in the living room, with towels, washcloths, diapers, buckets, and clean bedding. By sunrise the next morning, I had changed her clothes and bedding from the inside out six times. We were both exhausted. When I finally reached the pediatrician, she wanted me to bring Asia to the hospital to treat her for dehydration. I told her she was a --- ------ maniac, and she would never see either one of us again.

Asia was much too weak to drink, and her system could only handle small amounts of liquid, so I sat on the floor all day, giving her eyedroppers of water every fifteen minutes or so. By evening, I risked a little formula, and when that stayed down, we gave her very diluted chicken broth. Jerry came home in the middle of the day to help, and Meghann played nurse by bringing me whatever I needed, keeping me supplied with Coke, and reading to her sister.

When Asia was stronger, we took her to the pediatrician Dorothy took her children to. I refused to go back to the doctor who believed that Asia was doing this deliberately, the doctor whose remedy nearly killed her. I liked Dorothy's pediatrician immediately. He looked like he had stepped right out of a Norman Rockwell painting. He checked her for intestinal parasites and bacterial infections, and recommended that we take Asia, as soon as possible, to Minneapolis Children's Medical Center for an evaluation with a pediatric gastroenterologist. He made a quick phone call and scheduled an appointment two days later, and arranged for me to pick up copies of all of Asia's medical records to take with us. His calm, take-charge attitude both reassured me and at the same time scared me to death. She was really in bad shape, and there was no time to lose. That night we called Tom and Marleane

Callaghan and made arrangements for Jerry and Meghann to stay with them while I stayed in the hospital with Asia.

Jerry's sister Kim's wedding was just two weeks away. I was to be the matron of honor and Meghann the flower girl. We prayed that we would even be able to go.

Chapter Fifteen

?????

I PICKED UP all of Asia's records the day before we left and made copies of everything before leaving Duluth. Several of the clinics were reluctant to give them to me, a mere mom. What if I read them? What if I learned something? I ripped the envelopes open as soon as I got home, and read until dinner. Jerry took vacation days off work, and we drove down on Tuesday afternoon. During the three-hour drive, I read and reread the medical documents, in an effort to find an answer to Asia's illness. I read out loud to Jerry, hoping that something would register with one of us. We were both terrified that we weren't going to be able to pull her out of this one.

Early on Wednesday morning we met with the pediatric gastroenterologist, and after looking at Asia's records, and a brief examination, he arranged for her to be admitted to Minneapolis Children's Medical Center. Asia was too weak and sick to cry while being examined. It was another indication of how low she had gotten.

Jerry checked us into the hospital and stayed while the barium X-rays were done before taking Meghann to Tom and Marleane's. The irony was that in order to get Asia to drink the barium, we had to keep saying, "Come on, honey, take one more drink. Drink it all down now." She was so sick that I don't think she even noticed; and if she did, we could program that one out later.

The X-rays taken that afternoon showed that Asia's large intestine was grossly enlarged and completely impacted with stool. Her belly was huge. The first step, before anything else could be done, was to remove the impaction. All day Thursday the nurses tried laxatives, which did nothing. Thursday night they came in with something for Asia to drink that was supposed to be "heavy" enough to push the stool through. No amount of coaxing could make her drink the thick, clear liquid. All I could think of was Drano commercials. "Works through standing water to unclog that drain." Or something like that. Finally, using a nasogastric tube, they began pouring the awful stuff down. Asia's spirit may have been too weak to put up much of a fight, so her body took over. When less than half of the liquid had been poured down, up it came, just like Old Faithful, covering the nurses, herself, and me. She was oblivious to all of it, and just lay there while we cleaned her and changed her bedding.

By the time we were through, it was nearly 10 P.M., and the nurses decided she had been through enough. After they left, I called Jerry in tears, wondering if we had done the right thing by bringing her down here.

Asia was put on a liquid diet, with supplemental IVs to help keep her hydrated, and to provide nutrients her body had not been processing from her food. The following morning, the nurses arrived, armed with enema bags. Was there no end to their arsenal? "If this doesn't work, what's next?" I wondered. Luckily, by the end of the day, a second set of X-rays showed that her bowel was as clean as it was likely to get in this lifetime. Of course, being Friday, nothing could happen now until Monday, so we vegged out in the hospital. Jerry and Meghann came several times a day, and some of our friends from C.H.S.M came to wish us well. The torture was over for a while, and the IVs were doing their job, so Asia began to perk up a little when the visitors came. We took her out in a little wheelchair, the rolling IV stand trailing behind her like some weirdly thin robot. But mostly she slept, and we watched over her.

Monday morning she was scheduled for exploratory surgery to determine what was going on with her plumbing. The last time we had faced surgery, we had all been so hopeful, so sure that it would be the last.

About an hour-and-a-half later the doctor came to the room to report his findings. "We won't have any word about the biopsies we took for a few days, but the culprit would seem to be a huge bacterial overgrowth, which has caused her digestive system to stop processing her food. It's called malabsorption," he told us as we stood, gripping the rails of the bed. "The blow-outs happened when there was literally nowhere else for the stool to go. The biopsies will tell us if there are ganglion cells (nerve endings) in all the right places."

My Irish temper barely in check, I said, "But all of that was done in Duluth before her surgery. They said everything was fine. How could this have happened? Was it the milk? Should she have had special food?"

"I'm sure you were feeding her a good diet, but some of these kids need extra fiber. And even the presence of ganglion cells doesn't mean that there might not be other problems."

"Other problems? What kind of other problems?" I was frantic. The slender thread of rational thought was unraveling rapidly.

"Let's just take everything one step at a time and not borrow trouble. In the meantime I've prescribed Flagyl, a drug to get rid of the bacteria. We'll keep her on liquids and IVs until the biopsy results come back. Try to get some rest and --"

"--not to worry," I finished for him. These guys need new

writers, I thought. They've got to come up with some other lines.

The days seemed to crawl by as we waited for the test results. It was summer, and Minnesota summers were too short to waste in the hospital. Asia looked so pale, but she was beginning to come around a little bit. When she started to want food other than liquids, we knew she was getting better. The biopsies showed a normal amount of nerve endings. The doctor told us that we would know if the antibiotic was working if she began having normal stools when solid food was added to her diet.

The IVs were left hooked up until her first few days' worth of food began passing safely through. Fourteen days on the antibiotic, and gradually add soft foods, as if she were a flu patient. Constipation that prune juice didn't take care of would signal more bacteria, and require another dose of antibiotic.

We left the hospital just three short days before Kim's wedding in Rochester. Minneapolis was only an hour-and-a-half away, so we decided to stay with Tom and Marleane for a few more days to let Asia rest before the excitement and confusion of a family wedding. The Callaghans graciously allowed us these days of much-needed rest, sun, and good home cooking before sending us on our way. We relaxed by Marleane's parents' pool while Meghann swam until she looked like a prune and Asia floated in a tiny inner tube with a seat. Her swim suit, which had fit earlier now looked as though it belonged to someone four sizes larger.

We arrived in Rochester the day before Kim and Phil's wedding. I really tried to get into the spirit, but it was so hard. Asia was so thin and weak, and had to be carried most of the time. We took blankets with us everywhere, so she could lie on the floor. We made an appearance at every event, but usually had to leave early.

The wedding was spectacular, as only the florist daughter of a florists can be. Kim was a beautiful bride, with her tall handsome new husband, Phil. I remembered her as a teenager, taste-testing French fries in our Colorado kitchen. It seemed such a short time ago. And then, overnight it seemed, she was dating and then there was Phil and it was love. "Is that how fast the time is going to go with our children?" I wondered.

Meghann looked like something out of a fairy tale in her white hooped flower girl dress with a high lace neckline, wearing a halo of flowers in her long black hair.

Asia and I sat in the back of the flower-filled church, and halfway through the ceremony, Asia fell asleep on the pew beside me.

Later, at the reception, Jerry's Dad, Bud, carried Asia and danced to a waltz song with her. She was wearing a beautiful peach dotted Swiss dress with smocking in the front and a big pussy-cat bow in the back. The dress just hung on her thin frame. Her legs didn't even fill out the patterned white stockings. She had lost so much weight, she was almost as thin as when she had arrived from Korea. As much as I wanted to believe that a little antibiotic could make it all right, I had a sick feeling that even though she had begun to gain a little weight and strength and the color was coming back into her cheeks, this problem was going to require more than pills for ten days.

We had been away from home less than two weeks, but it seemed like months. Our garden was growing, but Asia's illness had cast a shadow over everything . . . like the daylight during a solar eclipse--still sunlight, but not quite.

Meanwhile . . . all four of our lives were about to be turned around and pointed south.

Chapter Sixteen

The Move

OUR NEIGHBORS ON the west, Lee and Rosemary Davern, had recently adopted a beautiful six-year-old daughter, Kim. Lee had traveled extensively to Korea on business for several years. We secretly felt that watching Meghann and Asia grow up next door had played a part in their decision. Kim looked like a pixie, with short black hair and large, expressive black eyes. We went to visit the day after she arrived. Kim knew no English and Meghann's Korean was limited to greetings, the names of foods, and a few songs, but there is a universal language between children, and they became friends instantly. Finally Meghann had someone to play dolls with. She and Kim were due to start kindergarten in the fall.

During the summer of 1985, Jerry's escalating dissatisfaction with his job at Engwall's coupled with my bargain basement lungs started us thinking about moving. I didn't really think that I could survive another **Minnesota** winter. Sometimes the ice would be so thick on the *inside* of the door that Meghann could write her name in it. One year there was only one month with no frost! I used to say that I knew it was cold outside when the hairs in my nose froze. My mother thought I was joking.

Jerry began to send out resumes to greenhouse-related companies around the country. He wanted to get into sales, and definitely had the personality and drive to do well in a sales position. Although it would have been nice to end up near one side of the family or the other, we couldn't be too choosy. As long as the job got us farther south!

In mid-July, Jerry received a reply from a company whose home office was near Cleveland, Ohio. The company, B.F.G Supply, flew him to Cleveland to meet with the President, Don Hornak. Even though Jerry had had no formal sales training, his natural enthusiasm and winning personality combined with the public relations skills he had learned in the Jaycees to create just the qualities B.F.G. was looking for. The company had an opening for a salesman in their office near Detroit. Jerry would be selling greenhouses and greenhouse supplies to growers in southern Michigan and part of Ontario, Canada. *And* they would hire a company to *move* us. What a concept--companies that do nothing but move people and their belongings from one place to another. Jerry and I were honor graduates of the Beverly Hillbillies School of Moving, and hadn't the vaguest idea how moving companies even operated.

Our excitement was dimmed only by the fact that neither one of us knew *anything* about Michigan, except for cars, Motown music and race riots. Oh well, we hadn't known anything about Duluth, **Minnesota,** when we moved there either. It was another adventure in our already action-packed lives.

B.F.G. wanted Jerry to be in Burton, Ohio, at the home office to begin his training at the end of August 1985. He gave notice at the greenhouse and we began to call moving companies for estimates. We had garage sales, talked to friends who knew anything about Michigan, and tried to sell our house. Actually, we had been trying to sell it for four years, but the bottom had dropped out of the housing market in Duluth right after we had bought our home, and had not recovered. We dropped the price and prayed. On August 16, 1985, the folks at the greenhouse had a going away party for us. Everybody brought food, and there was plenty of beer and wine. We ate, cried, promised to write, drank, and relived the good times with our friends. About 11 P.M. I left with Meghann and Asia and took a back road home to avoid traffic. Asia began screaming only a few blocks from the greenhouse and didn't stop. She had never liked good-byes anyway, and it was past her bedtime. Meghann had already fallen asleep. (Sleeping while Asia cried was, for her, like sleeping for someone who lives next to a busy railroad track: she just closed her eyes and tuned it out.) About halfway home, I turned around in a futile attempt to quieten Asia . . .

. . . and ran a stop sign--straight into high-speed southbound traffic. The oncoming car was unable to stop, and hit my car broadside. My station wagon flipped four times and came to a stop upside down. The last thing I remembered were the headlights of the oncoming traffic.

I came to outside the car, on my knees, and didn't know how I had gotten there. I couldn't move my left arm. I tried to scream, but couldn't. Meghann and Asia were still in the car. Disembodied hands tried to help me up, but my left leg wouldn't work. I could hear my daughters crying, hanging upside down in their car seats. Lights, sirens, and people were everywhere. Then we were in an ambulance. The girls had been cut loose from their car seats and were with me, and the wife of the driver of the other car was there too. She was pregnant.

Fade out . . . Fade in . . . We were in the emergency room of St. Mary's, where I had taken Asia for her hives, and where she had had her surgery. Meghann was on the gurney next to me and miraculously, there was Jerry. He alternated between Meghann, me, and Asia, while we were stitched, patched, and poked. Meghann had a broken clavicle, a piece of glass imbedded in her cheek, and her face was bruised. Asia, remarkably, came through it all with hardly a scratch. The wife of the driver of the other car was shaken and bruised, but she and her baby were (*thank God*) otherwise okay. My left arm was broken above the elbow, I had several broken ribs, my left thigh had a bruise the size of a dinner plate, and Jerry had arrived just in time to watch the doctor sewing part of my scalp back together. But no break or pain in my physical body could compare to the horror I felt at how carelessly I had endangered the lives of my own children, and a mother-to-be and her unborn baby!

Jerry took Meghann and Asia home, but I had to stay in the hospital overnight. I was taken to a bed in an otherwise empty four-bed ward, where I cried myself to sleep.

I was released at 11 A.M. the next day, and Jerry's brother, Bruce, and his girlfriend, Barb, took me home. My crying started all over again when I saw the cuts and bruises on Meghann's beautiful face.

Friends sent flowers and cards, telephoned and brought food. I wondered if they would have been so kind if they had known just how foolish, careless, and irresponsible I had been. Although not legally drunk, I had had one glass of wine too many, which had impaired my judgment and I could have killed someone with my stupidity. Physically broken in places and emotionally battered, it was a very low time for me. It was another demon drop on the emotional roller coaster ride from hell.

Jerry took the week off work and took over all the household and "kid maintenance" duties, while I slept. I felt like I had been run over by a Sherman tank, when, in fact, it was an American-made sedan. After seeing my car, I realized, only too well, just how lucky we all were to have walked away with so few injuries. I figured there must be a reason why I had been given another chance.

An orthopedic surgeon put my arm in a cast from my shoulder to my wrist, bent at the elbow, and gave me a padded sling to wear around my neck to support the weight of the cast.

Guilt, pain, and remorse aside, life had to go on, and I had to go with it. Before I showered while sitting on a chair, Meghann taped a black plastic garbage bag over the cast. Jerry's mother, Wim, arrived from Rochester to stay with us for a few weeks while he was in Ohio training and house hunting in southern Michigan.

The moving company told us only to pack what we would need for a few days and leave the rest to them. The mere thought terrified me!

Our wounds healed, and within three weeks, Meghann was doing cartwheels. Asia, however minor her physical injuries were, suffered in her own way. For weeks, she would grab on to the frame of the car to keep from being put inside, and scream when we put on the brakes.

Before leaving **Minnesota** for uncharted territory, there was one last professional visit to make. Asia's years of ear infection-generated teeth grinding had worn the enamel off two of her back teeth. One already had a cavity and the other needed to be capped if it was to be saved. Our dentist and friend, Carter Johnson, was the only choice, since Asia knew him on a personal level (his oldest daughter had shared birthday parties with Asia). We felt perhaps he would be less threatening than a complete stranger in Michigan.

Asia's recent illness and hospitalization had done nothing to improve her feelings about people in the medical/dental profession, and Carter, friend or not, was no exception. When the chloral hydrate and an adult dose of nitrous oxide failed to sedate her, Carter's assistant and I held her in the chair while Carter capped one tooth, filled another, and did a general cleaning. Behind that frail, weak exterior was a child with amazing strength, and when Carter was finished, we were all exhausted.

As I drove to Bruce's house in the rain, I couldn't help wondering how long it would take to establish the network of friends and professionals in Michigan that had always been our support system in Duluth.

Chapter Seventeen

Milan, MI 48160

THE DAY JERRY flew back to Duluth to drive with us to Michigan was bitterly cold, even though it was only September. I loaded up the car that morning with kids, dogs, birds, plants, and clothes to last us until the movers arrived with the rest of our belongings. Friends came with us to the airport, since we were leaving as soon as Jerry arrived.

I had no real regrets about leaving **Minnesota**. Sure, there would be people that I would miss, but I felt as though my purpose in living in that bitterly cold climate for seven years had been fulfilled with Meghann and Asia's adoption, and now we could move on to the next phase. The only thing I knew about Michigan was Detroit and cars, but it was south of **Minnesota**, so it had to be warmer, and maybe we could grow real tomatoes that actually ripened on the vine.

My Subaru station wagon had been totaled in the wreck, and we had bought an older Dodge wagon and two new car seats with the insurance money. The wagon was so big it was like driving an eighteen-wheeler. We made the trip in two days. It was like coming to another country. There were still leaves on the trees, small blue flowers blooming by the roadside, and people were wearing shorts. Jerry kept telling me that the people in Michigan drove like maniacs, and that I would have to learn how to drive all over again. I didn't care if they drove like Ben Hur in the chariot races, *it was warm here*!

We stayed in a small motel in Milan, Michigan, for two nights, until the movers arrived. Jerry had spent all of his free time for the past month looking for a home for us. After living in the country on two lakes with no close neighbors, living in a "neighborhood" would take some getting used to.

As we drove down the street, lined with huge, ancient maple trees that almost made a canopy, Jerry said, "I really hope you like this house. I looked at so many, and nothing seemed exactly right. Either the house was okay but the neighborhood was rough or the neighborhood was great but the house was too expensive. There's one community close by that I really liked, but the name of the town is the same as the last name of one of our least favorite people, and as silly as it sounds, I couldn't see having to write it all the time as our return address. I finally found this one, and I was so tired of looking and I wanted to get us all together again."

The house he had found was actually a duplex, and we had the lower half. It was a wonderful old house, with sliding doors between the rooms and lots of woodwork. It had easily twice as much space as our tiny house at the lake. There was a basement, and a small yard, and a screened-in front porch, and kids Meghann's age across the street. I loved it.

Asia had been anxious ever since the movers had begun packing everything days before. This was all too strange for her. We had kept out Touch and Tell, and the strawberry, and her plate and cup, but she didn't begin to really relax until she saw her things being unloaded from the truck, and the room she and Meghann would share begin to take shape. There was an extra room that Jerry would use as an office.

My mother arrived the day after the movers to help with the unpacking since my left arm was still in a cast.

The elementary school was only a few blocks from our new home, another plus, and I was able to car pool with two other mothers. Meghann started kindergarten, and Asia was tested by the school's psychologist to determine the appropriate preschool placement for her.

Asia still didn't handle small rooms with closed doors very well (did they remind her of doctor's offices?) but Joellyn Gutterman was kind and understanding, and left the door open during the two testing sessions. Joellyn recommended a pre-primary impaired class in a neighboring community. The school bus would pick her up at our door every morning and bring her home at noon. A bus? Asia? By herself? She was only four years old. Not to worry, there would be an aide to help. I thought maybe I should ride with her the first day. No, better not start something that would set the "way according to Asia" that things were to be done. No one knew better than I just how hard it was to reprogram that wonderful brain of hers. The way a thing happened the first time was the way it was supposed to happen every time after that. But I *did* call the school and the bus garage just to make sure there had been no trouble that first day.

In Duluth, we had lived so far from friends with children Meghann and Asia's age, until Kim Davern came along, that Meghann and Asia had depended on each other for companionship. No, that's not correct. Meghann depended on me, and Asia depended on no one. She was content to play by herself. Even when around other children, she would stay on the fringes of the group, maybe glancing at them occasionally, but for the most part, ignoring them in favor of a toy with wheels to spin. Other children's attempts to include her in their play went unnoticed. Asia would roughhouse and play chase with Meghann, but that was all. She only seemed to need us for the essentials: food and diaper changes. In all other areas, she seemed content within herself. Part of me believed that this was due to our isolation in Duluth, and once she was surrounded by children every day in school, she would begin to interact with them. The other part of me feared that she would continue to exist in her own world, with her fingers, cars with wheels, and Strawberry for companionship.

School was no different. Asia was beginning to use words, single words, to indicate what she wanted, but her speech still had the quality of a deaf person who had learned to talk. Well, with the amount of ear wax removed from her ears, she probably *had* been deaf for the early part of her life. Some people even thought that her strange accent was because she had only heard Korean for two years.

Asia would stop her wheel spinning if the teacher was working with her one on one, but only for a few minutes. And during story time, she would retreat to a quiet corner, away from everyone else, lie on her back on the floor, and flick the corner of a piece of paper gently against her eyelashes. This was a new habit she had acquired, and she would flick for hours if we let her. No piece of paper was safe from the flicking finger. Envelopes, paper plates, letter, photographs, all were potential "flickers."

Asia made no overtures of friendship to any of the other children; in fact, she barely acknowledged their existence, or the teacher's, unless she needed something. Once she was served her food, she needed no help feeding herself, so she totally absorbed herself in eating, blocking out everything else.

We began to insist on responses that consisted of more than one word, even if the other word was "please." Up, please; cup, please; down, please. "Change Touch and Tell, please," was her longest phrase, and the only long one. But she knew she had to say it to get what she wanted. Other people tended to look at Asia and think "Poor little girl," and would try to do everything for her, anticipating her every need and not insisting that she speak. I felt that I had to constantly explain my actions, because I'm sure that I seemed like a heartless b---- when I insisted on words from Asia. But I *knew* that if I gave in once, and gave her what she wanted without the words, that we would have to start all over again.

I knew that I would have to find pediatricians and dentists soon, and the prospect was not thrilling. I had sought out other adoptive parents almost immediately, to begin collecting medical supplies, diapers, and formula to send to Korea, and they recommended a group of doctors in Ann Arbor, ten miles from Milan, who worked with a lot of families with Korean born children. Dr. Blackman was thought to be the best, so I scheduled an appointment and warned the staff ahead of time about Asia. They all said they understood, but I don't think they were really prepared for the intensity of her terror, or the sheer volume of her screams. Once again, it served to get us in and out in record time.

After an initial examination and medical history, Dr. Blackman suggested that we take Asia to the University of Michigan Mott Children's Hospital for a consultation with Dr. John Wesley concerning the colostomy and the problems that had been plaguing Asia for the past year.

We had made it a practice to tell Asia when we were going for a doctor's appointment, even though we knew she would scream until we got there, and until we left. We felt that she needed to know what was going on in order to learn to trust us. Time really didn't seem to mean anything to Asia (tomorrow was just a word). If we told her a week ahead of time, she would just worry all day, every day for seven days, so we told her the morning of the appointment. Jerry had taken the day off to go with us. Asia screamed all the way, ten miles of driving in unknown territory, and then screamed through the parking ramp, a structure that was designed by a madman. She screamed through the hallways, which were so much like a maze that I felt we should leave a trail of bread crumbs to follow to get back outside. She screamed in the waiting room, and here it made no difference at all. We still had to wait an hour--an hour of Asia, terrified, screaming until she was hoarse and then screaming some more, and wringing wet with sweat by the time we were seen. The University surgeons have Pediatric clinic only one day a week, and even though appointments are made, they usually run longer than the allotted time. I learned fast--for the next appointment, I wanted to be first.

Even though we had brought all of Asia's medical records from Korea, Duluth, and Minneapolis, Dr. Wesley wanted to run all the tests again, including the barium X-rays and intestinal biopsies. Dr. Wesley didn't hesitate to prescribe chloral hydrate for Asia, which I was to give her just before leaving the house. It didn't really take effect until we got to the hospital, and then I strapped her into a wheelchair and navigated through the parking maze to the elevator. Asia must have an incredibly high tolerance for that particular medication, because she woke up halfway through the procedure, terrified and groggy, and had to be held down by two attendants for the rest. When the nightmare was finally over, Jerry took Asia while I went with Dr. Wesley to look at the X-rays.

"Your daughter's large intestine is like a circus balloon that has been blown up for too long and then all the air was let out. It's probably five times larger than it should be and has no elasticity at all," he told me. "There is no muscle tone to contract and push the stool through her system. But if it makes you feel any better, there is no way she voluntarily withheld stool. She had no control over this."

I had never believed the pediatrician in Duluth, whose opinion was that Asia was *voluntarily* withholding stool, so it was a relief to have *my* opinion confirmed by Dr. Wesley.

Her bowel would have to be empty before the biopsies could be done. Dr. Wesley sent us home with an enema bag, and blue hospital pads, and an appointment for the next week to see how we had done. This was not going to be pleasant.

I let the warm water flow from the bag into her rectum, and then sat her on the toilet. She couldn't push the contents out. Her abdomen was just larger and harder. I laid her back on the pad on the sofa, and drained the now watery stool out through the tube into the bag, and then emptied the bag into the toilet. It took three or four times before her bowel seemed emptier. After doing this every day for a week, we had managed to empty her bowel out enough for Dr. Wesley to schedule the biopsies.

Again we told Asia we were going to see Dr. Wesley, again we gave her the chloral hydrate, and again she screamed until the drug took effect.

The biopsies were done with Asia as an outpatient. At least she was under a general anesthetic for this procedure. Jerry and I waited in the family room for Dr. Wesley to come and tell us what he had found. Jerry took paperwork and I took needlework. I figure by now I've crocheted and cross-stitched my way through some of the best hospitals in the country.

After about an hour of mindlessly cross-stitching Christmas ornaments, I looked up to see Dr. Wesley walking into the room.

"Well," he began, "the good news is that there are nerve endings in her bowel at every point I checked."

"Why, then," I asked, "are things not working right?"

"Maybe the original problem started with the switch to cow's milk, or possibly because you were never properly advised of her dietary restrictions or needs. Or it could be something else entirely," he continued. "The bottom line is that you have to keep her intestines as empty as possible in order to allow the bowel to shrink to the proper size and regain its proper muscle tone."

"And how long will that take?" I asked, knowing that here came the bad news.

"How long is anybody's guess. We'll do barium X-rays every three or four months to monitor the shrinkage."

Not really wanting to hear the next answer, I had to ask, "Just how are we to keep her bowel empty?"

"By doing the enemas every day, three to five times a day, if necessary," he said. We left with more enema bags, a stack of blue pads, and surgical gloves.

Okay, I can handle this. It won't take that long, just a few months. We'll make the best of it. It won't be too bad. Yeah, right. It wasn't too bad, it was *barbaric.*

We tried having the T.V. on <u>Sesame Street</u> and <u>Mr. Rogers</u>. Sometimes Meghann would read to Asia. Other times Jerry played the guitar. It didn't matter, it was still frosting on s---. We tried to be positive. We were doing what the doctor said. And it was supposed to help. It *was* helping. We would see in three more months, two months, next month, next week, tomorrow. Yes, it had shrunk, but not enough. See you in three more months. Keep up the good work. (Keep up the torture, you mean.) The enemas became the focus of the day. Once they were over, we could relax and enjoy things. If we skipped a day, she become bloated. Sometimes doing the enemas took two hours or longer. Sometimes she cried and fought me. Sometimes Jerry had to hold her down. Sometimes I cried, after we were done, after she was cleaned up, when she was in another room. Sometimes I had Jerry take Meghann for a walk so she wouldn't have to listen to her sister scream, *"Be all done, Mommy! Be all done!"* Some of the worst times were when we had out of town guests staying with us. No one could have fun, because we all dreaded the enemas so much. I couldn't even think about anything else until it was done. Asia tried to be happy until she saw the enema bag and the blue pads come out, and then she would quietly start crying. Those quiet tears hurt the worst.

One afternoon after school, the bus driver said Asia had been crying on the way home and had acted as if she was in pain. We thought maybe she was getting the flu. Grandma Betty was visiting, and when Asia came in, instead of kissing Grandma, she just lay down on the floor. Suddenly she doubled up and screamed, and was writhing on the floor in pain. If this was the flu, it was worse than any I had ever had. We tried hot water bottles and heating pads, and nothing helped. I called the pediatrician's office and they said to bring her right in. With mother in the front seat and Meghann and Asia in their car seats in the back, I drove like a maniac through a blinding rain to Ann Arbor. My windshield wipers quit working in the middle of the trip, so I drove the rest of the way with my arm out the window, trying to keep the windshield clean with the snow scraper. I ignored Mother and the kids and cursed like a First Street sailor for ten miles.

While one of the nurses called Dr. Wesley, Dr. Blackman examined Asia. Blood and other tests ruled out appendicitis. She had no fever. She was not vomiting. Then, after nearly two hours, as suddenly as it had started, the pain was gone. Not gradually, just *gone.* She relaxed and her screaming changed from "I hurt really bad" screaming to "I'm in a doctor's office *again*" screaming, a small, but significant and recognizable difference. Just as the doctors were considering hospitalizing her. A bowel kink, they said. Not so uncommon, they said. With her bowel so stretched, and now empty because of all the enemas we had been doing for months, the intestinal loops just flopped around in her abdomen, and sometimes got hooked around each other, and there you have it, pain, PAIN, **PAIN.** Not so uncommon, could happen again. I drove home in a daze, wondering what other little surprises were in store.

Three more months passed, then four. I thought (prayed) that if we waited *just one more month* we'd hear the words we wanted so desperately to hear, "Let's try it without the enemas for a while." If God would just let us stop, I would do whatever it took, change whatever needed to be changed, to keep her from having to go through this anymore. But it was not to be. Yes, the bowel had shrunk some more. No, it was not enough, and the radiologist could detect no peristalsis when the barium was in the bowel. It was bad enough that we had to continue with the enemas, but these X-ray visits were no picnic either. Asia was so locked away in her terror that I don't think she even heard my words of comfort. The only thing that helped was when the lights came on and she scrambled to her knees as the nurses began to clean her up. Then she was giddy with relief. I had visions often during that year of Asia, twenty-one or so years old, as a young Sybil, in therapy trying to sort out the multiple personalities she had created to take away the pain she suffered as I, her mother, tortured her with enemas every day.

Jerry was the first to say that we couldn't go on like this

much longer. It was slowly but surely destroying my relationship with Asia, and the stress was taking its toll on Jerry and Meghann. After a year of this, there had to be another, better way. I vowed that our next visit for X-rays would be the last.

Dr. Wesley's alternative was another colostomy, and I took it.

Chapter Eighteen

Grilled Cheese Sandwiches

THIS TRIP TO the hospital was, in Asia's eyes, another in a series of betrayals. The day immediately following the surgery was the worst. Jerry *had* to go out of town to finalize a large sale. As much as he hated it, he had to leave for a few hours. The day of the surgery, Asia had slept all day and did not even know when he was there. But the day after, when she woke, she wanted her dad. She had been drifting in and out of sleep all day when Jerry arrived. When she was awake, she was a shell. The boss of the body had fled. Deciding it was all too much, she had checked out. For Jerry, this was almost worse than crying. At least most of the time when she was crying, she was *in* there. Each time it happened, we wondered if she would come back, or decide it wasn't worth it and just stay gone.

The day the nurses came in to remove the stitches, Asia learned to curse. She didn't really know any curse words, but she knew the emotions and emphasis behind them. The first staple came out and Asia screamed, "TREE-E-E-E!! at the top of her lungs. With the second staple came "APPLE!!" With each staple came Asia's version of expletives that should be deleted. Her vocabulary had increased.

With each day of her recovery came fewer and fewer of the "absence" spells, until they almost disappeared entirely once again.

The relief we all felt after Asia's surgery was a tangible thing. By comparison to previous operations, the surgery itself had been relatively simple. Dr. Wesley made an incision, cut the intestine on her left side, at the top, flipped the two ends to the outside, and stitched them down neatly. A nice piece of stitchery. The best thing about this trip to the hospital was that we could tell her that when she went home, there would be no more enemas. We had an elaborate ceremony to dispose of the hated items. Asia didn't use scissors yet, so we cut the blue pads up for her and let her throw them away, with the enema bag, into the outside garbage. She checked every day to make sure they were still there, as though the evil things would somehow creep back into the house to haunt her. (They do still haunt her memory.) If Asia is with me we don't tary long in the personal hygiene section of the grocery store these days, and we don't look at *anything* anywhere near the enemas. We walk as fast as we can down that aisle.

The new colostomy worked perfectly from the start, and in the intervening years the supplies had gotten easier to use. Now, *now,* we thought, she will finally be able to begin to develop normally. People live with far worse things than a colostomy.

Asia was five years old and had been with us for three years. She had made enormous progress, against incredible odds. She could now run and walk, feed herself with a spoon, hold and play with objects with her hands, and was learning to talk. But she still did not bite or chew anything. Every type of solid food was cut into bite-sized pieces. Occasionally I tried leaving the pieces a little too large, but they still went down whole, so I quit because I was afraid she would choke on something like a meatball. When no one was around at mealtime, we went through our chewing pantomimes, and moved her jaws with our hands, but she just didn't seem to get it. *Didn't seem to get it.* She had ground her teeth until she was three, and that was a chewing motion. The damaged teeth had been capped, so there shouldn't have been any pain. And she had bitten the paint off the guard rails of her crib. She could do this. Encouragement wasn't working. What we needed was incentive. A carrot, so to speak. Time for the stubborn Irish side of me to take over. I fixed chicken noodle soup for dinner one night (her favorite) and grilled cheese sandwiches. I served everyone their sandwiches first. Usually Asia's would have been cut into bite-sized pieces, but not tonight. Jerry, Meghann and I ate our sandwiches and I served the soup. Asia's sandwich was turning cold. *Once,* I said, "When you've finished your sandwich, Asia, I'll bring your soup." Only once, because I wasn't going to set myself up. We had been finished for over an hour and Asia was still sitting in her high chair, her sandwich solidifying on her plate. She didn't cry or scream, she just looked expectantly at me as if to say, "Didn't you forget something, Mom?" An hour-and-a-half passed, Meghann was working on homework, Jerry was in his office, and I was washing dishes.

"Down, please," she said.

"You can get down when you've finished your dinner, honey," I replied as I passed through the room.

Two hours passed, and the sandwich resembled butter coated fiberboard. Asia touched it with one finger and her face wrinkled in disgust (I didn't blame her). She gingerly picked it up with thumb and index finger (a first). She brought it to her mouth and we all held our breath. She opened her mouth . . . and put the sandwich down. Why didn't that surprise me? She was hungry, yes, but she didn't want to give in quite that easily. A few more minutes passed, she looked around to see if anyone else was watching, and very deliberately picked up the sandwich and took a bite. We all cheered and praised her, and I grabbed the camera. After she finished the sandwich, I served her soup, and then called the grandparents, Cindy, Dorothy, and anyone else who could appreciate what an achievement this was.

The next night, still feeling the rosy glow of success, I fixed fried chicken, and gave Asia the drumstick. Without hesitation, she picked it up, bit into it, and chewed with gusto. I had won another round, and even though she didn't realize it, so had she.

Meghann was enrolled in gymnastics in Ann Arbor and, with Mary Lou Retton as her idol, had her eyes set on the Olympics. She had been invited to join the competition team at the gym and we were all looking forward to Saturday gym meets. We wanted some form of physical exercise for Asia, something her own, where she would not be competing with Meghann. I had heard about a martial arts class in Milan at the same elementary school Meghann attended, and called the Instructor, Rodger Cole.

Mr. Cole taught Tae Kwon Do, Korean karate. Perfect. Jerry wanted to go too, so it was arranged that they would attend one class as guests. The class consisted of Mr. Cole and another instructor, Mr. Cole's son Jason, a fourth-grader at the time, and several other young boys near Asia's age. At first Jerry worked close by Asia, but as he progressed at a different rate, soon he was at one end of the gym and she was at the other. The class met on Monday and Wednesday nights for two hours, and Jerry and Asia practiced their forms every morning before work and school. Everyone in the class was patient with Asia, even the young boys. Asia seemed to pick up the Tae Kwon Do forms and movements quicker than school lessons. The physical movements came easier, and the memorization (history and organizational leaders, creed, etc.) came easier for her than reading and counting.

Jerry's work as a salesman required some out-of-town travel, occasionally with overnight stays. The Sunday after Thanksgiving in 1986 he left in the afternoon for a three-day stay in Canada. The weather was mild, and before Meghann, Asia, and I left to rent a video, we put Hurricane, our fifteen-year-old German shepherd, in the kennel. Hurricane had been our only dog for several years since Chinook, my elkhound, had been killed in Minnesota. We watched our rented movies and just before bed I went out to let Hurricane in for the evening. I unlocked the door and pushed it open. He didn't come to greet me. My heart froze, thinking he had died alone while we watched movies. I closed the kennel door and went inside for a flashlight. Hurricane was not in the kennel. It seemed that someone had opened the kennel, but when he wouldn't go with them, they closed the door and left. His hips and spine were too arthritic for him to have jumped or climbed over the six-foot wooden fence.

I put the girls to bed, locked the house and walked the neighborhood within sight of the house, calling our friend. At fifteen, he was partially deaf and had cataracts in both eyes. We felt he had become disoriented and couldn't find his way home. We ran ads, searched, and followed up leads for three months but never found him. It was a terrible time for all of us. He and Chinook had been in our wedding pictures, and we seldom left the house without him. Meghann had learned to walk holding on to his ears, and Asia had slept with her head on him as a baby. It was like losing a member of the family. And since we never found his body, it's still left unfinished.

In the spring of 1987, we were told that Asia would be too old to be classified as pre-primary impaired, and would need to be re-evaluated. The new label was "emotionally impaired" with a second classification of "speech and language impaired" According to the Stanford Binet IV Edition test, her test age was three years and six months. Her chronological age was six years. The gap was not closing. We would need to select a kinder-garten placement for her. Milan schools could take her later, but were not staffed for a child with her needs as yet. Her teacher, Mrs. Van Atta, recommended two schools in the district, and arranged for us to visit both of them. The first was in a small town about twenty-five miles from us. The classroom was beautiful, with computers and all the latest learning aids. The teacher was kind and knowledgeable, but Jerry and I both felt that Asia would walk all over her. I felt that she needed someone who had been a Marine drill sergeant in a former life, who could insist on certain behaviors, and follow through without wavering. Consistency was mandatory. Nancy LaPrairie, the teacher at Holmes School in Ypsilanti, fit my expectations to a tee. The classroom was for autistically impaired children (a label which I would not allow to be used for Asia), with a high emphasis on speech and language. There were only eight students in the class, with two teachers and an aide. The classroom was not as modern as the other one, but it had the elements I felt were important.

Once again Asia would be bussed to school, but this time it would take three busses to get her there! She would be on the bus for an hour each way every day, with the same bus aides as before. We met with the teachers and instructed them on colostomy care, and took Asia over to see the classroom she would go to in the fall. We knew that this change, like all the ones before, would be difficult. As much as we might have wanted to protect her, we had to prepare her for life, and life is change. Sooner or later, she had to realize that nothing stays the same forever.

The summer was warm and wonderful, and with the colostomy in place, Asia played in the water at a local beach until she looked like she'd been wrapped in a Band-Aid for a month. She was continuing to make rapid gains in gross motor skills, had worn out one exercise trampoline, and learned to ride a tricycle. I took Asia to speech/language classes at Eastern Michigan University several days a week, where she worked with graduate students directed by professors. Her small motor skills were developing more slowly. It was difficult to tell if she would be right- or left-handed, as she used them interchangeably, sometimes holding her spoon with her left hand, sometimes with her right. Early in the school year her teachers recommended a test to determine her "handedness" and to see if she had midline recognition.

Jerry and Asia had attended their Tae Kwon Do classes faithfully during the summer, and Jerry had already tested for and received his yellow belt, and Asia had mastered the three required forms to get a yellow stripe on her white belt. In October 1987, he was to test for his green belt, and Asia would be testing for her yellow belt. In addition to reciting the oath and creed, she would have to demonstrate five forms and recite their description, and break a one-foot-square, one-inch-thick board with her foot. The descriptions she rattled off so fast that if you didn't know what she was saying, you'd never understand. The forms she knew. She and Jerry practiced for weeks on breaking the board.

The testing was done at another school, and students from several classes were testing before the board of high-ranking Tae Kwon Do masters. All students were required to sit in position on the floor during all the testing. The lower belt colors were tested first. The gymnasium was packed with students, parents and well-wishers, many of whom already knew Asia, and had followed her progress. When Asia stood up, she looked so tiny in her white *do bak,* the smallest made and still hemmed five inches. She sailed through the oath and creed with no problem, and completed her forms with style. Then Jerry held the board, and the room held its collective breath, while I held the camera. Asia took her stance, gave a few practice kicks, and let fly with her right foot. As her foot connected with the board, it snapped with a resounding crack that was almost drowned out by the roar from the crowd as they jumped to their feet. Somehow I snapped the camera at the right moment, in spite of my tears. Asia gave a "not regulation" gazelle leap after a beaming Grand Master Eugene Humesky awarded her her yellow belt, accompanied by the cheers from the other students. Her picture was in the local newspaper, and she and Jerry were invited to do a demonstration for her class at school. The older students gained a new respect for their tiny classmate when she repeated breaking the board with her foot.

Chapter Nineteen

Shrinks

OUR RENTED HOUSE was sold in the fall of 1987, and the new owner didn't want to be a landlord. He intended to sell it, but we weren't interested in buying. When we eventually bought a house, we wanted enough land to have a garden, so we began looking for another home to rent or buy. Because we were so pleased with the Milan school system, we wanted to stay in the district, which restricted our house hunting area somewhat, but in short order we found a large older home on fourteen acres. It had been refinished inside, with new appliances and carpeting and had a large basement for the parrots which had become my hobby/job/obsession. I had been raising them for several years, handfeeding the babies and sometimes hatching the eggs in an incubator. We moved in February 1988, and now both Meghann and Asia rode the bus to and from school. Jerry had his office space, and we had the landlord's permission to plant a garden in the spring.

Raising and selling the birds and charging a fee for feeding babies for other breeders in the area had brought me a small income, which allowed me the luxury of staying at home. We felt strongly about consistency for Asia, and I wanted to be there to get the kids off to school and when they came home. In the fall of 1988, however, in an attempt to generate more income, I applied for and was hired by Eastern Airlines as a ticket agent at Detroit Metropolitan Airport. I had worked for Eastern in the late 1960s and for another airline and several travel agencies in the past, but still had to go to Miami for five weeks of training. Bud and Wim, Jerry's parents, came for four days after I left, and once again Grandma Betty came to the rescue to stay until I returned. I had never been away from my family and it was very hard for all of us, but our parents were the glue that held things together.

One of the benefits of working for an airline is the travel privileges for immediate family members, so Jerry, Meghann, and Asia were able to fly down for my graduation. I began work in November of 1988, working part time, four hours a day, with the promise of full time employment in the future. My shift was from 5 A.M. until 9 A.M., which was perfect, since Jerry could be home to get the girls ready for school. On days when I had to work in the afternoon, our ministers' daughter met their bus at our house and stayed until Jerry or I got home. My hours were too few and too erratic for any of the day care or latch key programs.

Having almost free airline travel allowed us to plan a much needed Florida vacation on an island with camping sites on the water. We arranged to ship all of our camping gear to friends near Tampa and rented a van after we arrived. We ate fresh seafood, swam, and collected shells and sand dollars, made friends with egrets, blue herons, and racoons, and caught chameleons to bring home. We slept in a tent, cooked over a fire and baked our brains out in the hot Florida sun. It was just what we all needed. On the way home, Jerry stopped in Atlanta for a few days to visit with friends. The airline passes made us feel wealthy when we were far from it (in money, that is).

Shortly after we returned, the schedules changed and my shift would be in the middle of the day. With Jerry on the road, I would have to have a babysitter, not only for my working hours, but an hour before and an hour after to allow for travel time to and from the airport. This expense, coupled with gasoline and parking costs, meant that not only was I *not* making any money, but it was costing me $20.00 more than my salary just to work. It didn't take a rocket scientist to figure out that this couldn't go on for long, so soon I was back to raising my birdies.

Asia had continued to make minimal progress in school. She exhibited many noncomplaint behaviors (she knew the rules, but chose not to follow them, or did just the opposite just to get a reaction) and only spoke in three- or four-word sentences. She still spun wheels and flicked paper, sometimes against her lips and the tip of her nose. She loved everybody, and wanted to touch them, their faces, hair, and hands. This did not endear her to the other children at school, especially the boys. We and her teachers constantly reminded her to keep her hands to herself. I used to say that she must go to sleep at night with the words, "Be appropriate, Asia," ringing in her ears. She could only sit still for a short time before jumping out of her seat and gazelle-leaping across the room. When she was upset or anxious, she would dig at the ring fingers of both hands until she peeled away layers of skin. She would take off any band-aids we put on, or just go to another finger. There were times when we taped socks on her hands to keep her from hurting herself.

By this time, she ate anything that didn't move when she bit it, and had to be stopped at two helpings of food at meals. She loved apples, and would have eaten an entire three-pound bag a day if we let her. Her appetite was phenomenal, yet she was thin as a reed. She had/has the metabolism of a fruit bat, and could eat six times her body weight in a day. Her need for sameness extended to mealtimes, and she would happily have eaten the same thing meal after meal, day after day, if we allowed. When she discovered oatmeal, that's all she would eat for breakfast for months, until I switched her to pancakes, and then that's all she wanted. She would have eaten macaroni and cheese forever.

She had no concept of what a stranger was, and would have

gone off with the meter reader if he had offered her food. This was one of my biggest fears, and one of the reasons we would later seek professional help.

Later that summer Asia wanted to learn to ride a bicycle like Meghann. Meghann was due for a new one, so we told her we would get it when Asia learned to ride the old one. We had no sidewalk, and the driveway was dirt, pitted, and on a hill, so we found a park with bike paths, swings (Asia's passion, besides food), and a stream for Jerry and me to fish. By the end of the summer, Asia had mastered the two wheeler, and flew like the wind around our driveway loop, her hair streaming back from her glowing face.

As the 1989-90 school year started, Asia was one of the older students in the class, and the administration decided that because of the large number of students in the autistic impaired classroom, to divide the class by age. Mrs. LaPrairie took the younger students and Maria Bolen would have the older kids. Mrs. Bolen was wonderful with Asia, and the change went smoothly.

In the spring of 1990, though, Asia's flicking took on dangerous overtones. She began to flick pencils against her eye-lashes, and when upset, instead of digging into her fingers with her nails, she dug with pencils or safety pins. She started hiding cars and other toys in her pockets and bringing them home from school. Mrs. Bolen began to frisk her before she left each day. Occasionally, when anxious or frustrated, she would pinch other students, or squeeze their wrists. We already knew that she didn't feel pain the same as others, and that temperature changes didn't affect her. She never slept under covers, and wore shorts in the winter if we let her. But this new self-abuse and aggressive behavior was alarming. We tried all the usual behavior modification, time out, taking away snacks, going to bed without dinner (usually the worst punishment we could inflict), but nothing worked. We saw subtler signs that disturbed us as well. Asia loved pictures, either in magazines, or photographs. We never gave her good ones, because they usually ended up as flickers and became unrecognizable. She began to scratch the eyes out of the faces. For some reason, that made the hairs stand up on the back of my neck.

We wondered if some of this behavior was the result of anxiety that she could not express any other way. In the fall she would be changing schools again, this time to Paddock Elementary School in Milan. She would be in a self-contained classroom and would have a full-time health care aide. Her teacher, Carol Vollink, was experienced and well thought of in the system. Asia seemed excited about going to the same school as Meghann. But maybe, deep inside where she checked out to sometimes, maybe she was really more worried about the move and had no language to express her concerns. So they came out in other ways.

Earlier that summer we had adopted two kittens and had been adopted by another. The one that had found us was a weak, sickly little thing that had probably been dumped by the side of the road by a passing car. We kept her on heat and nursed her back to health. Asia had not paid that much attention to the cats, but one night, when I heard the youngest screaming outside, I ran to investigate, and found Asia, holding the kitten facedown in a puddle and covering her with mud. My initial reaction was a sharp swat on Asia's bottom before sending her to her room, which, shamefully, I didn't regret at all. After washing and drying the kitten and calming myself down, we called Asia downstairs to try to find out what she was doing.

"Asia wash kitty," she said.

"But honey, kitties don't like baths, and what you were doing could have hurt the kitty," Jerry told her calmly. "You must never try to wash the kitty again." We never really knew how much sank in from these conversations, because when we asked her to tell us what we had said, Asia's stock reply was a blank stare. After she went to bed that evening, and I tried to squelch the nagging feeling of unease that the evening had left me with.

We knew that Asia desperately wanted to communicate, because she talked constantly, but very little of what she said had any relevance to what was going on. For example, in the middle of dinner, she would say, "Colostomy is red," or "High School, hives and fire," which she found hysterically funny. Many times she would laugh maniacally for no apparent reason. Out of the blue she would say, "Asia has pretty black hair." She always referred to herself in the third person.

After a second incident involving the kitten, we realized we needed professional help. Asia had put the kitten in a pet carrier inside another box and left it outside. We had called for it all day and checked the highway in front of our house for road kill, but found no kitten. Late that night, after the day's noises had quietened, I heard a faint meow from the back porch. I found the kitten, very dehydrated from the heat in the box, but alive. The next day I called our school case worker for a referral for help.

She recommended a child and family services center in Ann Arbor and I made an appointment with a female psychiatrist, whose name I'll not mention. We started our weekly visits in early August, and continued for nearly four months. Only once did she actually spend time with Asia, the child she was to evaluate. She talked with us *about* Asia and we answered questionnaires and brought in school reports. At one point Mrs. Vollink came in for a fifty-minute session with the psychiatrist, while I stayed out in the waiting room with Asia. In addition to the self-abusive behavior and agressive behaviors toward other children and the animals, we explained that Asia had next to no impulse control and the attention span of a gnat. To her, a stranger was simply someone she hadn't met yet, and she was determined to correct that at all costs. Basing her diagnosis on second- and third-hand information, questionnaires, and *maybe* twenty minutes actually observing and talking with Asia out of four months of sessions, she determined that Asia had attention deficit/hyperactivity disorder (ADHD), and prescribed Imipramine, a drug intended to treat depression or anxiety. Oddly, another use was to treat bedwetting.

Asia was to begin with ten milligrams of the drug a day, increasing by ten milligrams every three days. The doctor (and I use the title loosely), said everyone's therapeutic dosage was different, and she could possibly get up to one hundred milligrams or higher before her effective level was reached. We were told not to expect to see changes right away, as a certain level of the drug must be built up in the bloodstream. The typewritten sheet we were given (not the drug company insert) listed the possible side effects as numbness or tingling in the extremities (call the doctor), dry mouth, constipation, loss of appetite (*hah*), and inability to sleep. At the twenty-milligram dose, Asia wet the bed for the first time in four years. I should have seen that as a sign. At sixty milligrams we had seen no other negatives, and so far no positives, but we had been told it could take weeks to see the changes, so we waited.

Jerry and Asia had been continuing with their Tae Kwon Do classes every Monday and Wednesday, and were scheduled to test again on Saturday, October thirteenth. Jerry was testing for his blue belt and Asia was going for the green stripe on her yellow belt. She had perfected the seven forms and their verbal descriptions, although she still recited them in a 33 1/3 RPM monotone.

The Saturday morning dawned crisp and clear, a perfect fall day. We had breakfast, showered Asia, and gave her her medication. She was at seventy milligrams. We were to be at the school at 11 A.M. Asia waited quietly (*quietly? Asia?*) while the rest of us got ready, and then we all went outside to take pictures of Jerry and Asia in their crisp, white *do baks* amid the glorious fall colors. Asia was flushed and her pupils dilated, but said she felt okay. (This from a kid who hated doctors so badly that she could be bleeding from six places and say "What's for dinner?")

We drove to the school where the testing was to take place and Meghann and I took our places in the bleachers while Jerry and Asia joined the groups on the floor. There were padded posts for practicing body kicks and wrestling mats rolled up in the corner. Grand Master Humesky and the rest of the board of Masters sat at a long table at one end of the gym, with the students doing warm-up stretches on the floor in front of them.

The mother beside me was working on a cross-stitch picture. I could identify with that. Her child must be one of the last ones testing, I thought, as I got my camera ready.

Asia seemed disoriented and couldn't find her place with her group. When it was time to begin, everyone sat in position. Everyone but Asia. As she wandered around the gym, a knot began forming in my stomach. When called to come back, she looked at the instructor as though she didn't recognize him.

Finally she was seated on the floor and the testing began. Testing is always done from the lowest belt color, white, up to the highest, black. There were white belt students testing for yellow stripe, yellow stripe testing for yellow belt, and then Asia's group, yellow belt testing for green stripe. Several times during the other testing she got up and wandered dazedly, aimlessly around. Performances had to be stopped when she wandered too close to the students testing, until she took her place again.

Then it was her turn. She stood in front of the Masters with her hands hanging limply at her side and tried to recite the oath and creed. The knot moved rapidly from my stomach to my throat. She couldn't do it. This was not defiance or stubbornness. She was lost. She tried to walk away. Jerry brought her back and did the forms with her, something he shouldn't have had to do. Even then she turned left when she should have turned right as she sluggishly went through moves that had been sharp and clean the day before. She was a zombie child. When she finished I was glad I hadn't taken a single picture. What had we done to her?

Somehow we all got through the rest of the testing. Jerry did a beautiful job, and when the belts were awarded at the end, Asia received her green stripe, but only because of the performance the Grand Master had seen the week before in class, and because he knew the reason for her inability to function that day.

On the way home from what should have been an exhilarating day, Asia was confused, incoherent, and said she felt "like going round and round" (dizzy).

I called the pharmacist as soon as we got home to see what

the worst side effect would be if we took her off the Imipramine cold turkey. The possible flu-like symptoms for a day we could live with, but zombie-child had to go. Good-bye Imipramine; good-bye, Dr. You-Know-Who-You-Are. We called her on Monday to tell her of Saturday's nightmare, and that we wouldn't be back. Too bad, she said. She had wanted to try Haldol next.

Within a few days, Asia was back to normal (her normal), but we had been shaken to the core. We hadn't wanted to give her medication in the first place, but we were assured that this was one of the safest drugs, with the least side effects, and look what had happened. We vowed no more doctors or shrinks of any kind until after Christmas.

Chapter Twenty

Shrinks, Part Two

JERRY AND ASIA continued with their Tae Kwon Do classes, but Asia's behavior became more and more disruptive. Jerry was asked to take the position of assistant instructor, to work with some of the younger children, and he tried to keep Asia under control too, but it was almost a full-time job.

One evening in November, I was on the telephone with my back to the door when they returned from class. Asia came in crying, and said that a bee had stung her hand. I turned around to see Asia looking very much like she had in 1983, three days after her arrival, covered with hives. Her face continued to swell while I was looking at her. As best as we could tell, the bee had stung her hand as she bent to tie her shoes in the grass outside the class. In the dark car on the way home, Jerry couldn't see her swelling face. Her arm was so swollen that we couldn't get her coat on. Meghann rode in the back of the van trying to keep Asia calm on yet another white knuckle ride to the emergency room.

Jerry had called ahead, and we were met by nurses with a

wheelchair, who whisked Asia off screaming, while someone tried to steer me into a cubicle to fill out forms. "Give me the forms," I shouted, as I grabbed them in one hand and Meghann with the other. "I can't let her go in there by herself." She would have lost it completely if left alone with doctors.

Once again the epinephrine worked its magic, and we watched as the shiny swelling smoothed away, leaving her face recognizable again. Too bad they couldn't have tapped off some of my adrenaline--I had enough rushing through my body for three people. Asia and Meghann slept through a much slower ride home, and the following day the pediatrician prescribed an Epi-Pen kit (an auto injector), for any future bee sting emergencies.

Since our first venture into the world of psychiatric counseling had been such a bomb, we wanted to wait until after Christmas before pursuing any other attempts to seek counseling.

In the meantime, I spoke with other mothers and Mrs. Vollink, Asia's teacher, for recommendations. One psychologist came highly recommended, and we called for an appointment after the holidays.

Meanwhile, on the East Coast, Cindy and Steve had applied with the local adoption agency in Maine in January of 1990 and had taken the required six weeks of parenting classes. By March their home study had been done. Since they wanted to adopt an older child rather than an infant, and race or nationality was not an issue, the odds were in their favor for a domestic adoption. When she called early in December, there was no disguising the excitement in her voice. Her social worker had called. There was a little boy, almost three years old, in Texas. He and his eighteen-year-old Mexican mother had lived together in a foster home almost since his birth. His young mother had just recently made the difficult decision to make arrangements for his adoption. The agency had shown her several homestudies, and from them she had selected Cindy and Steve to be her son's new parents. The social worker asked if Cindy and Steve wanted him. *"YES,"* was Cindy's emphatic reply. The pictures and more information arrived a few days later, and Cindy immediately mailed off copies to us. The beautiful little boy, whose name was Preston, looked just like Steve! It was uncanny. They had the same hairline, eyes, and shy smile. The following week Cindy and Steve flew to Texas, and ten days before Christmas brought their son home.

Jerry and I were both present for the first session with the psychologist, and again related Asia's history as accurately as we could to date. (By then we had it memorized and could recite it in our sleep.) This doctor recommended a variety of tests designed to determine Asia's capabilities and liabilities. By this time I had come to hate all the acronyms for the different labels for challenged children. I felt that people looked at the label not the child. But, it was explained to me countless times, the labels are merely tools and nothing to fear.

Fifty-minute sessions once a week were set up for the initial testing. Asia has never tested well; her attention span was non-existent, she couldn't sit still for more than a minute, and was usually doing three or more things at once (watching TV, jumping on the trampoline, and running to the couch to draw). At least this doctor was spending time with Asia instead of with us.

Because we had mentioned, and the psychologist saw, the "absence-type" spells that were recurring, Asia was sent to a neurologist, who scheduled an EEG and a CAT scan, neither of which showed anything significant. I told the psychologist that Asia was bothered by certain sounds, the baby seat in the grocery cart, the vacuum cleaner, doors closing, etc., so a hearing test was ordered, which was normal (normal if all the test was designed to measure was hearing loss). The psychologist's colleague went to Asia's class and observed her in the school setting. He noted her extremely poor impulse control and poor social judgment, and recommended the continuance of an aide to help meet her educational needs.

The end result was a diagnosis of pervasive developmental delay (PDD), and it was recommended that she take Ritalin to help with her lack of impulse control. The neurologist would prescribe it if we decided to try her on it. We had recently attended a parent support meeting where *adults* with attention deficit disorder (ADD) were discussing how the drug had changed *their* lives for the better, how they were more in control and able to focus and could stay on task--in short, a lot of the things we wanted for Asia. But after our first encounter with drug intervention, we wanted to do as much research as possible.

One of the possible side effects could be tics (involuntary muscle movements, usually in the head or face, sometimes vocal, sometimes vulgar), and if tics were already present, the drug could aggravate or intensify them. I had read that Ritalin had been implicated in causing full-blown Tourette's syndrome in patients with preexisting tics. Asia's "absence" spells, as I called them, were believed to be a form of tic. She was already jumping enough hurdles; the last thing she needed was another. We questioned the psychologist and the neurologist repeatedly and both assured us that the likelihood of the tics occurring was minimal, and if any *did* develop, they would go away, especially when she was off the drug. She would take one tablet in the morning and another at lunch time if needed, but none in the late afternoon, since it could interfere with sleep. Another possible side effect was loss of appetite. *Ha*! once again, not a chance with this kid. As much as we hated the idea of giving her another drug, Jerry and I reluctantly decided to try the Ritalin.

We picked the prescription up on Friday afternoon. We had decided not to tell Mrs. Vollink, because we wanted an objective opinion of any changes. Saturday morning after breakfast I gave Asia the first pill. It was hard to do anything but watch her. What were we watching for? I don't know . . . anything . . . nothing . . . *something*!

An hour or so later I was washing dishes when Asia came up to show me a drawing. She was always drawing and seldom went anywhere without pens and paper, but the drawings were doodles, occasionally faces, almost always the same. This time she had drawn her bicycle, complete with handle bars, spokes, horn, and pedals. I was astounded. Then she wanted to know how to spell, and asked, in rapid-fire succession, for the spelling of words and names. Jerry and Meghann gathered around.

Giving her a fresh piece of paper, Jerry said, "Draw the TV, Asia." And she did it immediately, looking from the TV to her paper to get every knob in place. Then she wanted to draw the bathroom, of all things. Her perspective was from the ceiling, looking down on the toilet, sink, shower head, even the soap dish. She couldn't do things fast enough. She even ate lunch faster, if such a thing is possible. She was *busy,* involved, absorbed, absorbing, as we had never seen her before. When she asked questions, she looked *at* us. She went from project to project until the middle of the afternoon, when she began to wind down. We were astounded. How could one little pill accomplish *so much* when years of work by teachers, doctors, us, had just scratched the surface. We all compared notes and agreed that it had not been our imagination--for those few hours, she had been on target, right there, all the time. We couldn't wait until Monday to see what school would be like.

On Sunday morning, I gave her the Ritalin after breakfast, before we left for church. We were certain that friends at church would be able to see a change. Normally Asia couldn't sit still, burst out with comments which made no sense, or laughed loudly at nothing during the service. We went to the early morning service, when there were fewer people, and they all knew Asia. She sat quietly and attentively for the first half (a first), but midway through the service, I felt (or sensed) a change coming over her, and suddenly, quietly, she began to cry. She still had very little language, and it was especially difficult for her to express her feelings, particularly sadness. We spent hours sometimes asking, "Why are you crying, honey?"

"Sad."

"Why are you sad?"

"Tears on face."

"No, honey, there are tears on your face because you are crying. Why are you crying?"

"I'm sorry."

"You don't have to be sorry, honey. Why are you sad?"

"Eyes crying." Round and round we'd go, getting nowhere.

I put my arms around her and asked why she was sad. She couldn't even answer with her usual replies. Her face was flushed and contorted, and tears streamed down her cheeks. I took her outside to walk around in the warm spring morning and she finally seemed a little better. We thought maybe she realized that something momentous had happened the day before, and even though she couldn't tell us, she was glad. Maybe, just maybe, this monumental little pill had unlocked some internal door in our little girl, and she was overwhelmed at all the new sensations and feelings on the other side. We couldn't have been more wrong.

We went to the grocery store, as was our habit after church, and once again Asia began to cry, quiet, unbelievably pathetic tears. We comforted her as best as we could, with Jerry taking the lead so I could shop for the week's groceries, and by the time we got home, she was almost back to normal. We chalked the events up to emotions. We believed there had been a breakthrough on Saturday, and that once she became comfortable with the "new world," she'd be fine.

On Monday morning I gave her her pill, and sent her off to catch the bus. About 10 A.M. Mrs. Vollink called. I always held my breath when I heard her voice in the middle of a school day, and when she asked, "How are you?" as part of conversation, my reply was always, "It's 11 o'clock on a Monday morning, *you* tell *me*, 'How am I?' "

"Asia is crying inconsolably, and has been for about an hour. None of the usual remedies have helped--not talking, distraction, or music," she began. "We can't determine if she is in pain or sad or what. She doesn't even seem to know that we're there.

Marsha has taken her outside for a while to see if swinging will calm her."

I left immediately to get her. I, of course, got no further than they had at determining the cause, but told Mrs. Vollink about the Ritalin. As a special education teacher she had had other students on the drug without these particular side effects. We were both at a loss, but I wasn't willing to give up just yet. I had been shown a vision of what *could* be on Saturday, and I was going to cling to it. I couldn't believe that the pill that had wrought such an amazing change for the better in Asia one day could wreck her emotionally the next.

I took her home and within a few hours the crying subsided and finally quit entirely. This had to be caused by something else. But the next day, at almost exactly the same time, the scene repeated itself, right down to me driving into town to bring Asia home. We tried to identify an outside source. There was major construction going on in the school; maybe the noise was too much for her. Maybe it was frightening her. Maybe the drug had unlocked some long-repressed memory from her early years in the hospitals or in the orphanage, and she couldn't express the pain she felt. But whatever was causing the spells, they were over in a few hours and then she would be fine for the rest of the day.

By Wednesday we were able to tell by her expressions when one of the anxiety attacks was about to occur. First her eyes changed. It seemed as though she could see something none of us could see, way off in the distance. Then the skin on her face began to look puffy and flushed, and then began to contort, almost as if it was made of "electric putty" with the voltage on high. Then the quiet tears would start, and she would begin to wring her hands and dig her nails into her palms and fingertips. Her arms and legs would begin to twitch, and she would wrap them around each other like some grotesque parody of "Cross your fingers, toes, eyes, arms, legs, everything." We came to call this "the pretzel." Each time the attacks occurred about an hour after taking the Ritalin and lasted about four hours, the amount of time we were told that the drug remained in the system, which was the reason for the midday dose for some children. (Asia was never given more than one pill a day.)

On Thursday morning I sent her to school without the Ritalin, and the dreaded hour came and went uneventfully. No anxiety attack. No crying or "pretzeling." In the meantime, I called the psychologist and the neurologist's office to let them know how things were going (or not going, in this case). On Saturday afternoon I had left messages on their machines about all the exciting developments of the day. Thursday's call was somewhat less than exciting. Neither doctor thought that the Ritalin was the cause.

When I called the psychologist, he said, "This is very unusual. Surely there must be something else going on. Are there any other changes happening in her life?"

"Well, actually, yes," I replied. "We've bought a house in Milan and we're planning to move near the end of June. We've told Asia about our 'new home' and she was there with us many times while the purchase was being finalized. It won't involve a change in schools [something I had insisted on when we began the house search] and she will actually be closer to schoolmates. She's asked lots of questions, but hasn't seemed too concerned."

"But, knowing how she resists change, and how rootless parts of her past had been, maybe she's more worried about the move than she can express," he said.

And not having the language to express her fears, she turned herself into a human pretzel.

I called the neurologist's office and spoke with a nurse, who relayed the information to the doctor and called me back. "Doctor suggests that you cut the dosage in half for a few days to see if that will help."

"But if it's the move that she's worried about, how will cutting the drug dosage help?" I asked. But, hey, who's the doctor here? Who has the degrees and went to college and has all the proper letters after their names? And why was I falling for this again? You'd think I would have learned my lesson by now.

So we cut the dosage. School was nearly out and the kids had half-days. Asia got out of school at 10:45 A.M. and cried all the way home on the bus. I remember one of the bus drivers telling me how concerned the other children were, because, trouble-maker or not, Asia was always such a happy child, with sparkling eyes and a radiant smile for everyone. Who was *this* child, and what had they done with my Asia?

During the weekend we tried the half dosage and Asia went out to ride her bike. It was early summer, not too hot yet, and the rest of us were getting ready to work in the garden. In about an hour I saw her, across the driveway, straddling the bike with her back to me, staring off in the distance. As I walked up behind her, her shoulders began to shake as her body twisted into a knot. Her face was almost unrecognizable behind the sheen of tears. I tried to unknot her arms and legs to pick her up, but ended up carrying her, stiff as a board, and started back to the porch, screaming for Jerry. He ran to take her from me, trampling through the peonies, not caring, as Meghann came out onto the porch. We all four sat in a huddle, our arms wrapped around Asia, rocking and crying. She couldn't talk, wouldn't look at us. Her face twitched and grimaced as her body alternately curled and stretched and jerked. By the middle of the afternoon the worst had passed, and we tried 17,000 different ways of asking why she was had been so sad. We got 17,000 versions of no response. On one rare occasion, I asked her if she knew why she was crying and she replied, between sobs, that she didn't know. We began to notice that after the spells were over, facial and shoulder tics would remain, and more and more often her face would twitch or her shoulder jerk upward long after the medication was supposed to have worn off.

On Monday I called the doctors again. Try giving the pills every other day, they said. At school, Mrs. Vollink asked for permission to videotape Asia's behaviors. The camera was set up in a small room inside her classroom, where Asia spent time working one-to-one with Marsha Adams, her aide. Asia paid no attention to the camera. She chewed the ends of her fingers, her shoulders jerked, she hit herself in the head and under her chin with the heel of her hand, slamming her head back. She mumbled and babbled, "Jared has red hair." "What color my mom's hair?" She would jump up out of the chair, pace the perimeter of the room a few times, then sit down again. She poked at her fingers with a pencil. Marsha's patience never failed. During the worst times, when nothing else seemed to work, Marsha would take her outside to the playground swings. The physical release seemed to help, but sometimes she didn't even want that.

We were beginning to pack and clean in preparation for the move, and once again Asia watched solemnly as her belongings were hidden away in anonymous boxes. Maybe this *was* affecting her and she couldn't tell us. We tried to be supportive, to assure her that we were *all* moving together, that all her toys and papers and Touch and Tell were going with us. We tried to explain that she would be in the same school in the fall, with Mrs. Vollink and Mrs. Adams and all the kids. But we had no idea how much was sinking in. These pills should be helping her to deal with all this, not destroying her.

Moving day came and went, with trip after trip between the old house and the new, and Asia cried and twisted herself into positions a contortionist would envy. At the doctor's suggestion, we cut the dosage in half again.

Several days after we were in our new home, we set the video camera up on the tripod. I gave Asia what would be her last dose of Ritalin. I could have stopped right then, but I wanted a record of what happened. I felt that the doctors all thought we were exaggerating, blowing things out of proportion. No one could believe us unless they saw for themselves. We all walked around in a daze as the drug took effect and she began to draw in on herself. It had to be the pills; it couldn't be anything else. It couldn't be the move. We watched as she sobbed and twisted, oblivious to everything and everyone around her. We consoled and rocked and cried with her. She sat and tried to draw, but grimaced and cried, and stuck herself with her pencil. We took the pencil away. Between tears and sweat, she was soaking wet, her thick black hair matted slick to her head. She wouldn't eat, refused even macaroni and cheese. There was nothing we could do but wait it out. One-fourth of a tablet, in her system, lasted as long and had as devastating effect as a full tablet. God help us all if we had ever given her more than one. Finally it was over. She was back from whatever hell she had been to. Her smile returned, and with it her appetite, a sure sign that her spirits were improving. We heaved a collective sigh, flushed the remaining Ritalin tablets down the toilet, turned off the video camera, and tried to salvage the rest of the weekend. We had taped it, in part, to remind ourselves to try to stop anyone else who was told to put their child on this monstrous drug. And then we were done. We called the doctors and told them, and they assured us once again that the many facial and body tics would go away. *After all, the drug is gone from the body in four hours,* they said. The tics did not go away. She twitched and jerked like a puppet, with not one part of her body in sync with any other. She talked to herself. She clawed her arms and peeled the callouses off her ring fingers. She twisted her body as her face contorted uncontrollably. We watched in helpless frustration, paid the bills and took one more step away from the medical establishment.

Chapter Twenty-one
Re-Building

IN THE DAYS that followed, we watched Asia constantly, waiting for the magic time when the tics would go away as promised. But she had been altered, permanently, it seemed. We had all been altered during that terrible month, but for Jerry, Meghann, and me, the scars were inside. Asia wore hers every day. Sometimes her face was twitching so much, it was difficult to look at her. They weren't so much repulsive as they were distracting. We'd get so caught up in the motions of her face that we'd lose track of what she was saying.

There were other changes as well. Her sound sensitivity had increased. When we went grocery shopping, Asia would run to the other side of the store as I pulled out the grocery cart, or pull it out herself, very slowly, and hold the baby seat so it wouldn't slam down. If a baby was crying, Asia lost control. One of her chores was vacuuming, and she had been covering her ear with one hand and using her shoulder to cover the other for the vacuum noise. Now if the vacuum strayed from carpet to tile or wood floor, she flinched, or if something hard was sucked up rattling around inside (an unpopped kernel of popcorn, for example), she stopped entirely and backed away, grimacing. She couldn't tolerate the sound of the Salad Shooter, electric knife, or hand mixer. She covered her ears when we shut the door as we left the house, and went into another room when cupboard doors were closed. The doctors were puzzled, but not concerned--after all, her hearing tested normal, even better than normal. *It was just another of her quirks.*

The neurologist who had done the EEG on Asia suggested that we see a behavioral psychologist from his office once a week. I questioned her and her associate about the hearing sensitivity, but got only quizzical looks. I asked them about a procedure called auditory integration training (AIT). Earlier in the spring of 1991 B.R. (Before Ritalin), Mrs. Vollink had sent home a copy of an article from Reader's Digest entitled "Fighting for Georgie," by Annabel Stehli. In it, Ms. Stehli told of her autistic daughter, Georgiana and the miraculous treatment called auditory integration training, which had changed her from an eleven-year-old with an IQ of seventy-five into a thriving, intelligent, "normal" teenager. Georgie went on to graduate Magna Cum Laude from Hartford Art School. The treatment, detailed in the article, seemed amazingly simple. Georgie had listened to music filtered through headphones for thirty minutes twice a day for ten days. Even though Asia's "label" was not autism, the thing that caught my attention was Georgie's sound sensitivity. Barely audible sounds drove her to distraction. Could there be some connection? The first stumbling block was that the treatment had been done in France.

I began a phone search for more information on AIT. Local audiologists knew nothing. The University Hospital knew nothing. The local "autism specialist" pooh-poohed the idea as bogus. The Autism Society told me that the French doctor, Dr. Berard, had retired, and that his equipment was being used by a Dr. Stephen Edelson in Oregon. Well, never having been shy about using the telephone or calling up total strangers, I spent an evening searching for, and finding, several phone numbers for Dr. Edelson, and having a lovely conversation with his wife. Dr. Edelson, she said, was in the middle of his second grant study on the procedure, and already had over 1,000 volunteers. It seemed the treatment wasn't being done anywhere else. *Why* I didn't think to try to locate Annabel Stehli, I don't know. I "back-burnered" the idea of AIT, but didn't forget it.

I don't remember the exact wording, but the message was clear that the behaviorist felt the procedure was another way to encourage hope where there was none and milk poor, unsuspecting parents of their hard-earned dollars (which would be better spent on psychological counseling, perhaps?).

We saw the counselor, and throughout the summer we took notes, filling out hourly check lists on charts that she had prepared to record incidences of flicking, absence spells, and "the pretzel." The pretzel had been replaced by a newer, milder form which Asia called "fretting." The pose and intensity was similar, but didn't last as long. It did occur more frequently though. By late September we had learned absolutely nothing from these visits that we didn't already know--that Asia was a child with a lot of problems and perplexing behaviors and no easy answers.

One of the first tasks in our new home was to fence in the back yard. The lot was a long half-acre with a woody, swampy area at the very back. We wanted the fence to enclose a large area for the kids to play in, and for Sushi, our cockapoo-sheltie puppy, to run in. Outside the fence was still plenty of room for the garden and fruit trees. (I was amazed at how large one-half acre really is.) Jerry's parents were planning a trip through Michigan on their way south in September, and Jerry's dad offered to stay a few extra days to help put the fence up. A friend's son, Adam Edwards, would be here to help as well.

Each day they were up with the dawn, eating breakfast and waiting for the sun to burn off the mosquitos. While the men worked outside, I cooked and took care of critters, Asia rode her bike, and Meghann kept Grandma entertained with the soaps and game and talk shows. One of Wim's favorites was the Sally Jessy Raphael show. The second morning, I checked to see if anybody needed anything before going downstairs to work with the birds. Wim snagged me before I got to the top of the stairs. "Say, Adair, you might want to watch a little bit of this," she said. "It's really interesting. It's about kids with allergies." Yeah, right. I'm not the talk show type, and I never sit down to watch TV in the middle of the day unless I'm sick. But I stopped to watch a bit to be polite. The topic for the day was children with allergies that caused behavior problems. The guest was Dr. Doris Rapp, a pediatric allergist from Buffalo, New York, who had spent fifteen years studying the effects of food and environmental allergies on children. There were videos of the children before, during, and after the testing. Some of the behaviors were bizarre, frightening, and self-injurious. Depending on the child and the substance, the response could be as mild as red, puffy eyes and sniffles or as violent as self- or parent-abuse. We saw many things that reminded us both of Asia. It was downright spooky. I was hooked. We already knew that cow's milk had bothered her before the second colostomy surgery. But that was physical. Could the milk have other effects on her? Could there be other allergies as well? I ended up watching the entire program with Wim, and afterward, began a phone search for Dr. Rapp's new book, Is This Your Child? We found it, and Wim and Bud bought it for me for my birthday. I read out loud to Wim all afternoon, and to Jerry every time he passed through to go to the bathroom or get water. There were so many case histories of children that resembled Asia. None exactly, but bits and pieces here and there. It was like finding different puzzle pieces in different drawers, until you finally have a picture.

Dr. Rapp explained that allergies effect all of us in different ways, and effect the body's systems differently. The skin responds to an allergic substance by breaking out in a rash, the nose by sneezing, and so on. (I was already familiar with environmental allergies since my asthma was triggered by breathing certain chemicals or fumes.) The brain, as an organ, could also be allergic, and the response could be behavior changes. The more I read, the more convinced I became that this all applied to Asia. I began to call allergists in the area to find someone to test her for food and environmental allergies. I quickly found that the provocation/neutralization testing that Dr. Rapp does is not widely accepted by "traditional" allergists. (Why didn't that surprise me?) With the test, three drops of a dilution of the suspected allergen are placed under the tongue and held for twenty seconds, then swallowed (provocation). The child is observed for any changes for the next ten minutes. Sometimes handwriting samples are taken before, during, and after. If the child's behavior changes in a negative manner, then weaker solutions of the same allergen are tried until no reaction occurs. This is determined to be the neutralization dose. Many of the doctors I spoke with either didn't do this type of testing or didn't believe that food allergies could cause behavior changes in children. In other words, if it didn't make you cough, hack, sneeze, wheeze, throw up, or break out in a rash, then, "By golly, little lady," you weren't allergic to it.

Fortunately, Dr. Rapp's book came with a test that could be done at home. With the Multiple Food Elimination Diet, milk, wheat, eggs, corn, chocolate, citrus, sugar, peas, food additives, food preservatives, and colorings are eliminated from the diet for one week. This also meant any foods containing these ingredients. Milk (cheese, yogurt, ice cream), wheat (bread, baked goods, cereal), etc. You get the idea. My God, what can you eat? you may ask. Quite a bit, actually. Beef, chicken, turkey, fish (nothing breaded), and any vegetable, fresh or frozen preferably, canned if there are no additives, colors or sugar. The vegetable exceptions are peas and corn. Rice, potatoes (even French fries), and oats were allowed. Any fruit except orange, lemon or grapefruit was permitted. Eating out is difficult while doing the elimination diet, since you don't know how everything is prepared. Processed meats and TV dinners had to go, because of the additives, preservatives and colorings. The main thing was to keep the foods as basic as possible. Copious notes are taken as to behavior changes, *any changes,* during the week. The following week the foods are added back to the diet, one a day, and again notes are taken. If any negative changes occur, eliminate that food from the diet. If no changes occur, that food can be added. Continue adding a food a day and noting any changes.

We wanted to try it. All the food groups were there; the only challenge would be coming up with recipes with enough variety. I really felt we were on to something, so I took the book with us to the next visit with the therapist and left it for a few days. Their feeling was, once again, that we would be wasting our time. They were beginning to sound like a broken record.

Jerry and I read and talked and read some more. We could find no good reason *not* to try the diet. This was certainly less invasive than our more recent efforts. We had absolutely nothing to lose and everything to gain. We decided to go for it, but all of us, together, as a family. We couldn't stand the thought of eating Asia's favorite foods in front of her, and we might even uncover some hidden allergies in ourselves. We would only tell Mrs. Vollink and Mrs. Adams, since they would have to know about the "forbidden" foods for the week. Meghann found a library book on cooking for children with allergies. We were set. To hell with what the "specialists" thought. We would start on Saturday.

Chapter Twenty-two

The Cold-Turkey Diet

WE HAD EXPLAINED to Asia that we would be trying a new diet for a week to see if we were allergic to some foods, and that there would be some favorite foods that we couldn't have during that week.

"What about pizza, Mom?" she wanted to know.

"No, honey, no pizza, I'm afraid," I replied.

"Macaroni and cheese baked in oven, okay," she said confidently.

"I'm afraid not, honey. See, macaroni and pizza both have wheat in them, and wheat is one of the foods we might be allergic to. But we can have rice and potatoes and chicken and lots of other foods you like," I said, trying to sound upbeat.

"Baked zitis, okay, Mom?

"In a few weeks, after we're done testing, honey. See, zitis have wheat and cheese in them." I was really bombing out here.

"We still have popcorn at TV time, right, Mom?"

"No, honey, no popcorn either." I definitely wasn't selling this well at all.

"What having then, Mom?"

Think fast, Adair. "Well, you can have chips at TV time, and cream of rice for breakfast, and all the fruit you want," I ventured.

"*All* the fruit? How 'bout seconds?" She was yielding.

"Yes, all the fruit *and* seconds." *Now* I had her.

"Okay. What having for dinner, Mom?

I fixed a few of the *favorite* favorites on Friday night. Macaroni and cheese was a definite, and popcorn with T.V.

Saturday morning, breakfast without eggs, cereal, ham? Well, it's only for one week. We got through the weekend quite well, although Jerry really missed milk with meals. Asia wasn't too concerned yet, because with her, it's not so much *what's* for dinner, it's *how much* she can eat.

Weekdays were a bit more of a challenge. I had always fixed lunch for Jerry, Meghann, and Asia, so that wasn't new, but now I had to work without bread. Meghann, in the seventh grade now, wasn't thrilled, but was a good sport about not having a sandwich. Jerry, as a salesman, usually ate while driving between customers, so I had to send chunks of finger food, or he would go to a park and eat with a fork. Asia took her normal, linebacker portions of the allowed foods in containers. We tried not to let wishful thinking cloud our objectivity. We wanted something to finally work.

I kept a diary of what Asia ate every day, including snacks, and any and all behaviors. Mrs. Vollink kept up with the school/home notes. The reports were good, not spectacular, but good.

Probably the worst part of the diet was that, even though we could eat all we wanted of the allowed foods, we felt hungry all the time. I guess it was because we couldn't just grab a cracker or a slice of cheese whenever we wanted. We had to stop and think, "What's in it?" Shopping was also a challenge. I was fine with basic foods (meats, veggies, fruits), but I had to read labels on anything that came in a box, jar, or can. This added an extra thirty minutes or more to grocery shopping every week. It was quite an education, too, since I couldn't pronounce half of the ingredients, and the ingredient list was sometimes two inches of type on the label.

Meghann's best friend, Melissa Dertian was going to be staying with us for a few days while her parents were out of town, so she participated in the last few days of the test with us. On Friday evening we put Asia in our room with a movie while we all sat down and compared notes on what changes (or lack of them) we had observed in Asia. Everybody made their own list and then we compared them. It was really quite long, and included: calmer, less impulsive, less manic laughter, not as "testy," able to stay on task for longer periods. Mrs. Vollink and Mrs. Adams reported that she was more willing to work, had better concentration, was able to sit for longer periods, and had participated in group reading for the first time. They said that the Gypsies must have switched kids in the night. Now to start adding the foods back to our diets to see which were the culprits.

The first food we were to add was milk. "When do we get to popcorn?" Jerry wanted to know. The idea was to bombard the system with milk and certain plain milk products: cottage cheese, yogurt, white cheese with no additives. This was in addition to the foods eaten during the previous week. If any negative signs were seen, then that food would be eliminated again.

We already knew that the milk would give Asia diarrhea, but it also caused the tics to increase, she seemed confused, and her concentration was poor. The milk had such a sedative effect on Jerry that he slept all day. He ate breakfast (with milk and cottage cheese) and took a nap. Had yogurt and fruit for a snack and took another nap on the sofa. Ate cottage cheese and milk with lunch and went to sleep again.

Meghann's reaction surprised us the most. Normally agreeable and good-natured, Meghann was irritable, ornery, cranky, stubborn, and sometimes hostile. Melissa, who was still staying with us, mentioned that sometimes at school Meghann would be fine and in good spirits in the morning, but after lunch with *a half-pint of milk,* she would be edgy and irritable.

Meghann even recognized it in herself, but couldn't stop the way she was behaving. The milk didn't seem to affect me in any way.

On Sunday we added wheat. The book said it had to be plain, pure wheat, with no additives of any kind. They recommended Nabisco Shredded Wheat cereal, with milk, if milk was tolerated the day before, plain otherwise. I had to see for myself that this was the only plain wheat cereal on the shelves, and after reading the labels for half an hour, I found out it's true. Out of all those rows and rows of kid-appealing, advertised-to-the-hilt cereals, only Shredded Wheat is nothing but *pure* wheat. Asia had to eat it dry, which was almost as bad as making her drink the barium. She didn't like the texture or the taste, but she had to eat one-fourth of a cup before she could have anything else. Her activity level increased, but not unmanageably. She had another one-fourth cup before anything else at lunch, and it was another struggle to get her to eat it. We should have paid attention to her. Meghann, Melissa, Asia, and I went grocery shopping after lunch, and Asia was totally out of control. She kept running away from us down the aisles, laughing hysterically at nothing, grabbing things off the shelves, and talking a mile a minute. "Jared has red hair, what color Asia's hair? Colostomy is red. Mom is a nice lady. My teacher's name Mrs. Vollink," and on and on and on. Meghann and Melissa and I all looked at each other at once and said, "Gotta be the wheat." It was a challenge to get through shopping without tying her up with jump ropes.

We continued adding a food a day; sugar: egg, cocoa, foods with added coloring, corn, foods with added preservatives, citrus, peas. Sugar caused the expected "sugar buzz" in Meghann, but otherwise none of the other foods affected anyone but Asia. She had reactions to sugar, egg, food colorings, and preservatives. Mrs. Adams and Mrs. Vollink reported changes with each new addition, and asked us to send them the child they had had last week. The milk, wheat, and egg reactions eliminated macaroni and cheese, spaghetti and pizza right away. According to Dr. Rapp's book, we could try adding the offending foods on a four-day rotation to try to build up her tolerance. The other option was to find an allergist who treated food allergies with food extracts. In the meantime, we would totally eliminate wherever possible, and rotate where we could.

I took all my notes and charts to the next meeting with the behavioral psychologist. We were so excited. We felt we had found a course of treatment that would not be harmful, for once, and looked as though it might even help. Yes, it was more work than just giving her a pill, but *who cared?* There were *no* side effects, and plenty of positive changes, just in one week. The psychologist politely made copies of my notes and charts and promised to look them over later, but it was obvious to me that she was placating the "desperate mother" who was looking for answers to an unanswerable condition. The sentiment not expressed, but so eloquently evident, was that the only *true* way was their way, and all else was futile, wishful thinking-- hopeless, blind optimism. My eighth-grade history teacher once called me an incurable optimist, because I drew all my maps with ink. Well, I am stubborn and Irish to boot, and these poor professionals had no idea who they were dealing with. They couldn't possibly win. We just wouldn't go back there anymore. I had had all of their "etched-in-stone" labeling and predictions that I could take. None of the labels really fit Asia anyway. If anything, she was made up of bits and pieces from all of the different acronyms.

From now on, we were charting our own course, and if that meant leaving "traditional" medicine behind in order to find some of the answers we needed, then so be it.

We had continued for the last several years to take Asia for barium X-rays every four to six months, waiting for the magic day they would tell us there was peristalsis. I thought that the presence of the barium in the intestines would be enough stimulation, but I had been mistaken. Only digested food, in quantity, would stimulate the contractions. And that meant hooking up her plumbing--reversing the colostomy again. And then, if it didn't work perfectly, we'd have to use the enemas again, or go back to the colostomy. Jerry and I talked it over and decided that the trips to the surgeon were too stressful for Asia, and were telling us nothing useful. So why put her through them? The colostomy was functioning just fine, she was learning to change the bag herself, and having the colostomy didn't stop her from doing anything she wanted to do, including swimming (with special bags). We would wait until she was old enough and could understand what the reversal would mean. And then, if it was important to *her* to try again, we would. Until then, unless there was a problem, we would take her in for yearly check-ups with the surgeon and put the X-rays on hold for a while.

We worked with the elimination and rotation diets through October and into November of 1991. Then I began calling in earnest to find an allergist to do the testing and prescribe the neutralization drops. The one in Ann Arbor had a four-month waiting list and the doctor in Midland wasn't taking any new patients. I called Dr. Rapp's office in Buffalo, New York, and they gave me the name of Dr. C. F. Derrick in Trenton, Michigan, about forty-five minutes from here. I called on Wednesday and they were able to see her that Saturday!

The sign on the door of Dr. Derrick's office said that because of allergies, no perfume, cologne, hair spray or heavily scented soaps could be used, as they may bother other patients. The receptionist explained that no testing would be done on Saturday. Her history and symptoms would be recorded by the nurse and then Dr. Derrick would examine her. We had managed over the years to build up a certain level of trust with Asia where doctors' appointments were concerned. We told her exactly what was going to happen, to the best of our knowledge. We explained the level of her terror to any new doctors and received assurances that there would be "no owies" on the first visit. There had been enough "no owie" visits to prove us trustworthy.

With his shock of snow white hair, ruddy complexion, and

glasses perched on the end of his nose, Dr. Derrick looked like Father Christmas. His gentle, patient manner put even Asia at ease. He talked to us about food allergies and mentioned that environmental allergies could have contributed to Asia's school difficulties. With all the construction and renovation, there could be something in the new carpeting, paint, or flooring that she was allergic to. We hadn't even thought about that. He had a machine that would cycle the air in the school through a purified water and glycerine solution, and then a dilution could be made to test Asia with.

"Because of her many illnesses as a young child," he said, "and all of the antibiotics she was given, she probably has a yeast infection, which could cause some of the symptoms you're seeing. Many antibiotics kill the beneficial bacteria in our bodies as well as the ones which make us sick," he went on to say. "Without the beneficial bacteria present, yeast overgrowth can occur and cause many and varied problems. The first thing we must do is give her immune system a boost and get the yeast under control. Then we can begin testing."

We left his office with bottles of vitamin and mineral supplements to help rebuild her immune system and a prescription for Nystatin powder, to control and inhibit the growth of yeast. The actual allergy testing would begin in a few days, and would take several weeks, since only a few substances could be tested each visit.

We could choose the order of testing, and chose milk, wheat and egg for the first visit, since having neutralization drops for those foods would give us greater diet flexibility.

I had read the books and seen the tapes, but watching Asia's behavior change, within minutes of being given just three drops of wheat extract under her tongue was bizarre. Even more bizarre was watching her change back to the way she had been before each test began, once the neutralization dose was found. Her reactions to the different food extracts were exactly the same as her reactions to the foods themselves when they had been added during the second phase of the elimination diet.

We found that Asia was highly allergic to one of the foods that was allowed on the elimination diet. Asia had always loved oatmeal and had eaten it during the diet, but not to the extent that she had in earlier years. She was almost as allergic to oats as to wheat. We left that day with desensitization drops for milk, wheat, oats and egg. Over the next few weeks, we confirmed her allergies to oranges as well as food additives, preservatives, and colors and her mild allergies to corn and rice. We borrowed the air extraction machine and left it in Mrs. Vollink's room overnight. I picked it up the next morning and delivered it to Dr. Derrick's office. The originally clear liquid inside was now a frothy, milky color. What *was* in that air, anyway? The test confirmed that she was highly allergic to something in the school environment, so neutralization drops were prepared for school air. We had bottles made for home and for school. She was to have three drops from each bottle, one substance at a time, under her tongue every morning, hold for twenty seconds, then swallow. If the school air was bothering her or there was an allergic food in her lunch, Mrs. Adams or Mrs. Vollink could give her another dose.

The change was immediate and startling. Her notes from school came home consistently with smiling faces. Her behavior both at home and at school was calmer, with fewer and fewer "fretting" episodes, more compliant behavior, better impulse control. When people who didn't know what we had been doing could see positive changes in Asia, we knew it wasn't wishful thinking.

Chapter Twenty-three

Changes

A NEW ROUTINE was established. More time was allowed each morning to give Asia her vitamins and allergy drops. She handled all this very well, and was obviously pleased by all the attention she was receiving for her good behavior.

By all rights Asia should have gone to the middle school in the fall of 1992. But we felt strongly that she just wasn't ready for that challenge yet, either educationally or emotionally, especially since we had just found a procedure that had the potential for unlocking a lot of doors for her. Besides, she still hadn't gotten all she could from Paddock Elementary yet.

At her IEP on April 20, 1992, her label remained Educable-Mentally Impaired with a subclassification of Emotionally Impaired. The staff present agreed that she should stay as a fourth-grader in elementary school with Mrs. Adams as "health care aide for the colostomy, and to assist in instruction of appropriate and safe peer interaction and with adults." There would be much focus for the remainder of the school year on getting Asia ready for the move to middle school in the fall of 1993.

Mrs. Vollink developed a wonderful program called "Circle of Friends" for Asia. Asia had never really had a friend. No one came over just to visit Asia. Meghann had friends spend the night, and went to other girls' homes, but not Asia. Mom and Dad and Meghann received and made many telephone calls, but the only time anyone called just to talk to *Asia* was on her birthday. This was partially because Asia didn't seek people out very often, and when she did, her behavior was unpredictable at best. She still liked to touch people's faces and hair. Adults would tell her *no* but the children didn't always know how to handle it. Most of Meghann's friends were accepting of Asia's odd behaviors, some just ignored her, but one friend, Melissa Dertian, of all Meghann's friends, went out of her way to include Asia in activities, makeup sessions, dance lessons . . . girl stuff. The idea behind the Circle of Friends was to reintroduce her to her classmates, and enlist their help as peers, role models, and hopefully, friends.

Mrs. Vollink started by making a book about Asia, and she, Jerry, and I went to the different fourth-grade classes to meet the kids and introduce our daughter, through the book. Mrs. Vollink explained that we all have different circles of friends, starting with our family, outward to our special best friends, school friends, church neighborhood and so on. She told her attentive audience that Asia had the family circle, but beyond that, there were people she knew and who knew her, but no real friends. She ended by asking who in the class would like to be Asia's friend. Almost all the children raised their hands.

Each fourth-grade teacher made his or her recommendations as to the students they felt would be the best to begin the circle. They met at lunch time in Carol's room and spent time with Asia on the playground and at recess. Carol sent home wonderful notes about how well the group was doing. Hopefully these caring young people would provide a buffer, or security of sameness, for Asia when she went to middle school. When the Circle found out that Asia's birthday was in April, they started planning a party for lunch. They made a huge doll house out of poster board, and decorated all the rooms with fabric and paints. They had balloons and made cards for her. It was wonderful to see the pictures of her surrounded by kids who obviously cared for her. We just hoped the pressures of being teenagers wouldn't tear the Circle apart. We invited five of the closest friends over to our house for Asia's birthday party. Melissa Dertian came and we made banners and hung balloons, had pizza, and watched David Copperfield's magic on TV As hard as she tried, Asia still didn't know how to behave around the other girls, and in her frustration, with her face a riot of leftover Ritalin tics she ended up playing alone.

Asia continued to make progress in school and although I still didn't feel that she was ready for middle school, or that middle school was ready for her, it appeared that she would be going in the fall. In addition to her academic shortcomings, she had absolutely no social skills, her attention span was non-existent, and her impulse control was extremely poor. In spite of all this, all the teachers told us what a "neat kid" she was. And she really was. And we knew that there was more, much more to Asia than met the eye. We just didn't know which keys to use to unlock the doors to all her many mysteries.

She would become fixated on a person or a topic and worry it to death like a rat terrier. We had met a young boy at a friend's party the summer before. He was about five years old and had had some type of brain surgery, leaving a healing scar on his head. The family was from Brazil and spoke no English, but Asia hung around this little boy all afternoon. We knew that part of the fascination was the visible scar. We never even knew his name, but a year later she was still talking about "the boy with the scar on his head" and how was he, and he had black hair, and when would we see him again . . . over and over and over until we were ready to scream. Sometimes she would just pop out with it--"the boy with the scar"--just to get a reaction from us. Sometimes she used him as one of her "curse words" when she was angry. All of a sudden she would shout *The boy with the scar on his head!* Once we tried a new tactic. We told her she could talk about him for ten minutes on Saturday morning all she wanted to, but no other time. That worked okay, until she figured out that she could say "I can talk about the boy with the scar on Saturday, right, Mom?" So we had to qualify it. She could talk about him on Saturday *only* if she didn't mention him the rest of the week. Does this sound cruel and harsh? We didn't know. We only knew that it was making us crazy, like the teeth grinding years ago. Part of it, we knew, was her attempt to communicate and using the only things at her command. But part was perseverative behavior that I later learned is typical of autistic children.

She loved to draw and write names. She would draw pages and pages of faces. At first they were silhouettes, all in boxes, all different. Then she started to draw what Jerry called "the talking heads" because she wrote something about them around the hairline. She collected names the way other people collect stamps, and a reward for good behavior all week was for Marsha Adams to write down the names for her on Friday afternoon. She could print the names herself, but it was a special treat for someone else to print them for her. She was crushed if misbehavior caused her to lose the chance for Marsha to print her list for her. We never had to wonder what to get Asia for birthdays. If we ran out of ideas, we could always get her pens, pencils, crayons, paper or markers. She even dressed up as a blue crayon for Halloween one year.

She came to love certain movies, and would watch them day in and day out, day after day until another one caught her attention. She watched them until the tapes were so thin you could probably read the newspaper through them. The first was Dirty Dancing, then Ferris Bueller's Day Off, then each of the Karate Kid movies, then Amazing Grace and Chuck, and, most recently, Mrs. Doubtfire. Most of the time, if "her" movie was on, she would sit and watch it. Except for drawing, this was as close to "still" as she ever got.

She could sit and draw for hours, only intermittently getting up to jump on the trampoline or eat an apple or for mealtime,

her three favorite times of the day. Our house came complete
with a sidewalk, and Asia's boundaries for riding her bike were
the ends of the sidewalk in front of our neighbors' houses on
either side.   She would ride back and forth, over and over,
sometimes standing up with the wind whipping her black hair
behind her. She was tireless. Her energy knew no bounds. If she
raced with anyone, she always won, unless she got so far ahead
and stopped to wave and encourage the others on. Her appetite
has not yet been matched by any adult human being. (Possibly
she's from another planet?) We had to stop her at two helpings.
Her favorite dinners were pot luck, serve-it-yourself, all-you-
can-eat affairs. We still watched what she ate and gave her her
allergy drops. She ate every meal as though it would be her last,
or as though someone was waiting to rip the plate away from
her. And then if no one was looking, she would either lick the
plate or wipe it with her fingers and lick them. We had not yet
found a food that she didn't like. Not broccoli, cauliflower,
asparagus, peas, or spinach. She ate anything and everything,
but was still as thin as a reed. There was not an ounce of fat
anywhere on her.

We had been told that children who were nutritionally
deprived as infants often acted this way, having experienced
times of not knowing when, or if, another meal was coming, but
the pediatrician said that after ten years she should have
outgrown it. A friend suggested that we just let her eat, that
maybe the fascination was in the denial, and if we just let her go,
the thrill would be gone and she would begin to eat normal
amounts. What the heck, we decided, we'd try it for a weekend.
Saturday morning for breakfast she had three helpings *each* of
hashbrowns, watermelon, ham, and her one allowed egg before
we ran out of what I had cooked. She then had an apple. One
hour later a handful of raisins and a banana. For lunch, three
bowls of spaghetti rice (rice with spaghetti sauce)and three
salads. After lunch, more fruit three times, then for dinner,
turkey, mashed potatoes, green beans, Stove Top stuffing,
cranberry sauce--three or four servings of each. Sunday was a

repeat of Saturday. We couldn't afford to keep feeding her like that. I knew in my heart that she would not slow down, and would eat like that as long as we'd let her. If her metabolism ever changed and she continued to eat like that, she would look like the the Goodyear blimp. We went back to two helpings.

The second-worst punishment for Asia was to take away seconds at the next meal. The only punishment any worse was, of course, going to bed without dinner, which we reserved for the most heinous offenses.

She had (has) an amazing memory for events and people, their names, hair color, clothing. She could recall things that happened years ago in Minnesota, peoples names, what they were wearing. What seemed like minor happenings to us, like a cousin crying, were etched in her memory. Her love of names began to improve her spelling. If she could remember how to spell "Kiatkowski" she could remember how to spell "shoe." But she couldn't add 2 + 2.

The 1993 IEP was scheduled for April thirtieth at 3:30 P.M. Seventeen teachers--including the speech teacher, psychologist, art and gym teachers, Mrs. Vollink, Marsha, and the selected fifth-grade teacher, the Director of Special Education for the middle school, and Jerry and I attended. The large group was, in part, because Asia's MET (Multi-disciplinary Evaluation Team) report was being given just prior to the IEP. (Don't you just love all of these acronyms? You could start another language with them.) At the MET, a child's educational placement and label are determined, and the team consists of all of the above-named members. At this year's MET we would be deciding whether or not to change Asia's label from EMI (Educable-Mentally Impaired) to AI (Autistically Impaired).

For ten years I had fought against using the label of autism. It was okay to say that she had autistic-like tendencies, because even I could see that. But my biggest fear was that people would look at the label and stop right there. They would not see *Asia,* they would see a "plate-spinner," and they would never expect any more than that from her. The label would define the limits of the child's abilities, and would create a box from which she could never escape. No matter how much she achieved in her life, the label would be in the background, and could crop up at any time to stop her from attending a school or getting a job.

The social worker read the following summary of her evaluation:

> "Asia is a young lady with a history of developmental difficulties from before the age of two when she came to live with her adopting parents. She has difficulties in the cognitive, affective, psychomotor, and speech and language areas. Asia has impaired ability to relate to others, abnormal language patterns, and unusual responses to pain, as well as repetitive language and actions. These difficulties do not appear to be associated with schizophrenia. It is therefore recommended that Asia is eligible to receive Special Education services as a student with autism under rule 340.1715. An IEPC should convene to determine appropriate services."

There it was, the label I had been able to fight against so long, and now I had no choice but to accept it. The psychologist was able to show me enough examples of Asia's behavior that were consistent with autism. And as if that weren't enough, autism was the only classification which would allow for a full-time aide at the middle-school level. I knew beyond any doubt that, without an aide, Asia would fall through the cracks in middle school. She would be totally lost educationally and emotionally, and was in danger of being injured while unattended. It was absolutely critical that she have an aide. Everyone there sympathized with my concerns, but assured me that the label could be changed back or eliminated, and that her records would never be shown without our permission. Yeah, yeah, that all sounds good, so why doesn't it make me feel any better? The pen felt as if it were made of lead, my heart was heavy, and my brain felt numb as I signed my name to the agreement. Way back when, before Asia, when we had been asked by Children's Home Society what challenges we felt we could accept if we were to consider adopting a special-needs child, autism was one of them. But in the perfect world of my mind, I envisioned the child being lovingly enveloped by the school family, with no labels, no stigma. I knew nothing about the special education system or its acronyms, which paint such vivid pictures to those who can decipher them. I felt as if I had signed away her future. However, we would do whatever it took to see that she got the best education possible, and right now that meant having an aide. But the best possible news was that the aide would be Marsha.

Chapter Twenty-four

Mayhem at Middle School

ASIA HAD VERY mixed feelings about the move to middle school. She was excited about being in the same school with Meghann again, but sad about leaving Mrs. Vollink and all the other students in her class. Asia never liked for people to leave, and was always sad, crying for long periods, when visitors left, or when we came home from vacations with friends. We knew this was going to be hard for her, so we had to be strong and confident, and not let our concerns affect her.

We had an exciting summer planned. One of the benefits of the label change was a subsidy check which we would receive monthly, to be used in any way that would benefit Asia herself or the family as a whole. We decided to use part of it to buy her vitamins, which were not cheap or covered by insurance, and part for savings. With the extra money, we were able to send Asia to a summer camp for the first time.

Mary Ann Miller, of the Washtenaw Independent School District, sent us a list of camps for disabled (differently abled) children. We chose Camp Champ, operated by Ann Arbor Parks and Recreation. The camp ran for six weeks in the summer, four days a week from 9 A.M. until 2 P.M. It had structured activities, crafts, field trips, picnics, and swimming, and had a good camper-to-counselor ratio. They were equipped to deal with a wide range of challenges. Asia absolutely loved it. It was like school, which she loved, only camp was better, because she got to swim more often. She had learned to change the colostomy bag by herself and had her special bags for swimming days. She knew all the counselors' names the first day, and immediately added them to her name list. The six weeks flew by. There was a special party at the end for the campers and their families. All the students put on skits and at the end, the older kids performed a dance to the music from <u>Free Willy</u> by Michael Jackson. It was so beautiful that I cried.

Then we were off to Maine to visit Cindy, Steve, and Preston. They had a new, bigger boat, and we spent our days on the water, either ocean or lake. We ate lobster and crab fixed every possible way and relaxed with our wonderful family. Asia and Preston played like two puppies, chasing and splashing each other while we baked on the beach. We spent one day at Old Orchard Beach and Asia got her fill of amusement park rides, the faster and wilder the better. The week was over before we knew it or were ready for it, and we were on our way back home to Michigan. Back to the real world, with only a week to get ready for school.

Both of my babies would be in middle school! How could it be that they were getting older when I wasn't. I still didn't know what I wanted to do when *I* grew up.

We knew that middle school would be different, but there are varying degrees of different, all the way from just a *little* different to really, really different. Well, middle school was *really, really,* different. In fact, if Marsha had not been there, it would have been disastrous. Asia had a locker, and we had arranged for hers to have a padlock instead of a combination, figuring that a key on a cord around her neck would be easier for her to keep track of than numbers, which she hated. After the first few days, it was plain to see that the noise in the hallways between classes bothered her. So much so that she and Marsha left a few minutes before everyone else in order to get Asia settled before the rush and crush of students. Before and after school was a nightmare for her, with all of the kids laughing, talking, and slamming locker doors. Asia walked the hallways in the morning and afternoon with her ears covered any way she could. Within a few weeks it became obvious that changing classes so often was over-stimulating and Asia just couldn't shift gears that fast. Arrangements were made for Marsha and Asia to use an empty classroom as a "decompression chamber" when she reached critical mass.

The middle school had had comparatively few inclusion students in the past, and many of the teachers had not experienced a child with autism before. We offered to come in and do an "in-house training session" with Asia's teachers, but it didn't happen until much later. At the fall parent-teacher conferences, we were meeting with one of Meghann's teachers. He had finally made the connection between the two Korean-born students and commented to us, "Yeah, I wondered who the kid with the bodyguard was." It was crude and insensitive remarks such as that one that had us wishing that Asia was back in Paddock. Oddly enough, the one teacher we thought would give Asia a hard time had worked the best with her. We had to keep reminding ourselves that we had dreaded all of Asia's school changes so far, and every one of them had turned out to be positive. And after all, Meghann's middle school experience had been great so far, and we couldn't have been more pleased. But you can't compare your children's school experiences any more than you can compare your children. We would take it a day at a time and just be grateful that Marsha was there with Asia.

Asia became such a disruption in the classrooms that instead of sitting with the rest of the students, she and Marsha had a table to themselves, off to the side of the room. In some of the classrooms there were extra, small rooms in the back, so the two of them worked in there. Marsha adjusted the curriculum and adapted the lesson plans to suit Asia's abilities. Most of the teachers didn't have a clue how to deal with her. Marsha herself was a new commodity, and her role as aide sat somewhere in limbo. She wasn't a certified teacher, yet she filled that role better than anyone else could have. Next to Jerry, Meghann and me, she knew Asia better than anyone else. She had ridden through most of the bad times with us and had been there to celebrate the victories. I shudder to think what fifth grade would have been like without her.

Sometimes we all tend to get so caught up in the day-to-day grind that we miss something that is staring us in the face. Around Christmas time Asia's tics were becoming more and more pronounced, Richter scale sometimes. There was almost no time when her face was still. If we called her attention to the tics, and quietly asked her to "calm her face," she would snap back to here and now, briefly, as though unaware of what her face was doing. We didn't know how much control, if any, she had over the tics, and how much of this reaction was startle reflex. Finally it dawned on me that we should have her allergy tests repeated to see if her tolerance levels had changed, and to get the new school air tested. There might even be some new allergies that had cropped up. It was so obvious, once I stopped to think about it, that some of these behaviors could be allergy-induced that I beat myself up mentally for not having suspected it sooner. But, as I'm so fond of telling all my friends when they are looking back at a "should have, would have, could have," incident, "Honey, you better watch it or you'll 'if only' yourself right into the nut house."

On a more positive note, over the Christmas holidays Asia asked me to write words for her the way Mrs. Adams did. I decided to type them on the computer instead. She gave me the names and spelled them for me, and in twenty minutes she gave me one hundred and eight names. All were correctly spelled. There were no duplicates. If there were two "Jeffs," they had different last names. She knew if a name was spelled "Karl" or

"Carl." She gave me all the names from memory and used no other list to work from. I was absolutely astounded. The next day we typed again, and the list had other names. They were a combination of people she knew, relatives, school friends, teachers, local TV personalities, movie stars, and sports figures. We knew collecting names was important to her and wished we could link up her memory for names to other things, like math facts. In her world, however, names have significance, not numbers.

During the Christmas holidays we took Asia to Sears to have pictures made. Her school pictures had not turned out well. I curled her hair and we picked out several new shirts to wear for different poses. Other families had apparently had the same idea, because there was an hour wait, so we shopped until it was our turn. While we selected the backgrounds we wanted, the photographer got Asia on the table, posed with her hands folded in her lap. She stood about ten feet away from Asia with the remote button in her hand and snapped the first picture. The camera made a soft click and Asia jumped as if she had been shot.

The photographer smiled. "It's just the camera noise, Asia. It won't hurt you." She walked over and repositioned Asia's hands, which were covering her ears. "Here, let's try this again now," she said. She picked up the remote and Asia flinched, leaning away from the camera before the photographer even pressed the button. There was an expression of genuine pain on her face.

"Relax, honey," I said, as I gently pulled her hands from her ears and massaged her shoulders to relax them.

"Don't like noise, Mommy," Asia said.

"It's just the little click the camera makes when it takes your picture, sweetie. Now try to relax so she can take a great picture to send Grandma Betty and Grandma and Papa."

Luckily the camera allows the photographer to "freeze" a pose on a screen so the parents can decide if they want it or not, or we'd have been there until Valentine's Day. One hour and one exhausted but incredibly patient photographer later, we had five poses to select from. Asia grimaced, flinched and leaned away from the camera for every one of them.

We made an appointment for allergy re-testing in January of 1994. We eliminated testing oats since it was such an easy food to avoid. We had gotten a new video camera for Christmas as a combined gift from both sides of the family and ourselves. (The grandparents realized the value of home movies of the grand-children growing up so fast and far away.) We decided to record all of the testing, since more than once we had gotten raised eyebrows and weird looks, even from family members, when we described the effects some foods had on Asia. What better proof than to have it captured on tape?

We had asked Dr. Derrick before the testing began if he knew of anything that we could try, *not drug related*, that might help control the tics. He mentioned that magnesium taurate had been used with some success in people with Tourette's syndrome. It was available at his favorite pharmacy nearby. It was worth a try. He also suggested that we test her for sensitiv-ity to apple, since she ate so many (a serious understatement). He recommended testing for chlorine, formaldehyde (it's in everything from toothpaste to fabric), ethanol (an ingredient in all perfumes), our home air, and both beet and cane sugar, as well as baker's and brewer's yeast.

I took notes as well as videotaping, because we didn't want to miss a thing. Once again I was amazed at how quickly reactions occurred, how distinctly different the reactions to each substance were, and how quickly they were resolved when the neutral-ization dose was reached.

One day we had the opportunity to watch another child being tested; for what, I don't know. He appeared to be about seven years old and had received a Nintendo Game Boy for Christmas. He swaggered into the treatment room as only a seven-year-old boy can swagger, and plopped down on a chair to play with his Game Boy while waiting his turn. His mother sat working on a cross-stitch picture. (Sound familiar?) When the nurse was finished with Asia, she asked him to come to the desk, which he willingly did, and opened his mouth like a little bird, waiting for his drops. He was such a well-behaved little boy.

Within a minute of being given his drops, he got up from the chair and began pacing the room, faster and faster. Next he went to the white metal trash can in the corner and, using the foot pedal opener, began slamming the lid up and down, until his mother asked him to stop. Then he went over and kicked his mother in the shin. Twice. His mother grabbed him and tried to hug him, realizing that he had no control over his actions, but he wriggled away, went to one end of the room, and began to crawl on his belly like a snake across the floor. Jekyll and Hyde in Reeboks.

When the time was up and the nurse called him back to the chair, he didn't want to go, and had to be promised a treat when he and his mother left. The nurse gave him the next lower dose of the same substance, and again within a minute, he pulled his feet up into the chair, folded himself up as small as possible, and began to cry. His mother went over to comfort him and he wrapped his arms around her neck and cried quietly, without talking or leaving the chair. The third dose was given. His tears dried up, as if by magic, and he got up from the testing chair, walked to the chair next to his mom, and picked up his Game Boy to once again enter into the world of the game. His correct neutralization dose had been found.

I watched all of this with a combination of amazement, disbelief (although I *did* believe), and gratitude. Gratitude because I had been able to witness, in person not on TV, another child experiencing similar reactions to Asia's. It was confirmation of the purest sort. Asia had watched, too. Fortunately for all of us, she was being tested for something with little or no effect on her. She sat quietly, almost respectfully, as a peer went through the same things she herself had experienced. Maybe she felt better somehow, realizing that she was not the only one to react in this manner. Maybe it helped her to feel not quite so different. The little boy's mother was calm throughout all this, as though she'd been through it before. Our paths did not cross again during Asia's testing, but I felt a strange sort of kinship with her, almost as though we were warriors on the same side, fighting the same battle.

During this round of testing, which lasted about six weeks and included six visits, Asia reacted to milk, wheat, egg, apple, school air (although not as severely as to the Paddock air), rice and corn (rather mildly), chlorine, ethanol, formaldehyde, beet sugar, the house air (mildly), orange, and soy. She tested positive to baker's yeast but negative to brewer's yeast, (which meant that she could drink beer but couldn't eat bread--*just kidding!*) She has drops, some combined in the same bottle, for all but beet sugar and orange. (We found it easy to avoid those two items.) Her reactions included increased tics and grimaces, slow reaction time, dizziness, excess saliva, absence spells, feeling warm to the touch and saying that she felt warm, confusion, playing bongos on the chair, gazelle leaps across the room, spontaneous crying, agitated and antsy, manic writing and drawing, talking about slapping my face, hysterical laughter, and speed-rolling the chair across the floor.

One of the most unusual reactions was to formaldehyde. Because of the strength, formaldehyde testing starts with the third strongest dilution and proceeds from there. With the first dose, Asia became very solemn, staring around the room. This was a reaction we had never seen in testing. Usually it's just the opposite, with silliness and giddiness. We couldn't get her to crack a smile, and we got pretty silly ourselves just trying. (Wait a minute, who's being tested here?) After the fourth strongest dose was given, her face appeared puffy and flushed, and suddenly, quietly, she began to cry. Huge tears rolling down her face, she wiggled her finger for me to come over and she squeezed my wrist as hard as she could. She couldn't seem to speak, or didn't want to. It just about broke my heart. She wasn't doing the "pretzel" or clawing herself as she had done when taking Ritalin. She was just quietly crying and holding on to my arm. With the fifth strongest dose, she blinked a few times and was back to normal. It was chilling. It's so hard to explain to someone who hasn't witnessed it. There have been times when we've gotten glazed, blank expressions when we've tried to describe her food allergies to the unconvinced masses. Their looks say, "Yeah, sure, lady. They really saw you coming. Which bridge did you say you were buying?" But it's all right there on the tape.

The response to ethanol answered a lot of questions about why Asia had been having problems in speech class, which she loved. She adored her speech teacher and looked forward to the class three times a week, so we couldn't figure out why she acted up on some days. We asked the teacher what kind of perfume she wore, and Dr. Derrick said it was the one that most children who were allergic reacted negatively to. During spring break we did our own home test on two different perfumes that Marsha Adams wore. She soaked cotton balls with each and put them in separate Ziploc bags. I opened one just a little and passed it under Asia's nose. She blinked a few times and began slamming her head against the back of the chair. I quickly zipped up the bag and put both of them out on the porch. Enough mad scientist experimenting for me. Marsha doesn't wear that perfume to school anymore.

On the way home from the first day of testing we stopped at the pharmacy to pick up the magnesium taurate Dr. Derrick had recommended. I asked the pharmacist the same question--did he know of anything else that might help with the tics. He said that research had been done somewhere in California on DMG and vitamin B-6. DMG, or dimethylglycine, is legally classified as a food and is available through most health food stores. It has been shown to boost the immune systems of laboratory rats. In 1965 Russian investigators published a report which showed con-siderable improvement in the speech of twelve out of fifteen autistic children to whom DMG had been given. We bought the DMG and the B-6 along with the magnesium taurate and the pharmacist loaned us several articles to copy that he was saving for another customer with an autistic child.

I wanted to read while driving but the Highway Patrol frowns on that sort of thing, so I had to wait until we got home to devour the articles. The "somewhere in California" the pharmacist had referred to was the Autism Research Institute in San Diego, California, and the article was written by the director, Bernard Rimland, Ph.D. In another article by Dr. Rimland, he showed parent comparisons of the twelve most commonly used drugs for treating autism and similar behavior disorders and Vitamin B-6 with magnesium. The B-6/magnesium combination was rated twice as high as Ritalin for positive effects. In fact, the B-6/magnesium was the *highest* rated for improvements, with the lowest percentage of the parents reporting negative effects. I liked this study. I continued my reading. Another article, taken from a Canadian publication, was written by a parent and contained several more vitamins which had produced favorable results with his autistic son. My health food store shopping list was growing.

Everything I read had a solid ring of truth to it. It just felt right on target. There is a common thread linking many autistic or autistic-like children. Many have a history of allergies and chronic ear infections, prolonged crying spells as infants that could not be relieved by the usual means, supersensitive hearing, and self-stimulating behaviors. Well, that pretty well paints a picture of Asia, doesn't it? We knew we were already on the right track with the allergy treatment; now we wanted to see what happened when we added those vitamins to the mix.

In the course of my search for more information about the megavitamin therapy, I called another mother I had met several years before at a support group meeting. There are *no* coincidences in this world. When I asked how her son was doing, she replied, "Just terrific since he had auditory training." I almost dropped the phone. This was the treatment I had searched in vain for three years earlier. Her son had had the treatment done right here in Detroit. She gave me the telephone number, and I hung up without asking about the vitamins. Oh well, I could call her back.

This was just too fine. I finally felt as though things were beginning to come together. I spoke with Cindy Wilson, the Audiologist at the Children's Hospital of Michigan, who confirmed that, *yes,* it was the same treatment that Georgie had undergone in France, and *yes,* they were doing the treatment here, and *yes,* she would be glad to send me information about the therapy.

I was flying. I began beating up the postman again, waiting to get the information. In the meantime, positive reports were already coming in about Asia's behavior in school, and we hadn't even completed the allergy testing yet.

When we read in the local newspaper a reporter's account of a school board meeting at which a parent had objected to inclusion students,saying that they took teacher time away from "regular" students, we called for a meeting at the school. We went prepared with folders for everyone, including all of the information on the allergy testing, vitamin therapy and the auditory training we were planning for the summer. We brought our videos of Asia when she was taking Ritalin, and Mrs. Vollink's videos. We showed them where she had *been* so they could better appreciate where she was now. This was the meeting we had wanted to have in the fall to prepare the staff for her coming.

We explained that Asia was a lot like water poured through a piece of lava rock--she'll take the path of least resistance. They could help by insisting on complete sentences and correct pronunciation just in conversation. We encouraged them to coordinate all their efforts through Marsha, since Asia's concentration levels and capabilities were changing daily. Jerry's analogy is that Asia is like a child racing along in knee-deep water while all the other children are running on the beach. Most of the time she's running as hard or harder, but it takes her longer to get to the same place. We shared our hopes and goals for the 1993-'94 school year. And we voiced our concerns over the parent complaint at the school board meeting, when we had heard nothing from the teachers. We discovered that the school superintendent had addressed the complaining parent by saying that all students, whether in regular or special education programs deserve the best education in the least restrictive environment. We closed with pats on the back in advance for their handling of this latest challenge and thank-you's to those teachers already voluntarily interacting with Asia. We realized that any smoothing we did for Asia now would ultimately help the inclusion students who followed her.

With all the positive changes we were seeing in Asia, we found another use for some of the subsidy money. While the doors were opening, we were going to stuff as much through them as we could. We called the high school and asked for recommendations for a student to tutor Asia at least one afternoon a week. Danette Talbot, whose brother Chris was in Asia's class, began working with Asia for an hour each Wednesday, and became another ally in the ongoing battle for Asia. She volunteered to go with me to turn the rope for Asia on March seventeenth at Jump Rope for Heart.

For those of you who don't have this event in your community, Jump Rope for Heart happens here every March at the elementary school. The students collect pledges for jumping and receive prizes for the amount of pledges they collect. The money is sent to the American Heart Association. The day of the event they jump--individually, in pairs, or teams for an hour and a half, with fruit and juice breaks every twenty minutes or so. It's loud, raucous fun, and Asia had jumped for the last two years. Even though she was in middle school now, she wanted to come back to jump. Who could turn down dedication like that? She collected her pledges, jumped to the music, and earned her T-shirt. She was ecstatic.

Meanwhile, the information had arrived from Cindy Wilson, the audiologist at Detroit Children's Hospital, and after reading it, we knew this was something we would have to investigate. Cindy explained that her husband, Ken, was a speech-language pathologist in private practice in Berkeley, Michigan, and that he did AIT also. Ken apparently had better luck getting insurance companies to pay for the AIT, so we decided to call him. I liked his voice before I met him. It was confident, reassuring, and encouraging. We scheduled an appointment for an audiogram and speech-language evaluation at the end of the month. To keep us busy until then, Ken sent us a behavior checklist and developmental questionnaire.

Both Jerry and I answered the questionnaire, in different colored inks, because, while we agreed on most of the answers, there were some that we had different viewpoints on. As I read through the questions, I was mentally saying, "Yep, that's her all right." Ken said that the behaviors we described and the obvious sound sensitivity indicated that Asia would be a good candidate for AIT, but the proof would be in the audiogram. He offered an easy solution to the noises in the hall--soft foam ear plugs. I bought them that afternoon. Asia balked at first--she didn't like *anything* in her ears--but finally agreed to try them one time. I hid outside and walked into the school behind her, out of sight, and watched as she walked down the hallways swinging her arms, not covering her ears for the first time all year.

From then on, she used the ear plugs in between classes, when the band played for assemblies, and after school on the way out of the building. We went to hear Meghann play in the band's spring concert and the only seats were near the front. This would be a true test of the ear plugs, since a number of the songs had cymbals. I watched in awe as Asia sat through the entire concert, swaying to the music and clapping. Once when she saw the percussionist raise the cymbals, she raised her hands at the same time, but went back to clapping when she realized that it didn't hurt. I called Ken the next day, so grateful for the help before we'd even met him. Such a simple thing, these ear plugs. Why hadn't we thought of them?

Asia and I met Jerry at Ken's office the day of the testing. Basic audiograms had been done through the schools, so she was used to the earphones. The test showed peaks at 1,500 and 8,000 hertz, the frequencies that hurt. She also had up to a five-second time delay in her right ear, which meant that she heard things up to five seconds later in that ear. Look at your watch to see how much you can say in five seconds. I could say my name and most of my address. No wonder she was confused. Her brain would receive a sound in her left ear and then seconds later the same sound would reach her brain from her right ear. Sounds would be tripping over each other and nothing would connect. Imagine living with that most of your life! It would be like living in an echo chamber. It explained so much.

Although he could make no promises or offer any guarantees, Ken definitely felt that Asia would be a good candidate, and would benefit from AIT. I felt that if we could eliminate the sound sensitivity and balance her hearing, the money and the drive would be worth it. Anything else we got would be sauce on the sundae.

Ken scheduled Asia to begin therapy on June sixth. In order to facilitate insurance coverage, he asked Dr. Derrick to write a prescription for speech-language therapy and included it with his diagnosis of Asia's problems. We sent this to the insurance company with a cover letter from me, requesting prior approval before beginning the treatment. But my mind was made up. She *would* have this treatment, insurance or not.

Something was freed up in Asia that day. It was now all right for her to talk about sounds that hurt. She realized that not everyone was bothered by the sounds that hurt *her* ears. On Friday night, Jerry and Asia were watching TV, and Jerry set a plastic glass down on a stone coaster.

"Don't put it down loud, Dad, it hurts my ears. Put it down like this," Asia said, showing him how to put it down gently. He had put the glass down normally the first time, I thought. The next morning he put his orange juice glass down on the same coaster and Asia said, "Come on now, Dad. We talked about this last night, remember. Put it down like this." We both raced to get the cork coasters.

On a whim that same morning, we turned off the TV and asked Asia what she could hear. Sitting on the sofa in the living room, she could hear bacon frying in the kitchen, a faucet dripping in the basement, a dog barking several blocks away that I could barely hear even outside on the porch, and a tiny "whoosh" sound from the fax machine across the room that I could scarcely hear sitting next to it.

She showed us how to close the cupboard doors so the sound didn't hurt her ears, and she began to use the ear plugs when she vacuumed.

A few days later in speech class, Asia suddenly covered her ears and yelled, "Make it stop! Stop it right now!" Her teacher, Ms. Larson, asked her what was hurting her ears and took her into the hallway to find the source of the discomfort. Ms. Larson heard nothing out of the ordinary or unusually loud. Asia led her to a room two doors down where a copying machine was running, and pointed to the machine. *That* was what she had heard through the walls dividing two rooms with the space of the library in between.

I knew I shouldn't be wishing my life away, but I couldn't wait until June sixth.

Chapter Twenty-five

AIT and Annabel

DURING THE COURSE of one of our many conversations over the next few months, Ken, suggested that I'd probably enjoy reading *The Sound of a Miracle,* by Annabel Stehli, the full-length book that the <u>Reader's Digest</u> article had been taken from, and *Hearing Equals Behavior*, by Dr. Guy Berard, the French doctor who had treated Georgie. I immediately ordered both books. Jerry read *The Sound of a Miracle* after I finished it, while I read Dr. Berard's book. We then ordered copies for our parents and an additional copy we could loan out. We both felt as though we knew Annabel Stehli. I mentioned that to Ken one day, and he said, "Why don't you call her?" Who, me? Call a famous author? I wouldn't know what to say. Gee, Ms. Stehli, I really liked your book and I feel like I know you. Sounded kind of cheesy to me, but what's the worst that could happen? She could laugh and hang up? I didn't really think she sounded like that kind of person.

So I called. And she answered. Herself. No servants or answering service. And we talked, and it *was* as if I knew her. I told her all about Asia, her colostomy, and the allergies and AIT, and how I'd read her story years before but couldn't find anyone to do the treatment. Once I got rolling, it wasn't hard to talk at all. Famous or not, she's another *mom* who could talk the talk because she'd walked the walk.

She said she was writing another book. This one would be a collection of stories written by parents of children with a variety of learning disabilities, and all the steps they had taken to maximize their children's potential. These were parents who re-fused to give up or take the easy way. Many, if not most, had become disillusioned by the medical profession and its tunnel vision. Many had gone against traditional medicine, seeking non-traditional methods of treatment for their children. Annabel had established a network of parents across the country who were willing to share their experiences with other parents who were still groping around in the dark, not knowing what questions to ask or who to ask them of. It was a game of chance called "Kids by Braille," and the stakes were enormous. There's nothing like talking to someone who's been there and knows what you are going through. It was from these parents that the stories came.

A few weeks later, Annabel asked if I would like to send her a condensed version of Asia's story for consideration for her book. "We don't have any Korean-born autistic girls with colostomies, allergies and all of Asia's '-isms' yet," she said. (We always knew she was one of a kind.) If she liked what I wrote, maybe she could use it. I had long ago given up hope of ever seeing the story I had started before Asia arrived appearing in print. Even if she couldn't use it, the fact that she wanted to read it thrilled me. And certainly, if it appeared in her book, maybe our experiences with Asia could help another family. That certainly gave me something else to think about besides AIT for the next few weeks.

Jerry's parents were driving out from Minnesota for the long Memorial Day weekend and we were in the middle of a combination of basic spring cleaning and mad, insane, "oh my

God, the parents are coming" cleaning when the insurance company called to say they had approved twenty-seven sessions of speech-language therapy for Asia. (We only needed twenty.) We danced around the living room with mops and brooms and called Ken to tell him we were still on for June sixth at 8:00 o'clock in the morning.

School would not be out yet, but the last few days were half-days, so I didn't feel too bad about taking Asia out early. Dr. Berard recommends that, if possible, someone receiving AIT not work or attend school until the therapy has been completed. Ken had taken the treatment himself to see what it was like, and so he could better explain to parents and children what was going to happen. He said it was one of the most exhausting things he had ever experienced. Just sitting and listening to music for thirty minutes, twice a day? Didn't sound all that tough to me. Call it brain exercise. Annabel had coined a word for it--neurobics.

Monday morning we were up by 5 A.M. and ready to leave by 6:30. We were headed into Detroit suburbs where I'd never been and the traffic at that hour would surely be horrendous. I had the video camera and tripod along as well as my notebook and a pocket tape recorder, just in case anything happened during the six hours we would be spending in the car each day.

We arrived in plenty of time for our 8 o'clock appointment. Ken let Asia choose where she would sit, the straight-backed chair or the bean bag. She chose the straight-backed chair. For thirty minutes she would have to sit, quietly, not reading or coloring, or doing anything but listen to the music. Ken has a wide selection of music of all types to suit any taste. Usually he let the patient choose, but he selected for Asia, adjusted the machine and put the earphones on her. He set the volume at a moderate setting, and after a few times of lifting one side up to hear what we were saying, she sat and listened. The sessions have to be separated by at least four hours, so we drove home to feed the birds and drove back for the 1 P.M. appointment. During the afternoon session Asia was swaying to the music. That evening she spontaneously picked up a book and read it to us. Up to that point, Asia had never read for the sheer pleasure of reading.

Ken had explained to us that we might see side effects, such as sleepiness, anger, hostility, or irritability during the treatment, and certain signs were likely to appear at particular points.

Asia's first real stress occurred during the sessions on Wednesday, when Ken increased the volume. During the morning, he and I gently held Asia's hands to keep her from plugging her ears. By the middle of the afternoon session she was snapping her fingers, and even adjusting her snapping to match the rhythm of the music. That evening she began experimenting with closing doors without covering her ears.

Thursday and Friday her moods alternated between anxious and comfortably teasing. The midpoint audiogram showed that the peak at 1,500 Hz was gone and the time delay in her right ear had been reduced to two seconds. Still to work on was the peak at 8,000 Hz and a smaller one that had appeared at 3,000 Hz. That evening Asia began slamming doors in earnest, beginning with the cupboard doors. Jerry had gone for a bike ride but was due back soon and Meghann was at a friend's. I had started the oil for popcorn when Asia came running through the house slamming doors.

"Come on, Mom," she yelled. I left the stove and followed her to the bedroom where she slammed the door and laughed. "Look, Mom, look. I hear it and it doesn't hurt." We both ran, laughing and crying, to the front door to see if her ears hurt when she slammed it. No pain. But out of the corner of my eye I saw a flash in the kitchen. I had forgotten to turn the stove off, and the oil I started for popcorn had caught fire! The flames from the pan were leaping toward the ceiling. I ran for the kitchen and tried to slap the lid on the pan, but it was too hot. I tried to beat out the fire with a towel, but failing that, tried to get the pan out of the house. The breeze from the window was blowing the flames back in my face and I dropped the pan. I finally succeeded in smothering the pan with a towel and the fire went out. I lifted the pan to find two black scorch marks on the tile floor--a reminder of the night that slamming the doors didn't hurt.

Ken told us that Asia's habit of covering her ears in anticipation of painful sounds would be a tough one to break, but we kept reminding her that "Ken was fixing her ears" and encouraged her to try to listen without plugging them. More often than not, she found, to her pleasant surprise and our great joy, that the sounds didn't hurt anymore. That weekend she was very ornery and loudly proclaimed, "I don't like (you, popcorn, the fair, etc.). It had always been Asia's form of self-punishment when she was upset or angry to say, "I don't like . . . "then she'd fill in the blank with something she really did like. We theorized that she was chastising herself by taking something she liked away. We had been told to expect behaviors like this.

By Tuesday of the second week she was napping regularly both on the way home in the morning and on the way back to Ken's office in the afternoon. Asia normally only naps when she's sick, so it's a good thing we had been warned about this possible side effect. Tuesday was an especially testy day. Asia repeatedly did things that she knew not to do, refused requests, complained of a headache, and listed things and people she didn't like, including me and potato salad. That afternoon she started wrapping the cord of the earphones around her finger. Ken tried several times gently to get her to stop. When the "evil eye" from Mom didn't work, I threatened her with the loss of her afternoon Doritos. That day seemed to be the turning point.

Wednesday morning she was up, dressed, and ready to go in record time, with no prompting from me. A definite first. She finally discovered the bean bag chair in Ken's office and, sprawling out, perfectly comfortable, she listened to the music without complaint for the full time. Her sense of time was incredible; she almost always knew, without a watch or clock, when it was time to end the session. While we were home for lunch that day, she vacuumed for the first time without the ear plugs or covering her ears. That afternoon she listened with no protest to what Ken considered the loudest piece of music he had. She loved it. Our advice for the day from Ken was to observe her conversational skills--self-monitoring or fixing conversational errors, staying on topic and initiating conversations. On the way home she corrected a previous pattern of speech twice. Luckily I was at a stoplight and could write them down.

Thursday evening she had a nice conversation with Jerry's parents. Jerry's mom said, "You know, that's the first time I've talked to Asia on the telephone without one of you [Jerry or I] translating or prompting her with the answers."

Friday morning, there was not even a flinch from Asia as Jerry put the pots and pans away in the kitchen. She was Ken's first patient ever to ask him to "turn it up louder." The final audiogram that afternoon showed that the time delay in Asia's right ear was gone, as well as the peak at 3,000 Hz. in her left ear. The peak at 8,000 Hz. was still there, but the distance, or valley, down to 6,000 Hz. had decreased. In fact, the line from 1,000 to 6,000 Hz. was completely flat. From a purely audiometric standpoint, Ken considered the treatment to be a success.

Chapter Twenty-six

After AIT

THE TWO WEEKS of auditory integration therapy were stressful as well as exciting. The drive was an hour to an hour-and-a-half four times a day. Meghann still had one week of school left, so Jerry took her to school each morning. I was back in time to pick her up after Asia's second session. The time between the morning and afternoon sessions was spent feeding adult birds and cleaning cages and feeding baby birds at least twice, fixing Asia's lunch, answering phone messages, and, if time permitted, running errands. When we got home in the afternoon, babies had to be fed again and dinner fixed for the human family, plus any last-minute grocery shopping. Then I packed Jerry and Meghann's lunch for the next day. I tried to stick to meal schedules as much as possible, because if dinner was later, so was bedtime, and with my schedule with Asia, Meghann's final exams, and Jerry's work, we all needed plenty of sleep.

I didn't really mind the drive. Ken loaned me several tapes from previous conferences he had attended, so I was able to listen to Georgie, Annabel, Dr. Rimland, Dr. Temple Grandin, who's a story in herself, and others, while driving. The tapes answered questions and raised others. One of the tapes I listened to was about sensory integration, and explained how it is now thought that people with autism are either hyperacute or hypoacute in one or more of their senses. Exercises which stimulate the vestibular system in the brain can be beneficial. Swinging, rocking, jumping, and spinning have a calming effect on individuals with autism. This explained Asia's fascination with the trampoline (she's worn out five or six so far), the rocking chair, and swings at school.

The hour a day while Asia was listening to music, Ken was preparing me for any behaviors we might see during and after AIT. I was encouraged to keep up with my notebook, since behaviors may change daily, and it's easy to forget. No guarantees had ever been made, beyond Ken's assurances that the hearing abnormalities could be corrected, and I would have been thrilled with that. The way Jerry and I looked at it, if the sound sensitivities were eliminated, Asia would be more relaxed in her world, and learning would come more easily. If the time delay was removed, then she would hear language in a more normal manner, allowing speech to make sense for the first time. That had to have a positive effect. We were encouraged not to let past limitations stop Asia from attempting new things. Something she couldn't do a month ago, she might be able to do now.

Ken told us that there would probably be a regression period, and there was no predicting when it would happen, or how long it would last. In some children, the regression was so brief it was scarcely noticed, while in others it lasted much longer. For the support other parents can give, Ken and Annabel put me in touch with other people whose children had completed AIT.

We were told that it might be three months or more before changes were noticed, and they might be so gradual that they would be apparent only after a while. Ken would send us progress questionnaires at three, six, nine, and twelve months. We were not to get discouraged.

The week after Asia completed the AIT, the fair came to Milan. After the parade, as we walked through the midway with all of the loud music, screaming riders, and engine noises, I watched to see Asia's reaction. She was grinning from ear to ear, pulling us to the different rides. She didn't want the tame, baby rides, oh no, she wanted the Gravitron, the Tilt-a-Whirl, and the Sizzler. The noises didn't seem to phase her. She went back on two other days and rode until she should have been sick, but she wanted *more*. More of that vestibular stimulation. The only sound that bothered her were from the fireworks.

The following Sunday we were re-watching <u>Free Willy</u>, and Asia asked, "Mom, is there a <u>Free Willy II</u> like <u>Home Alone II</u>?" Later, when her bed time rolled around she asked, "Can I stay up to see the whales at the end and hear the music like at Camp Champ?" On Monday she said, "I don't like the fire engine noise in the parade, but I do like the band." These were more complete and well-thought-out sentences than ever before.

Every day, it seemed, we tried new sounds "to see if it hurts." She seemed happier and was volunteering to help around the house, even using the hand mixer and salad shooter. The facial tics and grimaces, a constant reminder of the Ritalin prescribed three years before, were decreasing. This was a bonus we had never expected. I thought it was my imagination until Ken mentioned it one day.

"I hadn't really wanted to say anything, because I didn't want to get your hopes up. Some time ago I treated a young man for sound sensitivities who also had Tourette's syndrome and his tics improved after the AIT," he said. "No one knows why. No one really knows why any of this works. The procedure is just now being researched, and the results measured and charted."

It would be two more months before we could try the lockers at school, but in the meantime, we would take each improvement and run with it.

Things were rolling along so well that, when the predicted regression occurred, it caught me completely by surprise. It was about two weeks after AIT, and Asia was going to Camp

Champ. When I picked her up in the afternoon, the head of the camp met me at the door, with Asia in tow. She had scratched a little girl's leg so badly it bled, with no apparent provocation. It had been years since she had hurt someone else intentionally, and she could offer no explanation. As I apologized to the little girl's mother, and hurried Asia to the van, my head was spinning. This was the beginning of a downhill slide that lasted about two weeks and, before it was over, had us convinced that any progress we thought we had seen had been our wishful thinking. As her behavior deteriorated, the sound sensitivities returned along with the tics. Gone was the helpful, cheerful child of last week, and in her place was an irritating, aggravating, rebellious pain in the butt. She pestered her sister to distraction, threw pens and pencils across the room, left her bicycle in the middle of the driveway . . . any little thing she could do to get under our skins. We were depressed and drained emotionally. We talked to each other constantly, trying to muster our optimism, reminding ourselves that this was probably the regression and it would soon be over.

"But what if it isn't?" Jerry asked after the first week. "What if she is the one child in 5,000 [?] who regresses and stays that way forever? What if she gets stuck in reverse, like a car with a faulty transmission, and can't go forward anymore?" What if . . ? What if . . . ? What if . . . ?

None of the "what-if's?" ever happened. We were probably only hours away from the ends of our badly frayed ropes, when, just as suddenly as it started, the regression became progression again. The only thing that could have amazed me any more than the gains at the beginning was the speed with which she came out of the regression.

We spent our vacation in Rochester, Minnesota, with Jerry's parents. Jerry's sister Kim had arranged for our niece and nephew, Brandie and Bryce, and their mom, Terry, to come over for the day. With Kim and Phil's two daughters, Alyse and Andrea, it was the first time all six Renning grandchildren had been together. We managed to sneak off for a few hours and have portraits made of the grandchildren to give to Bud and Wim for their anniversary. I marveled at how much Bryce and Brandie had grown; Bryce--who smiles with his whole face and has eyes like his dad, and Brandie, a beautiful young lady, the perfect blending of her two parents. We laughed and cried and recalled old times and swore not to let ten years come between us again. We visited Jerry's Grandma Thiede in the nursing home, and with that special bond that is so often there between the very old and the young, she and Asia connected again.

When school started in the fall, Asia was in the sixth grade and Meghann a freshman in high school. This year was going to be different; we were sure of it. Marsha was now a veteran middle-school aide, and that she was a pearl beyond price was surely evident to the tenured teachers.

Her home room teacher was a bit apprehensive about having an autistic child (there's that label again) in his class, but at a meeting an the end of the previous year, we had encouraged him to look past the label and get to know the child. We were pleased and pleasantly surprised to receive "Happy Grams" a few days after school started, telling how well Asia was doing. One morning her home room teacher even called to tell us how much he was enjoying working with her. Her schedule needed to be adjusted, and once again she and Marsha were given a "decompression room" at the end of the sixth-grade hallway. She brought home the same spelling words as the rest of the students in her class. She now walked in the hallways without covering her ears. Math remained a problem, so she was introduced to the calculator. Things were not perfect, but armed with vitamins, allergy drops, and AIT, Asia was much better equipped to meet the middle-school challenge than the year before.

I had sent a thirty-page condensed version of Asia's life to Annabel, and our telephone friendship grew as I kept her updated on Asia's continuing gains. It still amazed me that a treatment as noninvasive and potentially beneficial as AIT was relatively unknown in a community as medically advanced as Ann Arbor, with the prestigious University of Michigan hospitals. More and more I was hearing that this child or that was being put on Ritalin for attention deficit disorder. ADD/ADHD and dyslexia were only two of the many disabilities which AIT had been used to treat. Why, I asked myself, would anyone choose a *drug* over this treatment? The answer seemed simple. They either didn't know about it or, worse still, were being discouraged from pursuing this course of treatment by their child's doctors. Doctors have their own agenda, I've discovered, and AIT is threatening to them. I was, with my usual zeal, shouting from the rooftops the benefits of allergy treatments, vitamin therapy, and now AIT.

In one of my conversations with Annabel, she mentioned the speaking tours she had gone on several years before. I asked if she would be willing to come to Michigan if I organized a conference. And it was that simple. This was the way to give other parents a chance to hear about some of the treatments that had been so beneficial to Asia. Just like the Little Rascals, when they wanted to raise money for baseball uniforms . . . let's put on a show! And so, like the Orphan Benefit Dinners in Minnesota, I began making plans for the Michigan Conference on AIT. I called Ken and Cindy Wilson to see if they would be presenters with Annabel, and contacted Weber's Inn in Ann Arbor for available dates for their Grand Ballroom.

We were long overdue for a visit to North Carolina, and decided to go for Christmas. It had been seven years since we had been home, and my cousins' *children* had children. Asia remembered *everyone* from the previous visit, which had been made during a time when we had no idea how much information was being processed and saved, and how much was just flying around inside her head, looking for a place to land.

We spent one evening with forty or so relatives, feasting on wonderful Southern home cooking--whole tables full of food-- Asia's favorite kind of meal. While the adults were taking videos and catching up, Asia was able to play appropriately with the other children, something that would not have been possible a year before. Meghann radiated beauty, grace, and poise. The house rang with the sound of children's laughter and Asia's face glowed with happiness. On the way back to Mom's house, Asia sat quietly in the back of the van for a while, and then we heard the sound of quiet sniffling.

"Honey, what's wrong?" I asked.

"Mom, can I be sad?" Asia wondered.

"Why are you sad, honey?"

"Can I miss all the people?"

"Of course you can, honey. But we'll see them again soon," I assured her.

"Can I miss them and still miss our home in Michigan?" she said, still sniffling.

"Sure, but we'll be back home in Michigan soon."

"These are happy tears too, Mom. I love the people."

"I know, honey."

Asia cried quietly all the way home. She kept saying, "Look, Mom, look at my eyes. I still have tears."

Six months before, this conversation would never have occurred because Asia would not have been able to tell us *why* she was crying. She has always had such a deep well of feeling for everything. It had always surfaced spontaneously, triggered by the music at a concert, a movie, or simply a visitor leaving. The difference is that now she is beginning to acquire the gift of language to express these deep emotions. In the past, these same emotions were expressed sometimes in self-abuse, scratching and clawing her arms and digging holes in her fingers.

We spent a wonderful Christmas Day, first at Mom's and then with her friend Peggy's lively family for lunch. And all too soon, as usual, it was time to go home.

We all came back to Michigan with colds. On New Year's Eve, Jerry, Asia, and I were still under the weather and elected to stay home. Meghann was with her boyfriend's family. We rented movies and ate, and Asia sat on the floor between our chairs writing the list of names she calls her School Picture Wallet.

The best (and the kindest) description for Asia's printing up to that point would be *uncontrolled*. The letters were large and rounded, and she tended to wrap them around and down the side of the page if she ran out of a line. There was very little distinction between upper- and lowercase letters. Never was a space unfilled, nor did any scrap of paper go unrecycled around here. No piece of paper was sacred. In her mind, it *all* belonged to Asia. With the School Picture Wallet list, she printed the names in columns of a sort, but there was seldom any space to speak of between the columns. And like everything else she did, she wrote with incredible speed.

As Jerry and I watched <u>Schindler's List</u>, Asia wrote quietly for a long time, then whipped a piece of paper back to me. On it were neat, precise names, all with appropriate upper- and lowercase letters, printed within the lines, in perfect columns with ruler-straight left edges. It didn't even remotely resemble her previous printing. Was my daughter possessed? Was this the automatic writing I'd read about?

While Jerry and I marveled at the crisp precision of the letters forming words which anyone could read, not just the privileged few, she was producing another, equally perfect sheet. And another. And another, as we watched, spellbound, until it was time for popcorn. Before, even when asked, she couldn't produce anything as fine as this. Could this be another manifestation of the benefits of AIT? I could hardly wait to ask Ken.

When school started after Christmas, for the first time in three years, Asia didn't have a problem with the school air. In the past, the first few weeks back were a nightmare. In the beginning we thought it was just readjustment, but as we learned more about environmental allergies, we came to believe that her reaction was a negative response to all of the cleaning solutions used while the school was closed for the holidays. We knew floors were waxed, carpets cleaned, bathrooms scrubbed, and who knew what else. I could hardly breathe in there myself when I walked the hallways after Christmas. Her allergy drops were current, so in January of 1995, she had no problem. Thank you, Dr. Rapp and Dr. Derrick. I couldn't help but wonder how many other children were similarly affected, but were treated as trouble-makers.

We were now less than a month away from the Conference, and I had met a group of exciting, energetic parents in the process. We arranged for publicity and began taking reservations in earnest. By the day of the Conference we had over two hundred reservations from parents, teachers, speech pathologists, doctors, and lawyers. They represented children who carried various labels: autism, PDD, ADD/ADHD, dyslexia, and hyperlexia, to mention only a few. The parents I had spoken with in making reservations were hungry for the information that was going to be available. They were anxious to take an active part in helping their children be the best they could be. They were open minded and attentive, and we believe they left with hope. *That was our measurement of the success of the event.*

Annabel charmed everyone with her easy "over the backyard fence" conversational style. Her Parent Network has joined a nation of parents with special children together with a common cause--to spread the word. *Never give up!*

Ken and Cindy Wilson's knowledge and experience working with children with a variety of learning disabilities made their presentations meaningful for all who attended.

The panel of adults who shared their stories and those of their children brought to life the hope we wanted to inspire, and gave it faces and names and personalities.

Annabel had set the conference date as a deadline, and she sold out of the first-run copies of her new book, *Dancing in the Rain.* Asia's was one of the twenty-two stories in the book.

Traditionally the sixth graders at middle school go to an environmental camp for four days each year. This year's class would be going to Camp Storer, the YMCA camp in Jackson, Michigan in April. We had not really considered sending Asia. We were still not quite ready to let go that much yet. But when her tutor, Danette Talbot, offered to go as a cabin aide, we began to think that it just might work. We worked out the kinks with the school and camp staff, and it was arranged that Marsha would go up during the day as well.

As the time to leave for camp grew closer, Asia vacillated between intense, almost unbearable excitement, and mortal fear. Never, since her arrival twelve years ago, had she spent one night away from us. When she was in the hospital, I stayed with her. When I was in Florida training with Eastern Airlines, Jerry, Meghann, and Grandma were with her. At an age when most teenagers routinely spend nights and entire weekends at friends' homes, Asia had never spent the night without at least one of us near. This was due to a sad combination of facts. We did not believe that Asia would behave appropriately without one of us riding herd on her. Few people we knew had teenagers who might run out into the street or go up to a passerby, a stranger, and strike up a conversation. One of our biggest fears was that she was a walking target for anyone with naughty thoughts on his mind. Letting go simply wasn't a risk we were ready to take yet. The other reason was that, even with all the good to come out of the Circle of Friends, spending the night with one of the girls wasn't one of them.

On the one hand, Asia wanted desperately to go to camp with all of the other sixth graders, but on the other, she was terrified. She began to misbehave in school, and at one point asked Marsha, "If I'm really bad, do I still go to camp?" She was looking for a way out. But it showed a new depth of thought, and the connection between responsible behavior and rewards.

The days grew closer and she was giggling with excitement. The night before she could hardly sleep. We had packed all her gear, clothes, sleeping bag, colostomy supplies, vitamins and drops, etc., on Monday and were at the school at 8:30 A.M. on Tuesday. It was pouring rain and the atmosphere was charged with teenage energy. They would assemble in their classrooms before boarding the buses to leave. I had given the teachers five copies of six typed sheets of instructions regarding diet, colostomy, vitamins, behavior, and allergies, as well as three land phone numbers, one car phone, a fax number and a pager to reach Jerry or me anytime of the day or night. This was a monumental step for all of us.

The week flew by. I'm almost ashamed to admit that I expected the phone to ring any minute, and on the other end would be an irate camp counselor demanding that I come pick up my out-of-control daughter. The house was quieter than at any time in the past twelve years. No one asked, "What's for breakfast [lunch or dinner], Mom?" We could eat whatever we wanted, guilt-free. There was one less person constantly interrupting telephone conversations. We missed her terribly. We missed her thundering down the stairs in the morning. We missed, "Can I have an apple?" And most of all, we missed that often imitated, but never duplicated, infectious laugh of hers.

The child who stepped off the bus on Friday was not the same one I had put on the bus on Tuesday. There was a new maturity and confidence about her. She came home and went immediately around to check on all her papers and her room, and then went to our water bed and lay down. "What's up, kiddo?" I asked.

"Just thinking about camp, Mom."

"Oh, anything in particular?" I asked.

"No. Just stuff, Mom. Mom, can I go to camp next year?"

"No, honey, the camp is just for sixth graders," I said.

"But Danette and Jennifer were there, Mom," she said as she sat up. "They're in high school." I couldn't argue with that.

"I know, honey, but they went as cabin leaders."

"I'll be a cabin leader leader in high school, Mom, okay?"

"That would be great, Asia."

"Mom, what's for dinner?" Then I knew she was home.

It took a week to get all the details, but to say that she had a good time is a classic understatement. She rode a horse, went through the obstacle course, kept her cabin mates in stitches, and earned the admiration of some of her fellow sixth graders for all of the things she *could* do. The week is now immortalized forever in a photo album she carries with her papers.

My mom came out in May this year, and Asia stunned her the first night by sitting at the computer that lives on the dining room table and typing her School Picture Wallet list. Quietly, her face set in a determined expression, her fingers flew over the keys. She whipped out two pages, three columns each, a total of one hundred and fifty-nine names.

That night we went to the high school band's spring concert to hear Meghann play, and Asia sat through it, leaning forward on the back of the chair in front of us, to catch every note. Mother and Asia had actual conversations, you know, where one person asks a question, and the other one answers and so on, back and forth. This was another of her new abilities. Mother was treated to new surprises every day, and went home with a number of fresh 'Asia stories' for all of the relatives in North Carolina.

Asia is currently mastering the calendar, so she can keep track of who's coming when and when appointments are, and when camp starts, and how long it is until yearbooks come.

We are now at the end of the school year. A few days into the week, I came up from feeding the birds in the basement and Asia said, "Mom, Janice called." I stood looking at her as if I had lost my wits. "I told her you were feeding birds. She said call her soon." This from a child who, for twelve years, has never answered the telephone, no matter if it rang fifty times.

I shook the cobwebs out of my head and looked around for the hidden camera. "Really?" I said. "Thank you, honey." And I hurried to call Janice.

The first words out of Janice's mouth were, "What the heck's going on over there? Asia just answered the phone." Before I could reply, she said, "And she did so well. I asked to speak to you and she said, 'Name, please.' I told her it was me and she said, 'Oh, hi, Janice, Mom's in the basement feeding birds.' I told her to have you call me and she replied, 'Okay, but let's talk first.' I couldn't get her off the phone." Janice, needless to say, was flabbergasted.

Last weekend two neighborhood children who went to school

with Asia last year stopped by to pick out one of our kittens. The girls had gone with us to Major Magic's for pizza for Asia's birthday in April. As they were leaving, they asked Asia to spend the night on the last night of school. We are definitely entering into a new phase here.

Chapter Twenty-seven

The Last Chapter

"How are you going to know when to stop writing?" Teri Bell asked during a phone conversation on Monday.

"When there isn't any more to say," I replied.

"But you *always* have more to say," she said. "If that's your guideline, you'll be writing until you're fingers are nubs."

"Yeah, but too many great things happened this summer, and they need to be in here. But this is *really* going to be the last chapter." Jerry says he's heard that one before.

Today is August 30, 1995 and it is the first full day of the new school year. It is a beautiful, mild and sunny day, and with the new school scheduling this year, everyone, including Jerry, was out of the house by 7:30 A.M. I have the house to myself, having just returned from taking Asia to the middle school. I had to help her carry her bag inside since it was filled with about twenty pounds of spiral binders, notebooks, pens, pencils, markers and folders, the tools of the trade for a seventh grader. She's wearing her new running shoes, since this afternoon will be her second day of training with the middle school cross-country team. Monday, the first day of practice went well. The team jogged the one-half mile through town from the high school to the park where they practice, and I drove, one block away, watching to make sure street crossings went smoothly.

It was our typical busy, hectic summer. While Asia was enjoying her days at Camp Champ, Meghann was attending drivers' training. She received her permit to drive with a parent last month and now *I* have a chauffeur instead of being one. I can't believe that it has been sixteen years since I first saw her picture.

This was the best year yet for Asia at Camp. She brought home "Catch 'em being good" notes every day for behavior and participation. Part of the reason, we believe, is because of new additions to her vitamin regimen that were added this summer They were the beginning of a program designed to correct a problem that has affected her in more ways than one for at least six years.

Asia's beloved Dr. Wesley had left the University hospital several years ago and his cases had been assigned to various other doctors in the pediatric surgery unit. Late in the fall of 1994 I contacted Asia's newest surgeon concerning several problems. One of the problems confronting Asia for the past six or more years had been intractable flatulence. And now she was old enough and aware enough to be embarrassed by it. Most of the children in school were tolerant, even coming to Asia's defense when there were substitute teachers. But there was occasionally cruel teasing, and it broke my heart for her.

I called the surgeon for advice, and he referred me back to her pediatrician, who recommended stool tests to detect the presence of intestinal parasites. None were found. Since we had had more contact with the surgeon than the pediatrician regarding colostomy concerns, I found myself continuing to direct my questions to his office.

"I would match her appetite against any three players on the University of Michigan football team," I began. "She was born without a "full" gauge. You're looking at me as though you think I'm exaggerating, but you simply have no idea the volume of food this child can consume. But she's thin as a reed. I'm concerned that she may not be absorbing her food properly. And the constant flatulence is causing problems for her at school. Aren't there some tests that will give us some answers?"

"If you want to talk flatulence, Mrs. Renning, I can take you into any locker room in the state for comparisons," he began.

I could barely control myself. "But we're not talking 'locker rooms,' here, we're talking about a thirteen-year-old girl in the sixth grade, who is already facing more than her share of challenges and certainly doesn't need any more," I said.

"Look, I don't think malabsorption is a problem because her weight is fine," he said calmly. But, as you pointed out, she *is* a teenager, and teenagers eat a lot. If you want a referral to a pediatric gastroenterologist, I'll give you one, but I don't think that's where your answers are."

I wanted to ask, "Then where the heck are they, 'cause they certainly aren't here." But I kept quiet, for a change, and left feeling defeated and patronized.

A few weeks later, however, the problem recurred with a vengeance, and I called the surgeon's office for help. An assistant we'd dealt with since our first days at the clinic answered our call, since Asia's doctor was out of town.

"I can sympathize with you, Mrs. Renning. This is frequently a problem with kids who have colostomies," she said. "The doctors often prescribe Flagyl to help control the odor. I'll discuss this with one of the other surgeons and see if they will call in a prescription for Asia."

"When Asia took Flagyl earlier, I thought it was an antibiotic," I said. "But in birds it's used to treat intestinal parasites, and Asia's tests were negative for parasites and their eggs."

"I know, but it also works for this, too," she replied. "What pharmacy do you use and I'll see if I can get someone to call in a 'script?"

In the past when Asia had taken Flagyl, she had had no side effects, so I wasn't too concerned about a reaction. Amazingly, three days later, the problem was gone, completely gone, much to everyone's relief. And it stayed gone for the entire month she took the drug but reared it's ugly head during our Christmas visit in North Carolina. Fortunately my mother's doctor was familiar with Asia's history, through Mom, and was willing to prescribe Flagyl for Asia there.

Sadly, after that prescription ran out, we soon needed another. Asia was scheduled for her annual check-up with the surgeon, and I asked him, "Why isn't the Flagyl correcting this problem?"

"Sometimes it takes more than one round of the medication," he answered.

"Is there a problem with Flagyl killing beneficial bacteria and setting up a breeding ground for a yeast infection?" I asked. My experience raising birds had taught me that anti-fungal medications are frequently prescribed at the same time as antibiotics to prevent candida albicans (yeast) overgrowth.

"That won't be necessary," he said. *"Flagyl has actually been shown to inhibit the growth of yeast.* And what it does to control the flatulence is amazing. I don't have a problem keeping her on Flagyl for an extended period."

Well, I did. But again I kept my mouth shut. A few days later Annabel called to give me a report on a conference she had attended. When I related our latest encounter with doctors, she said, "What's bothering her has a name. It's called "Leaky Gut Syndrome" and I'll give you the numbers of some parents to call for more information about it." Here's an example of parents networking again, arriving just in the nick of time like the Cavalry.

I was dialing Marie Robinson's phone number in Virginia before the telephone had cooled from the last conversation. Marie, who is an Auditory Training Practitioner herself, had organized the conference Annabel had attended. She began researching Leaky Gut Syndrome in the summer of 1994 and had written to Dr. C. A. Kotsanis of Dallas, Texas, who developed the protocol for its treatment. Dr. Kotsanis found disordered digestive patterns in 100% of the children with autism who were part of his study. 75% suffered from gut permeability or Leaky Gut Syndrome.

Marie gave me telephone numbers for Dr. Kotsanis and also a lab in North Carolina which does a test which determines the health status of the digestive tract, and promised to send me more information gleaned from her search for answers for her twenty-nine year old son with autism. Marie's son's story also appeared in *Dancing in the Rain.*

Leaky Gut Syndrome. The name triggered that tuning fork in my brain that is my personal "ring of truth." It was so descriptive of many of Asia's digestive symptoms. We fed her enormous amounts of food which never seemed to satisfy her, she was thin as a rail and it was normal for her to change a full colostomy bag three to five times a day.

My mom was visiting, and to her questionable fortune, got to watch her daughter in action on the telephone, on a mission, *again.* I called Dr. Kotsanis' office the next day and spoke with Chris Harjes. Dr. Kotsanis' approach to treating children with autism is to treat the entire child, beginning with the digestive system, and including sensory integration, visual retraining, as well as auditory training. Chris is the audiologist. Chris likened Leaky Gut Syndrome to a lawn overgrown with weeds. A digestive system out of balance because of illness or antibiotic treatment becomes a breeding ground for yeast and opportunistic bacteria, which grow rapidly in an environment no longer equipped to fight them. The bacteria and yeast alter the digestibility of foods and create weak, thin spots in the bowel which allow molecules of undigested food to pass through. "It would be like giving yourself a "milk shake I.V.," Chris explained.

The good news was that in most cases these imbalances could be corrected and proper digestive function restored. And like the lawn full of weeds, after the correct nutritional ingredients have been added, the system is then capable of keeping out the "weeds." After speaking with me at length about Asia and her various "plumbing problems," he promised to send me more information about their clinic, and gave me the telephone number of the lab in North Carolina to find out which doctors in our area used their services. (The telephone company and the postman were going to just *love* me .)

Two days later a large envelope arrived from Great Smokies Diagnostic Laboratory in Asheville, North Carolina. To my great relief, Dr. Derrick, Asia's allergist, was listed as already using their services. If I had had to persuade someone that I wanted this test done on Asia, Dr. Derrick was the only one I felt I would have had a chance with. I arranged to pick up a test kit for a Comprehensive Digestive Stool Analysis (CDSA) from his office the next day. The stool analysis would, hopefully, provide answers to many of our questions.

Soon Marie Robinson's information came and shortly after, another large envelope from Dr. Kotsanis's clinic. As I read about the clinic, which includes facilities for many of the interventions we were using, but all under one roof, I thought, "What a wonderful resource for parents with children just recently diagnosed; they can go to one place for answers instead of being like the ball in a pin-ball machine--careening from one post to another in their search.

The instructions were to send the stool sample by Federal Express to the laboratory and the results would be sent to Doctor Derrick, who would then discuss them with Dr. Kotsanis, and a treatment protocol would be developed especially for Asia.

Dr. Derrick kindly sent me a copy of the test results as soon as they arrived. It was like no other lab report I've ever seen. It was prepared in a manner that both parents and professionals alike could decipher. And as I read it, I wanted to cheer. Not because I had been right, but because we were finally getting to the bottom of some problems that should have been addressed long ago.

The tests showed that Asia had no parasites. (How could she?) She had moderate growths of E. Coli and Klebsiella, two potentially harmful bacteria. While the report stated that an optimum level of lactobacillus was +4, there was *no lactobacillus* present in the sample taken from Asia. Lactobacillus is one of the "friendly" bacteria that *should* be present in the intestinal tract of a healthy person. It is critical for proper nutrient absorption, and helps prevent the growth of bacterial and yeast infections. Her digestive enzymes were severely out of balance and there was evidence of maldigestion and malabsorption as well as a "substantially greater than normal amount of yeast, which represented an overgrowth condition."

The Dysbiosis Index, which represents Leaky Gut Syndrome, is rated from zero-to-three as *normal*, four-to-six as *slight*, seven-to-ten, *moderate*, and ten or more, *severe*. Asia's score was *eleven*. The report went on to say that "The Dysbiosis Index score is elevated and strongly suggests that a state of disordered bowel flora ecology exists and is contributing to altered gut metabolism."

As strange as it may sound, I almost felt relieved, because now the previously unknown demons had names. They were names I was familiar with and they could be fought. I left a message with Dr. Kotsanis' office to call me if he needed any further information about Asia that Dr. Derrick might not be able to provide. Much to my surprise, he called me the following morning.

He was very concerned about Asia's CDSA report, although in most respects she seemed to be quite well. "It will be three weeks before I will be able to speak with Dr. Derrick, as I am leaving today for a lecture tour," he said. "In the meantime, I would like for you to have some specific blood tests done and have the results sent to me, to be here when I return."

"That certainly is no problem, but isn't there something, anything, that we can do in the meantime?" I asked. "I feel as though this test has given us so many answers, and I don't want to wait almost three weeks to begin. This has gone untreated for too long as it is."

"It is not possible for me to prescribe for Asia without having seen her or discussing her condition with her doctor. The fact that you are in another state is an additional complication. However, if you will notice on the yeast sensitivity chart, the yeast is very sensitive to garlic, and odorless garlic tablets are available at most health food stores. Lactobacillus products are also readily available there. Another product that would be beneficial is called Vital-Zymes. You should be able to find a health food store that carries it as well. These should be taken with each meal. If you think of the digestive system as similar to a compost pit, the Lactobacillus and Vital-Zymes will be the fuel to promote the proper decomposition. The garlic will help control the yeast overgrowth until Asia's system is functioning properly on it's own."

After thanking him profusely for his time and help, I hung up and called Jerry. "Dr. Kotsanis just called from Texas. He's read Asia's CDSA report and wants some blood tests done before he works up a complete treatment plan with Dr. Derrick. The good news is there are some things I can get at Whole Foods today to get started."

"I have a chiropractor's appointment this afternoon, right around the corner," he said. "Give me a list and I'll pick the stuff up on the way home."

I called Dr. Derrick to get a request form for the blood tests, and then sat back to re-read the report, to absorb some of the terms I was unfamiliar with.

Jerry brought home the lactobacillus and garlic tablets but the Vital-zymes were not available at the health food stores we shopped at. However, Dr. Derrick's office carried that brand and arranged to mail a bottle for Asia. By this time Asia was so used to taking vitamins that adding a few more to the routine didn't faze her. These additions were to be taken immediately before, at the mid-point, and at the end of the meal for a "layering" effect with the food eaten. I laid them out by her plate and explained the process, cautioning her that Dr. Kotsanis wanted her to chew her food more slowly. Though she dislikes them intensely, Asia has a great deal of respect for what doctors say.

The next day she was careful to remind me to give her her "mealtime" vitamins.

On Friday the Vital-Zymes arrived from Dr. Derrick's office. All three new additions were in place.

Three days later we noticed the first change. So many things that happen during the day become so routine you don't notice them until they *don't* happen. Asia was typing when she noticed that the seal was ripping on her colostomy bag, which was unusual. As she went in the bathroom to change her it, I asked her, "Honey, when was the last time you changed your bag?"

Very matter of factly, she said, "Last night at shower time, Mom."

"Are you sure?" I asked. "You didn't change your bag all day?"

In her exasperated 'Aw, come on Mom,' voice, she said, "Yes, I'm *sure,* Mom. I changed my bag at shower time last night and that's all."

"Okay, honey, just checking," I said, thinking it must be a fluke. She normally changed her bag three-to-five times a day.

The next morning, wording my question carefully so as not to set off any of her alarm bells, I said, "Asia honey, let me know when you change your bag today." Normally she only says something if she needs supplies.

"Why, Mom? What'd I do?" A note of concern had crept into her voice.

"Nothing, honey. I'm just trying to keep track of how many bags you use so I know how many to order next time." I hated to lie, but if I said anything about it being unusual (the number of times she changed her bag) she would immediately think that it meant a visit to the surgeon's and all her internal panic buttons would go off at once.

That night before bed, I asked casually, "Asia, have you had to change your bag today?"

"No, Mom."

"Not at all?"

"I told you, Mom, no."

"Thanks, pal. Just let me know next time you change it, okay?

"Sure, Mom."

It was a full twenty-four hours between bag changes. The last time she went that long between changes it signalled a bowel kink and a lot of pain. But that wasn't the case this time. Her system was finally absorbing the food. It was the beginning of a series of changes in her digestive process that was miraculous.

It was customary for me to buy at least two, sometimes three, three-pound bags of apples a week, plus bananas, pears and whatever other fruits were in season. Granted, some of them went into bird food, but most of them went into *Asia*. The first week after starting the new "vitamins," Asia didn't eat *a single apple*. Not one. And I knew for sure, because I had only bought four fat Red Delicious apples for Jerry's lunches since I didn't need any for school lunches. No raisins, grapes, or bananas were missing either. Her appetite at mealtime was unchanged--she still ate two helpings--but, whether she realized herself or not, she was not *compelled* to eat almost constantly between meals. The first week was going so well that during the second week, I decided to conduct my own personal "blind study." Asia was supposed to take one-250mg. tablet of Flagyl three times a day. I eliminated them all. It was a gamble, but it was summer time, and I just *knew* that she didn't need them anymore. I didn't tell Jerry or Meghann for two weeks, and then I casually asked if they had noticed any change in the gas, or lack of it.

"Nope, everything seems fine to me," Jerry said.

"I haven't been around all that much," said Meghann, "but I haven't noticed any.

"Well, guys, she's had no Flagyl for the last two weeks. Just the garlic, lactobacillus and enzymes." Not only was she having to change her colostomy bag less than half as often, but her incessant craving for food had dramatically decreased, and all of this was occurring without the constant stigma of the flatulence. It would be difficult to say which of the three changes excited us more. They were all significant and equally dramatic.

To me, it seemed perfectly clear what was happening. The garlic was attacking the yeast overgrowth, the lactobacillus was creating colonies of "friendly" bacteria in her digestive tract, and the Vital-zymes were helping to balance her own insufficient enzymes. And all of this combined was allowing her body to finally absorb the nutrients from the massive quantities of food she ate. Consequently, her food cravings lessened. The proper absorption of nutrients and more correct balance of intestinal flora eliminated the breeding ground for bacteria which caused the gas. Every day that passed I held my breath. Occasionally she would ask for a piece of fruit for a snack. Once in a while she would change her bag more than once a day, but the flatulence was gone, blessedly gone. And the most amazing thing was that the *full treatment hadn't even started yet,* and wouldn't start until Dr. Kotsanis returned from his lecture tour. After he had a chance to review the blood tests, he would confer with Dr. Derrick and get back in touch with us.

I took Asia to the University Hospital for the blood tests Dr. Kotsanis had ordered and we went about the business of summer; Asia in camp, Meghann learning to drive, Jerry doing "garden therapy," and me writing.

Asia had always loved to swing, and on playgrounds would make a bee-line for the swings as soon as she was out of the car. This summer after the class picnic, the substitute aide met me at the car with a very distressed expression on her face.

"Mrs. Renning, Asia has blisters on both of her thighs. She was on the swings at the Nature Park for almost two hours. One of the blisters popped and has a Band-Aid on it. We didn't know until she got off the swings."

The aide was so upset, as though it was her fault. "Don't worry, she doesn't feel pain the same as other kids," I reassured her. "She was in a state approaching total bliss on those swings. The blisters will heal, and she'll still have good memories of the swinging."

We used to think of the swinging as some kind of obsession. But the more we learned about Asia's altered sensory perception of the world around her, the more the swinging made sense. Like rocking in the rocking chair or jumping on the trampoline, swinging stimulated the vestibular system and had beneficial effects. Yard sized trampolines were too expensive, so we had gotten Asia a swing for her birthday--the rope kind that is supposed to hang from a tree branch. The only problem was there wasn't a straight branch anywhere on our property. We got a heavy gauge nylon rope to hang it with and selected the closest-to-horizontal branch we had (at a thirty-degree angle) and hung the swing.

"Fix the swing please, Dad," Asia politely asked after her first trial. "Doesn't work right." It didn't swing straight.

"That's the best we can do, Asia," Jerry said. "We don't have any straighter branches."

She came inside. "Mom, tell Dad to fix the swing," she said. "It swings funny."

"He can't fix it any different, honey. Just try it like that for a while."

"Then ask Jeff to fix it." Janice's husband, Jeff, is a "wood wizard," so Asia expected him to work miracles with thirty-degree-angled branches. "And if he can't fix it, get one that goes like this and like this and like this," she continued, drawing in the air with her hands.

"All right, honey, but we may not see Jeff for a while, so just try it, okay?"

"Ask Janice when you talk to her tomorrow." The kid knew me too well. And she sure was a persistent little cuss. But I had to love that language, reason, and persuasion!

The branch was on a tree right outside the back door, and the next morning, I could see the end of the branch waving madly, bouncing up and down, but there was no wind. I looked around the corner and there was Asia, swinging perfectly straight, legs pumping and black hair flying. She had learned how to adapt her swing to allow for the imperfect angle of the branch. She was in heaven.

She wore blisters on her hands the first week and we bought

gardening gloves for her to wear while swinging. The weather was much to hot for long pants, so the blisters came back on her legs. Soon the rope began to wear through the bark of the tree, and I told Jerry that we would have the only branch in town that was sawed off by a rope. Jerry wrapped a carpet square around the branch under the rope. A month later the rope was so frayed it had to be replaced. I had visions of it snapping mid-swing, sending Asia flying across the fence into the neighbors' yard. Now the rope is slipped through a piece of garden hose and the branch is wrapped with a new carpet square. We'll see how long this combination lasts.

She is out there in the morning and at night before she goes to bed. I only have to look out the kitchen window to see if the branch is bouncing to know where she is. We know that the swing, like the trampoline before it, is satisfying a sensory need in Asia. Next on the list of interventions we want to explore for Asia is sensory integration, as well as having her eyes examined by a behavioral optometrist to see if visual retraining would benefit her.

As my writing progressed, I began thinking about titles, introductions and all the things that take this from being a stack of type filled sheets to being a real book. Ten years ago the title was *She Will Be Pretty Like Flowers.* Last year, when I wrote the chapter that appears in *Dancing in the Rain,* the title became *Seoul Food.* I played around with several other possibilities, not really happy with any of them. After delivering Meghann to drivers' training one day, I saw Asia's aide, Marsha Adams, visiting with her for few minutes before taking Asia on to Camp Champ. When I told her about Dr. Kotsanis and Leaky Gut Syndrome, she said, "You know, Adair, it's really incredible how you keep finding out about these treatments. First it was the allergies, then the vitamins, then the AIT, and now this."

"Yeah, I know. It's sort of like being on a scavenger hunt," I said. "We get a clue that leads us somewhere and pick up another clue that takes us somewhere else. Hopefully at the end of *this* hunt the prize is a child who can function on her own."

We said our good-byes and hurried off in different directions. As I drove Asia to camp, the phrase 'scavenger hunt' kept running around in my head like a gerbil on a wheel. It really had been the ultimate scavenger hunt. And then I knew I was close to the title of the book. I was so excited I called Jerry with the idea when I got home. He suggested *The Ultimate Scavenger Hunt: Finding the Child Inside.*

I liked it, but changing the title from *Seoul Food* was like changing a child's name. It was not something I took lightly. I called the members of my "Board of Advisors" who were available: my Mom, Annabel, Marsha, Joan Matthews, Kathy and Janice. Everybody liked it, but the image called up by the word 'scavenger' bothered Annabel.

"It makes me think of buzzards and carp. It has a negative connotation to it," she said.

"Okay, so what else do you do that's like a scavenger hunt?" I asked. "Some game where you get clues that lead you around until you find the treasure." *Treasure.* I called the "advisors" back and they all whole-heartedly approved of the change. Then when I thought it was all settled, Jerry and Meghann decided they didn't like it. Jerry still liked the original title and Meghann thought "The Ultimate Treasure Hunt" sounded silly. All my explanations of how perfect I thought it was fell on deaf ears, but in the end they agreed that it was my book and I could call it what I wanted. Now I think they've both come to like it.

Deciding who should write the introduction posed another set of questions. Annabel, on whom I've come to rely heavily during this project, felt that the introduction should be written from the perspective of the adoption of foreign-born children with special-needs. Several people immediately came to mind. One of them, if I could even find her, was Teri Bacall, the social worker who had found Asia in the orphanage.

A quick call to Children's Home Society in St. Paul and a lovely conversation with Mrs. Han gave me the information I needed to reach Teri (who is now Teri Bell.) She was no longer with C.H.S.M., but was continuing to do what she does so well--

locate and find families for children with challenges.

I would love to have been able to see her face when I identi-
fied myself. The agency she is currently with, Americans for International Aide and Adoption (AIAA) has an office in Birmingham, Michigan, and Terry would be there two weeks later. As
we talked about Asia and her changes and challenges and the
various treatments we had tried, Teri said, "So what you're
saying is that these symptoms have organic origins and can be
fixed with these different methods. Is that right?"

"Well, I don't know about the origins, but the conditions
themselves can certainly be improved by these interventions," I
said.

"What do you know about attachment disorder?" she asked.

"Absolutely nothing. Why do you ask?"

"There's another mom I'd like you to talk to before we get together in two weeks. She and her husband adopted a little boy
from Romania, and we're finding that a lot of these children exhibit many of the symptoms you've described in Asia. I'll send
you her newsletter and phone number. You two deserve to get to
know each other." (Funny, Annabel had said the same thing
when she gave me Marie Robinson's phone number.)

I arranged to send her a copy of my manuscript to read before
agreeing to write the introduction and we made plans to meet at
her office in Birmingham later in the month.

Although the newsletter Teri promised arrived in two days, it
was several more days before I could sit in one place long
enough to read it. Jerry's opportunity came first, and contrary to
his usual inability to read and concentrate with the television on,
he sat, totally absorbed in the newsletter, until he had finished
all six pages, front and back. He handed it to me and said, "This
is it. This is Asia, right here. You have to read it right now."

Right now didn't actually happen until the following morning
when everyone was gone. It was a wonderfully hot summer day,
just the kind I love. I finished feeding all of the birds, washed up
breakfast dishes, grabbed a glass of tea and sat under the ceiling
fan to read.

The newsletter, called *The Post,* is published by The Parent Network for the Post-Institutionalized Child. Thais Tepper, one of the four co-founders of the group was the mother Teri wanted me to talk to.

The opening paragraph began:

"The Network was created to connect families throughout the United States and Canada who have children who came from maternity hospitals, orphanages, or institutions for "street children," or economically deprived children. Many of the children who came from these circumstances are exhibiting a variety of problems, particularly emotional and psychological disturbances (such as agressive or passive behavior, autistic-like behavior and attachment/ bonding problems), developmental delays and learning disabilities (such as hyperactivity, expressive, receptive, and articulation language disorders, and cognitive disorders), as well as medical problems like Hepatitis B and D."

Well, I thought to myself, as opening paragraphs go, that one certainly did pack a powerful punch. I continued reading.

"The effects of bleak caretaking environments were studied by Rene Spitz and William Goldfarb in 1945. Spitz was a consulting doctor at a foundling home whose infants wasted away   and died from a condition called *marasmus.* He discovered that despite hygienic surroundings and nourishing diet, the babies received minimal stimulation from the social and physical environment. Spitz showed that mothering is essential to healthy psychological development and to life itself.

Dr. Goldfarb's continued studies of children removed from orphanages and adopted showed that these children suffered from long term effects of *privation*-the absence of appropriate stimulation--as manifested in

indiscriminate affection, extremely demanding
attention-seeking behavior, social unrelatedness with
peers, autistic-like behaviors, hyperactivity, aggression
(including acts of cruelty), temper tantrums, no cause-
and-effect thinking, and no concept of time, past or
future."

I sat glued to my chair, oblivious to everything around me,
the birds, the telephone, the doorbell. In spite of the heat of the
day, I was chilled to the bone. This newsletter contained a "word
picture" of Asia. After refreshing my tea, I continued.

"The DSM III (Diagnostic and Statistical Manual), the
psychiatric reference book describes the symptoms of
Reactive Attachment Disorder in Infancy and Early
Childhood as including: lack of weight gain (failure to
thrive), poor motor development, failure to make eye
contact, poor muscle tone, failure to establish vocal
communication, feeding disturbances, sleeping disturbances, hypersensitivity to touch and sound, persistent
failure to initiate or respond in an age-expected manner
to social interaction, indiscriminate sociability
(excessive familiarity with strangers and displays of
affection), repetitive behaviors that are non-functional
(body-rocking, head-banging or biting oneself, teeth
grinding, eye poking, thumb or finger sucking),
repetitive non-functional vocalization (animal noises,
trilling, screeching) creating self-stimulating behaviors,
and susceptibility to infection. (Note: In the DSM IV the
symptoms listed for this diagnosis have changed
slightly.)"

I was beginning to wonder why I had never heard any of this
mentioned by any of the professionals who had ever treated
Asia, (except for Teri, of course, who questioned Asia's ability
to bond with a family until she observed her with the Choi
family). Then I read that today's pediatricians and psychologists,

unaccustomed to seeing institutionalized children, fail to recognize the characteristic behaviors, and that mis-diagnosis was not uncommon. The one thing all of the professionals agreed on was that Asia was not "classically" anything; not *classically* ADHD, or *classically* PDD, or *classically* autistic.

Later on in the newsletter, Asia's story, from *Dancing in the Rain* was referred to, saying it ". . . tells the story of a post-institutionalized adoptee from Korea" who was helped by AIT.

When I finally looked up from the newsletter again, my eyes were blurry, both from fatigue and tears. Finally, someone had given her a label that fit, and that I could live with. I felt so foolish and naive, remembering my firm conviction that if I just "got her home to her family she would be just fine." We had known that she had been nutritionally deprived and understimulated. We knew that she had received medical treatment when necessary, but suspected that there had not been one consistent caregiver in her life until Teri placed her with the Choi family. It had never occurred to me that no amount of love from the age of two on would *ever* make up for all that she had missed from birth *until* two. Those two years had been stolen from her, and could never be replaced. Once again, I grieved for her loss. There were gaps in her life, and consequently her development, that we could not fill in. We could only hope to bridge them. None of what I had just read changed how I felt about Asia or our adoption of her. She is, was, and always will be our daughter. But I could feel myself slipping into a well of depression and guilt and "if only's"--*if only* a foster home could have been found sooner; *if only* Teri had seen her sooner; *if only* we could somehow have learned of her sooner. *If only* . . .

We will never know what Asia's life would have been like if just one thing were different. If she had not needed the colostomy, for example, perhaps she would have had a foster mother immediately, as Meghann had. But that was not the course her life was to take, and that line of thinking was a waste of time. This was a revelation that required immediate action. We were on the verge of new and exciting discoveries about

Asia, discoveries that did not allow time for "if only-ing" myself into the nuthouse. We were on our way to another clue in the treasure hunt.

I flipped to the front of the newsletter where Teri had written Thais' phone number and picked up the telephone.

After I introduced myself, she said, "That's strange, I had my hand on the telephone to call you." Teri was right. I did need to talk to Thais. I had a lot more questions.

Our first conversation lasted well over an hour. As she told me about her son, and the children of other members of the group, suddenly all of the television specials and news broadcasts I had seen about the horrors of Romanian orphanages (warehouses) came flooding back--the children with large, dark haunted eyes, the dim, windowless rooms filled with rows and rows of cribs, some holding more than one child. The rooms were so crowded that the children may as well have been stacked like cord wood. These children were now with parents and families who loved them, parents who were living today what Jerry and I had been experiencing for the last twelve years. The difference was that Teri and the staff at C.H.S.M. had given us every scrap of information available about Asia, and had gone to great lengths to try to prepare us for what problems the future might hold. Thais and other families currently adopting children from Romania and Russia today had apparently been much less fortunate, and their agencies less realistic (less honest?) about the possible outcomes for their children.

One thing became clearer as we talked. The reason the information available about these children is thirty to fifty years old is due to the fact that the research was done during a time when orphanages were common, and as with all things, there were good ones and bad ones. The children who survived the "bad" ones were the statistics the journals and texts had been written about, and around whom the diagnoses were developed. Then came "The Pill," and legalized abortion, and suddenly the well from which these unfortunate children sprang dried up, and with it, the studies into attachment disorder and post-institutionalized behavior. The future for those children was bleak, according to Thais. They usually ended up back in institutions, either mental or correctional.

Now we have a new generation of attachment-disordered children. But to their good fortune, and ours, the parents who love them, there are interventions available which directly address the problems and challenges facing them. Among these interventions are some of the very things which we have found to work for Asia, and others we want to try, including AIT, sensory integration therapy, visual retraining, and food and environmental allergy testing. We already know that the children are benefitting from these treatments. What the future holds for them remains to be seen.

Thais and I talked again the following morning. I was so grateful for her newsletter which had finally given me answers that I had searched for for twelve years. And, once again, the answers had come from another parent. In addition I had found others that are as committed as Jerry and I to sharing any and all information we have gleaned in our search to help other families. Thais' group is especially dedicated to providing this vital information to families intending to adopt children from institutions in other countries, and encouraging the placement agencies to give accurate, honest representations about the children to those potential parents.

Summer moved along, too fast, as good summers do. Asia was still completely off Flagyl and having no problems with gas. When she was inside, I found that we were able to have conversations. Mostly they centered around current and future events, but the repetitive speech was fading. She was developing a sense of humor and began laughing appropriately at television shows. One morning, while I was fixing breakfast, she called out to me. "Mom, come here. Look at this!"

By the time I got into the living room the scene had changed, and I saw nothing spectacular. But as soon as I turned back to the kitchen, she said, "There, look at that!" She was really excited about whatever it was. I turned around, but again not fast enough.

"What is it, honey?" I asked. "I don't know what you're looking at."

She thought for a minute, her forehead wrinkling. Then she burst out with, "Power pole swing! It's a power pole swing."

While I was puzzling over what a "power pole swing" could possibly be, the scene switched again to a ski lodge, and in the back ground was a ski lift, Asia's "power pole swing."

"What a great way to describe it, Asia. It's called a ski lift, and it takes people to the top of a mountain so they can ski down," I explained.

"Can we get one Mom?"

(Why not, I thought. Every back yard should have one. We'll be the envy of the neighborhood.) "No, honey, they're much too big."

"Listen to me very carefully, Mom. Just get a little one then," she reasoned.

About that time Jerry walked through the room. "She'll be a great lawyer someday," he said, laughing all the way to the garden.

Later that same day, as Jerry was preparing the barbecue grill, I started making hamburger patties. Asia came into the kitchen, looked at the package of ground beef and said, "Ground Chuck? Mom, who's Chuck?" I laughed every time I thought about it that night.

She started watching cartoons, something she had never done as a young child, and began developing favorite T.V. and radio stations. She lost the obsession with particular movies. Her mealtime appetite stayed the same, but her need to be eating continuously between meals was gone. Her swing replaced the trampoline and riding her bike back and forth from mailbox to mailbox as favorite pastimes. She began typing her name list on the computer while I cooked dinner, but first she had to add to her diary, which she had started at the beginning of the summer. She wrote about camp, what she ate, who she saw, who was coming over; her feelings about dentists' and doctors' appointments as they occurred. She loves our dentist, Dr. John (Wehr), and has no fear at all of appointments with him. He and his wonderfully patient staff have taken her from the screaming child who had to be strapped to a papoose board for cleanings to a child who, two years ago, had two teeth filled without me even in the room.

A recurring theme in her diary is that she doesn't want to "keep the colostomy in high school." She had told Marsha at the end of school last year and told her to "tell my Mom," but it wasn't until later in the summer that she told me herself. The last time we had discussed having the reversal done the surgeons could offer us no guarantees of total successful bowel function. And unless everything worked perfectly, they said, Asia would be faced with the possibility of enemas again. It was at that point that we put everything on hold until such time as a medical miracle could improve the odds. We had said that we were content to wait until it became important to *Asia* before even discussing it again. Well, now it was becoming important to her, so the effectiveness of Dr. Kotsanis' treatment became even more critical.

It occurred to me one day that perhaps one of the reasons the first reversal surgery had failed was because of the same problems that had been affecting her lately. We knew that she had been on antibiotics numerous times for a variety of infections while still in Korea. And the discovery of her ear infections here necessitated eight months of treatment. At no time that we know of was she ever given anything to prevent or control yeast overgrowth. We also knew that her body could not digest milk. What if other digestive enzymes had been out of balance even then? And if that much of my hypothesis were true, could we have prevented the need for the second surgery by altering her diet, adding enzymes, and creating digestive harmony in her system?

Just so I don't confuse you, *these* "what if's" aren't the same as the "if only's", or the "could've, should've, would'ves." *These* "what if's" can take you places, teach you things, and open your mind. The others are negative and only serve to drag you down.

What if we were able to correct the imbalances? Would her digestive system then function correctly? There was reason to think that, if this were true, the reversal might work this time.

Continuing on with this line of thinking, I began to consider the implications of the word malabsorption. In our Random House College Dictionary, the fourth definition for *absorption* is: "passage of substances to the blood, lymph, and cells, as from the alimentary canal or from the tissues." The prefix *mal-* means bad or wrong. If Asia was suffering from malabsorption *and* maldigestion, then it didn't matter how carefully I planned our meals or how much she ate, her body was not using the nutrients properly, and not only was her body suffering, but her brain was missing out as well. So *what if* we correct the malabsorption and allow her digestive system to finally make proper use of the nutritious meals I prepared? If her brain began to be nourished, doesn't it stand to reason that it will begin to function better? Since we had already begun to see positive changes, things should only continue to improve when the full treatment was started, I reasoned.

In the meantime we were preparing for the second session of AIT to start the second week in August. The conference in January had generated so much interest in AIT in the Ann Arbor area that Ken agreed to come here to treat a group of young people for two weeks. We were lucky enough to be able to be part of that group. Although Asia was having no problems with sound sensitivities, I felt that she would benefit from another series of treatments. Joan Matthews son, James, had shown improvement in social skills and peer interaction after his second treatment, and Ken had told us that everyone he had treated a second time had shown additional, often different, gains.

Asia was looking forward to seeing Ken again, and also the Doritos rewards on the ride home. We arrived the first day and she sprawled out on the bean bag chair in typical teenage fashion, arranged her hair around the headphones and ordered Ken to "turn it up" Last year she had sat stiffly in the straight backed chair until almost the last day. She appeared serious most of the time that morning and wanted me to sit by her. That evening she alternated between demanding and silly and all but refused to go to bed.

The second day, during the morning treatment, she again wanted me by her, holding hands the whole time. That afternoon she was cute and almost flirty, constantly trying to get our attention without talking. We could tell that something was happening when she began pounding on the bean bag chair with her fist and then retreated behind the "dead fish look." That evening, after repeatedly slamming her head back against the chair, she asked if she could watch T.V. in the bedroom. About an hour later she was quite relaxed.

Every day seemed to be a treat for Ken as he saw changes in her from a professional point of view that indicated growth since last year.

On Thursday evening she entered "cheerleader mode", cheering for everything and everyone, from the cat to Jerry Seinfeld, and she stayed that way through Friday morning's session.

Friday afternoon we left for Cleveland for BFG's Employee Appreciation Weekend, and Asia talked the entire trip. It was all appropriate talk about what we were going to do, who we would see and other things that interested her. There was little, if any, perseverative behavior or obsessive talking.

The next day, at the Cleveland Zoo, we walked as a family, without one of us having a death grip on Asia to keep her from drifting away into the crowd. Of course she remembered everyone from previous years and addressed them all by name, using her latest favorite phrase, "So, what's up?"

We were strolling through the new Rain Forest exhibit and Jerry pointed to a glass enclosure and asked Asia, "What are those?"

"Goods," she replied.

He blinked a couple of times, shook his head, laughed, and said, "No, honey, they're Bats." (Not goods--bats . . . get it? It's a joke. Her first.)

That evening, at a baseball game, she cheered with the best.

On Monday morning, driving to the Methodist Church where Ken had set up his temporary AIT room, Asia began giving me directions, telling me correctly when to turn and in which direction. When we got to the next town I asked her which way to the pet store where we shopped and she knew. Up until that point I hadn't known if she could have found her way home from the center of Milan, even though she could repeat our address. That afternoon she paced and clapped for the entire half hour. The next morning she took the bean bag chair out into the hallway, where she preferred to sit for the remainder of the treatments. The mid-point audiogram was very nearly perfect.

Ken had cautioned me in the beginning that the reactions to treatment could be the same as the first, including one or more regressions after the therapy was completed. We saw the behaviors pretty much on schedule, including fatigue, although this year her new-found maturity added a new perspective.

The remainder of the therapy went smoothly, until the last day, when Asia tried running with a bag of vegetables we were taking to Ken. She dropped the bag, and the squash, cucumbers, eggplant and melons went sliding across the pavement, leaving gashes in their previously perfect surfaces. I was angry at her carelessness and she knew it. She was so upset and anxious, even after I calmed down, that I think it affected the outcome of the final audiogram. We'll drive out to Berkley and recheck it later.

That was Friday, August twenty-fifth and school and cross-country training started the following Monday.

It is now September eighth and Jerry, Asia, Meghann, and Jess, Meghann's boyfriend are at a football game. Last Friday the remainder of the ingredients making up Dr. Kotsanis' treatment protocol for Asia arrived. Now in addition to Vital-Zymes, garlic, and lactobacillus with every meal, she will be taking preparations designed to soothe and heal her bowel. Some she will take for only two months and some for a year. At some point we will send for another CDSA test kit to see how well things are going from a clinical stand point. We know it will take time, because, after all, her system didn't get this way over night. But Chris assures me that we will begin to see behavior changes as her system begins to function more normally.

School has been in session for two weeks now and several teachers have already commented to Marsha on how well Asia is doing. Her schedule was adjusted slightly to allow for chorus and a living skills class.

Cross country is her passion now, and after sitting in on the first three practices, we now drop her off at the gym at 2:30 P.M. and pick her up at five P.M., just like the other kids. The coach says she can run with the fastest of the middle schoolers, some who participated in cross country last year. Their first meet is on Saturday, September sixteenth. Jerry's parents will be here to cheer her on with us.

Earlier this week, while I was in the kitchen preparing corn to freeze for the winter, Asia was typing at the computer. Suddenly, she yelled, "Now, just what are you doing?"

Thinking she was talking to me, I replied, "Cutting corn off the cob, honey."

"No, Mom, I wasn't talking to you, I was talking to the computer," she said. I could relate to that. I talk to it all the time.

A few minutes later I heard, "Will you stop that, please?"

"What's it doing, honey?" I asked.

Pointing at the screen, she said, "It moved this down here and I used the arrows but I can't get it back up there where it's supposed to be." All of this was said with perfect inflection.

I waited, wanting to see how she would play this out. In a few more minutes she said, "Now how am I supposed to type when you do that? Mom, can you come help me with this, please?"

As I dropped the corn to go help her, I couldn't help but think, *'This is so normal.'* And this is just the beginning.

Jerry, Meghann, Adair, and Asia,
Christmas, 1983

Asia and Meghann, Mother's Day 1983

Jerry and Asia
on her
Naturalization Day

Asia with Touch
and Tell

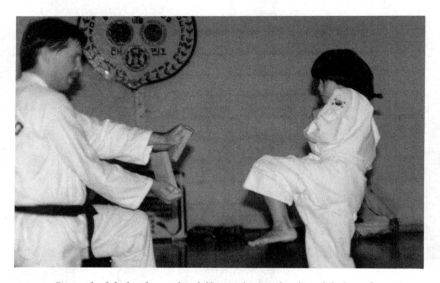

Jerry held the board while Asia broke it with her foot

First day of school, 1994.

Afterword

To help a child achieve beyond what might have been expected is to embark on the ultimate treasure hunt. The paths to
such discoveries are rarely easy, nor are they direct. Parents
often face "wrong turns" and "dead ends" in their searching, as a
result of no advice or bad advice from professionals and others
who are well intentioned. Sometimes they try treatments or
therapies that simply don't work. It takes an immense amount of
love, perseverance, and energy for parents to help their children
achieve the goals they know in their hearts are possible.

Adair Renning is the kind of parent who possesses love,
stamina, and tenacity in sufficient depth and quality to make the
"impossible" happen. She responds to situations that would
represent an extreme crisis for some persons as challenges from
which change must arise. When I first met Adair in the Spring
of 1994, and we discussed Asia's candidacy for auditory
integration training, I was impressed with the depth of understanding Adair had as to the nature of Asia's symptoms,
especially those related to her dysfunctional auditory skills. I
was equally impressed with her energy, the research she had

done, and the cohesiveness of her family. All of them understood the nature of the problems Asia faced and all were dedicated to helping make things better for her. Asia's treatment in the Summer of 1994 was successful in many ways, and during the months that followed, Adair contacted me frequently with updates on Asia's growth and with questions about her behavior. On several occasions, Adair commented that not enough parents knew about AIT, and that there needed to be a way to get the information out. Being solution oriented, she decided to put on a workshop to share what we knew about AIT. In a matter of six months from concept to completion, Adair put together a working board of parents, made arrangements with a local inn, and created a program which included a nationally known author, two local auditory integration training providers, and a panel of parents and others who had direct experience with auditory integration training. She announced the coming workshop to hundreds of people, and not surprisingly, it all came together in January 1995. In a way this illustrates Adair's ability to meet and deal with issues and see them through to the end.

Adair and I have discussed in detail many alternative therapies and treatments as they relate specifically to Asia's behaviors. These discussions, in turn, have enabled me to more effectively counsel other families. It is important that parents take the time to carefully evaluate these alternatives and the persons who provide them. It is equally important that parents have the strength of their convictions and not be afraid to consider alternatives outside the realm of traditional medicine and clinical practice.

Kenyon Wilson, MA CCC SLP
Speech-Language Pathologist
Berkley, Michigan 48072

What to Read and Who to Call

All parents of challenged children are involved in their own personal quest for information that will help them develop a program to bring out the best in their child. Here is a list of the books, organizations, and individuals who were helpful in getting us started. I hope the reader will find it helpful. Each one will lead you to another, and that's how the Treasure Hunt starts.

BOOKS:
Is This Your Child?
Doris Rapp, M.D.
William Morrow & Company

The Sound of a Miracle: A Child's Triumph Over Autism
Annabel Stehli
Doubleday

Hearing Equals Behavior
Guy Berard, M.D.
Keats Publishing, Inc.

Emergence: Labeled Autistic
Temple Grandin
Arena Press

Dancing in the Rain:
Stories of Exceptional Progress by Parents of Children With
Special Needs.
Annabel Stehli
The Georgiana Organization

ORGANIZATIONS:

The Parent Network for the Post-Institutionalized Child
Box 613
Meadowlands, PA. 15347
(412) 222-1766

The Georgiana Organization, Inc.
P.O. Box 2607
Westport CT 06880
(203) 454-1221

P^{2}REP^2
(Parents and Professionals Re-educating Parents and
Professionals)
37785 Greenwood
Northville, MI 48167

Autism Research Institute
4182 Adams Avenue
San Diego, CA 92116
(619) 261-7165

Great Smokies Diagnostic Laboratory
18A Regent Park Boulevard
Asheville, NC 28806
(800) 522-4762

INDIVIDUALS:

C.F. Derrick, M.D., P.C.
1821 King Rd.
Trenton, MI 48183
(313) 675-0678

Kenyon Wilson, MA, CCC, SLP
2766 W. 11 Mile Rd.
Suite 8
Berkley, MI 48072-3051
(810) 544-0560

Cindy Bazell-Wilson, MA CCC-A
Audiologist
Children's Hospital of Michigan
3901 Beaubien Boulevard
Detroit, MI 48201-2196

C.A. Kotsanis, M.D.
Baylor Medical Plaza
1600 W. College St.
Suite 260
Grapevine, TX 76051
(817) 481-6342

Sharon Hurst, M.S.
Auditory Training and Education Center
Atrium Center Suite 223
Carol Stream, IL 60188
(708) 682-8101